Highley

FAMILY, SEXUALITY AND SOCIAL RELATIONS IN PAST TIMES

GENERAL EDITORS:
Peter Laslett, Michael Anderson and Keith Wrightson

Western Sexuality: Practice and Precept in Past and Present Times
Edited by Philippe Ariès and André Béjin
Translated by Anthony Forster

The Explanation of Ideology: Family Structures and Social Systems
Emmanuel Todd
Translated by David Garrioch

The Causes of Progress: Culture, Authority and Change
Emmanuel Todd
Translated by Richard Boulind

The English Noble Household, 1250–1600
Kate Mertes

An Ordered Society: Gender and Class in Early Modern England
Susan Dwyer Amussen

Porneia: On Desire and the Body in Antiquity
Aline Rousselle
Translated by Felicia Pheasant

Medieval Prostitution
Jacques Rossiaud
Translated by Lydia G. Cochrane

Highley: The Development of a Community, 1550–1880
Gwyneth Nair

FORTHCOMING

Wet Nursing: A History from Antiquity to the Present
Valerie Fildes

Illegitimacy and Society in Eighteenth-Century Scotland
Rosalind Mitchison and Leah Leneman

Mobility and Marriage: The Family and Kinship in Early Modern London
Vivien Brodsky

The Country House Society
Jessica Gerard

Highley

The Development of a Community
1550–1880

Gwyneth Nair

Basil Blackwell

Copyright © Gwyneth Nair, 1988

First published 1988

Basil Blackwell Ltd
108 Cowley Road, Oxford, OX4 1JF, UK

Basil Blackwell Inc.
432 Park Avenue South, Suite 1503
New York, NY 10016, USA

British Library Cataloguing in Publication Data

Nair, Gwyneth
   Highley: the development of a community,
   1550–1880—(Family, sexuality and social
   relation in past times)
   1. Shropshire. Highley. Social conditions,
   1550–1880
   I. Title II. Family, sexuality and social
   relations in past times
   942.4'59
   ISBN 0–631–15338–1

Library of Congress Cataloging in Publication Data

Nair, Gwyneth,
   Highley: the development of a community, 1550–1880/Gwyneth
Nair.
   p. cm.—(Family, sexuality, and social relations in past
times)
   Bibliography: p.
   Includes index.
   ISBN 0–631 15338–1
   1. Highley (Shropshire)—History. 2. Highley (Shropshire)—Social
life and customs. 3. England—Rural conditions—Case studies.
4. Villages—England—Shropshire—Case studies. 5. Rural
development—England—Highley (Shropshire)—Case studies.
DA690.H702N35 1988   88–4337
942.4'59—dc19.   CIP

Typeset in 11 on 13pt Garamond
by Cambrian Typesetters, High Street, Frimley, Surrey.
Printed in Great Britain by
T. J. Press Ltd, Padstow; Cornwall

To my Mother

Contents

List of Plates

Station. The arrival of the railway in 1862 widened social
and commercial horizons.

Acknowledgements

I should like to thank all those who have helped and encouraged me in the preparation of this book. In its initial form as a Ph.D. thesis, the study owed much to the support of the late Professor Christina Larner and the guidance of Dr. Derek Sayer and Dr. Lionel Glassey, all at that time of the University of Glasgow. Their continued advice has been invaluable, and their patience greatly appreciated. I am grateful too for the constructive comments of Dr. Keith Wrightson, Professor Michael Anderson and Dr. David Hey, who read the manuscript in either its original or final form and whose suggestions have been most helpful.

Archivists and staff at the County Record Offices at Hereford, Shrewsbury, Worcester and Gloucester, at the Birmingham and Shrewsbury Reference Libraries, at the Bodleian Library and Christ Church, Oxford, the Public Record Office and the British Library have given me every assistance, both personally and by answering numerous postal inquiries.

I should also like to thank those residents of Highley, too many to name here, who generously supplied information and lent or took photographs. Finally, my thanks go to Mohan Nair for all his support and encouragement during the project's long gestation.

Gwyneth Nair,
University of Glasgow

Abbreviations

B.L.	The British Library
B.R.L.	Birmingham Reference Library
Ch.Ch.	Christ Church, Oxford
G.R.O.	Gloucestershire Record Office
H.R.O.	Hereford and Worcester Record Office at Hereford
P.R.O.	The Public Record Office
S.P.L.	Shropshire Public Libraries, Local Studies department, Shrewsbury
S.R.O.	Shropshire Record Office
T.S.A.S.	Transactions of the Shropshire Archaeological and Natural History Society
W.R.O.	Hereford and Worcester Record Office at Worcester

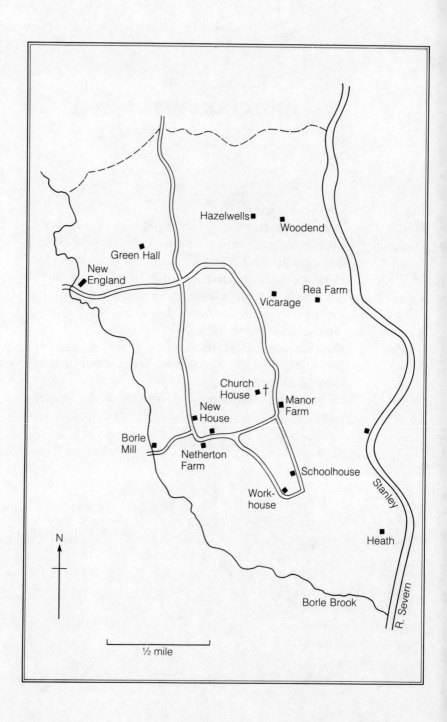

Hazelwells■

■ Woodend

■ Green Hall

New
England■

■ Vicarage

Rea Farm
■

Church
House■ †

Manor
Farm■

New
House■

Borle
Mill■

■
Netherton
Farm

Schoolhouse
■

Work-
house■

Stanley

Heath
■

Borle Brook

R. Severn

N

½ mile

Introduction

Highley is a small, roughly triangular parish in the south-east corner of Shropshire, bounded on its two longer sides by the Borle Brook to the west and the River Severn on the east. Thus the centre of the village sits on a ridge, with the land falling away to the watercourses on either side. The nearest towns are Bridgnorth, eight miles to the north, and Bewdley, nine miles to the south. The county town, Shrewsbury, is over 25 miles away.

Highley and its immediate neighbours are situated on the Coal Measures which overlie the Old Red Sandstone: the area provides coal, ironstone and building stone, all of which have been worked in the past. It is, however, a predominantly agricultural area. Only Highley and its neighbour across the Severn Alveley retained coal mining after nationalisation until final closure in 1969.

To the south and west of Highley are the large parishes of Kinlet and Stottesdon, characterized by scattered farms and shrunken hamlets. Billingsley and Chelmarsh, to the west and north, are like Highley itself more strongly nucleated, but nevertheless have outlying farmsteads. Yet this was an area of open-field farming until enclosure began in the late sixteenth century, although the settlement patterns were very different from the classic fielden type.

Enclosure happened at an early date in this part of Shropshire, and has in the main left little documentary evidence. In Highley most of the activities of enclosure took place in the second decade of the seventeenth century. Since written records relating to the community become abundant from about 1550, there is a period of 70 years or so where the old agrarian order can be examined. Then followed a post-enclosure period when agriculture remained virtually the only occupation of the villagers. Finally, from the

1780s, Highley's mineral resources began to be exploited and in the early nineteenth century its population more than doubled.

This opportunity to examine social and economic change over a long time-span and in three distinct phases makes Highley an interesting case study. The survival of records relating to it is good, although very little is in print. The parish registers begin in 1551 and are complete thereafter except for a short gap in the 1740s which can be bridged by the Bishop's Transcripts. There seems to be some under-registration of marriages in the early seventeenth century, but otherwise the quality of registration, while not exceptional, is adequate. There was no organized Nonconformist worship in Highley until 1815 and so registers before that date are little affected. Even when a Methodist chapel was built, numbers attending were for the most part small.

Records of parochial administration survive from the 1680s, and considerable use has been made of the Easter Books where payments of Easter dues to the vicar from 1679 to 1832 were recorded.

The other major classes of records used were national fiscal returns, such as Lay Subsidies and Hearth Tax returns; records of courts, both lay (Manor Courts, Quarter Sessions) and ecclesiastical; wills and probate inventories; and census returns from 1841. These were supplemented by the use of Parliamentary papers; deeds, leases and estate surveys; glebe terriers and other diocesan material; coroners' inquests; and some printed sources such as trade directories of the nineteenth century.

Secondary sources relating to Shropshire are still relatively few. The landscape and its evolution have been explored by Rowley.[1] The industrial development of the county, concentrating mainly on Coalbrookdale, has been traced by Trinder.[2] The south of the county, with the exception of Ludlow, has been the subject of far less research than has the north. Hey has followed Richard Gough, whose early eighteenth-century work was the precursor of modern parish studies,[3] in providing a detailed study of Myddle in north Shropshire.[4] Otherwise the major research on Shropshire is

[1] T. Rowley, *The Shropshire Landscape* (London, 1976).
[2] B. Trinder, *The Industrial Revolution in Shropshire* (London and Chichester, 1973). *The Most Extraordinary District in the World* (London and Chichester, 1977).
[3] R. Gough, *The History of Myddle* (London, 1981).
[4] D. Hey, *An English Rural Community; Myddle under the Tudors and Stuarts* (Leicester, 1974).

contained in unpublished theses and in the volumes, published and in preparation, of the Victoria County History.

Thus, while it would be useful to set events in Highley within a local south Shropshire context, it is rarely possible in the absence of detailed research to do so.

So, why another parish study, and why of Highley? There are of course limitations to the legitimate aims of a single-parish study: Finberg warns that 'one cannot hope to establish a thesis of general application by writing the history of a parish'.[5] On many topics, however, it is only through several such local studies that it can be hoped to form and test a general thesis.

Any study of a single parish is open to the criticism that it in fact deals with an arbitrary administrative unit, a 'community' only in convenience. In fact, although Highley villagers had considerable links with the surrounding area, there is evidence of a strong sense of community and identification with the parish. In Highley more than in any of its neighbours geographical and administrative units coincided: the manor, the village and the parish were virtually identical in terms of geography and personnel. The parish was small and centralized, and its separate identity was hightened by the fact that all its boundaries except that to the north were formed by waterways which had to be crossed by bridge or boat. Agriculture, social control and poor relief were all locally organized. Villagers were obliged to gather regularly at the parish church, to pay local tithes and poor rates, to abide by local manorial or parochial customs, to serve as parish officers. Many villagers left sums of money to the parish church and to the poor of the parish. 'Highley', whether as manor, parish or village, clearly had an empirical force and significance for its members.

No student of a parish can afford to ignore the overlapping 'communities' of which his or her place of study forms a part – those areas and groups from which business contacts and marriage partners were drawn, the local market towns which exercized an influence and provided a focus, and the wider area over which contact with relatives could be maintained. Nevertheless, in dealing with Highley we are not giving a wholly spurious significance to what happens to be a convenient unit of study.

Another problem of the parish study is in identifying agents of

---

[5] H. P. R. Finberg, 'Local history', in H. P. R. Finberg and V. H. T. Skipp, *Local History: Objective and Pursuit* (Newton Abbot, 1973).

change at local as opposed to national level. Doubtless much of Highley's experience was shared with other communities in Shropshire, and indeed in the whole of England. But the precise timing and course of social change can frequently be attributed to purely local factors, although the separating of national and local trends and agents is necessarily problematic.

A 'microhistory' of one parish, then, has attendant difficulties. It can also have considerable rewards. Local studies have helped to explode some of the myths of social history: that geographical mobility in the past was much less than today, for instance, or that marriage age was much lower. They have also given rise to new orthodoxies about the size and structure of households before the nineteenth century. Many of the larger questions of social history – such as the chronology of the development of a class society – call for the kind of depth and subtlety that can only be achieved, at least initially, at local level.

Highley was chosen as a subject for study for several reasons. First, it is in an area which as we have seen is little researched: it is well not to confine our picture of social life in England to the south-east of the country even if, as yet, the local context for parish studies in remoter areas is less accessible. Importantly, Highley's experience of enclosure and industrial development means that in a span of three centuries it is possible to examine three economic systems and their impact on social relations in the village. Highley is a small parish: to link a wide range of sources in order to chart and integrate changing social and economic experience in this way would be impractical over a comparable time-span in a larger parish. Furthermore, it is important to remember that a majority of the population of England before 1800 lived in small rural communities of similar size.

If the small size of the parish allows a long-term perspective, it also presents problems in demographic analysis. Highley would hardly generate samples of sufficient size for a purely demographic study. Demographic profiles of the community are here presented as background to the course of social change in the village, and no large claims can be made for their more general significance. This is the other side of the coin, the roundabout to the swings of long-term perspective and the synthesis of data from many sources to reinforce and supplement each other.

In the series of trade-offs involved in any choice of research area, then, Highley emerges rather well. And of course there was an additional advantage: I was born and brought up there and was able to offer personal knowledge of local people and conditions, geography, agriculture and dialect.

The study is structured around two major forms of change – enclosure and industrialization – and thus divided into three chronological sections. This must not be taken to imply, however, that these periods were in themselves wholly homogeneous and static. Social and economic change was a dynamic process: in identifying the two most crucial agents of change there is no intention to deny the evolutionary process for which they provided the focal points. There were trends in village society which were not caused by enclosure, for instance, but which enclosure certainly speeded up and highlighted.

In each of the three sections, the local economy is examined, as well as the salient features of demographic and social realities. The final chapter attempts to draw together some of the major threads in the course of social change in the village community over the period of more than 300 years.

PART I

The Manor
1550–1620

1

Farming in Common

The methods of agriculture practised in Highley in the sixteenth century are of paramount importance in any study of the community, for virtually every inhabitant was involved in farming. The great majority of men earned their living solely from the land, as yeomen, husbandmen or labourers.

Where other occupations existed, they were concerned with the provision of local services: there were at various times tailors, a miller, a blacksmith and a mason. There is little sign of production for a wider market, although the Severn provided a convenient link with Worcestershire and Gloucestershire, and in 1569 Thomas Lowe recorded his occupation as 'waterman'. Such local tradesmen as there were also farmed land, and combined at least a smallholding with their trade. Even the village priest was active in farming his glebe lands. Thus every member of the community was directly affected by the prevailing system of agriculture; and until about 1620, that system was farming in common.

Because it enclosed early and largely without formal documentation, south Shropshire has not always been recognized as an area of open-field farming. Gray, however, pointed out that such a system had operated in the area,[1] and Rowley cites further evidence both of the existence of open arable fields and of their piecemeal enclosure during the sixteenth and seventeenth centuries.[2]

The manor of Highley had belonged before the Dissolution of the Monasteries to Wigmore Abbey in Herefordshire. After a brief period in the hands of the King, and of a London merchant called Cupper, it was sold in 1546 to John Littleton of Frankley in Worcestershire.[3] The manor was almost, but not quite, coterminous

[1] H. L. Gray, *English Field Systems* (Cambridge, Mass., 1915), pp. 123–7.
[2] T. Rowley, *The Shropshire Landscape* (London, 1976), pp. 137–44.
[3] *Letter and Papers, Foreign and Domestic* Henry VIII, XXI Part 1, No. 970.

with the parish. There were actually three holdings which lay within the parish of Highley which did not form part of the manor. A small area of woodland in the south-east near the River Severn had been granted to the Priory of St Wulstan at Worcester in the 13th century, and this passed at the Dissolution to Christ Church Oxford.[4] More importantly, the water mill on the Borle Brook, together with a virgate of land, had belonged to the White Ladies Priory at Brewood in Staffordshire. This was acquired by the Throckmorton family of Coughton in Warwickshire.[5] Finally, a farm in the south of the parish called Ardens was sold to John de Arderne of Kinlet in 1470, and by the sixteenth century had come into the possession of George Southall of Kinlet.[6]

Thus there were two holdings which were not part of the manor; the mill, which was bought by its occupant Thomas Lowe in 1579; and Ardens which was the home of Thomas Strefford the village blacksmith.

Otherwise, the whole of the parish belonged to Littleton. It comprised a manor house and demesne lands, already leased since 1521 to a sitting tenant, and at least 25 tenancies, a few freehold but the majority held by lease or copy of court roll. There were open arable fields, closes of meadow and pasture, and a wood of 137 acres where tenants had rights of common.

The arable land lay in four open fields. Since an extent of 1332 described a three-field system, a fourth field had been added at Netherton, a settlement to the west of the village centre.[7] This was known as Netherton Little Field, and does seem to have been smaller than the other fields, stretching along the higher slopes of the Borle valley. The larger, older fields were Rea Field, north and east of the village; Cockshutt Field, north and west; and the self-explanatory South Field. That Netherton Little Field was a later addition to a three-field system is further suggested by the absence of any glebe land here. Possibly it was assart land, taken from the woodland of the Borle valley, although other assarts in the north of the parish seem to have become enclosed pastures rather than common arable lands.

Whatever its origins, Netherton Little Field raises questions

[4] *Letters and Papers, Foreign and Domestic* Henry VIII, XXI Part 2, No. 648.

[5] A. T. Gaydon (ed), *The Victoria County History of Shropshire*, II (London, 1973), pp. 83–4.

[6] S.R.O. 3320/16: Kinlet Collection, leases 1397–1649.

[7] P.R.O. E142/68: Inquisition Post Mortem, 6 Edw. III.

about the nature of Highley's open-field farming in the sixteenth century. The vicar, and probably other tenants too, held no land here. There are indications that a disproportionate number of strips in this field were held by men whose homes were in the Netherton township – and who therefore would have had a correspondingly small stake in one or two of the other fields. It is difficult to reconcile this with the classic pattern of open-field farming, with its reliance on a rough equality of holdings in all fields to allow for the fallowing of one field each year.[8] This was by no means always the case in Highley by 1570; and it begins to look as if the process of exchange and consolidation of holdings which was to lead to enclosure in the seventeenth century was begun with the creation of this fourth smaller field.

Otherwise the lay-out of arable land in the parish was as one would expect: the fields were laid out in strips, locally called rudges, which were grouped together in furlongs. Individual tenants occasionally held single strips, but more usually blocks of anything up to a dozen. These strips seem to have been much smaller than the 'text book' one acre; smaller even than those of Wigston, where Hoskins found three strips to the acre.[9] The only firm evidence of their size is in an important glebe terrier of 1625, which shows strips of between a quarter and a fifth of an acre.

The earliest survey of the manor which permits a computation of the total arable acreage in Highley dates from 1603, by which time several farms, including the demesne, had been sold, and so we do not know what percentage of the parish total acreage of 1527 acres was under the plough in this pre-enclosure period. In 1603 there were 184 acres of arable out of a total of 738 still belonging to the Littletons.[10] If this proportion was reflected in the remaining farms of the parish, and there is no reason to believe that it was not, this represents a very different state of affairs from that more accurately assessed in the mid-nineteenth century, where of a total of 1350 acres farmed, 780 were arable.[11] The importance of pastoral farming to the pre-enclosure economy was clearly considerable.

Not all pasturing was on commonly-held waste land. By the

[8] W. E. Tate, *The English Village Community and the Enclosure Movement* (London, 1967), p. 36.
[9] W. G. Hoskins, *The Midland Peasant: The Economic and Social History of a Leicestershire Village* (London, 1957), p. 151.
[10] B.R.L. Hagley Hall MSS. 357347: Survey of Highley, 1603.
[11] S. Bagshaw, *History, Gazeteer and Directory of Shropshire* (1851).

middle of the sixteenth century there were numerous closes of pasture, held in several, many of which represented woodland clearance on the fringes of the parish. By the time of the 1603 survey, every farm listed had some pasture of its own. Indeed some farms consisted entirely of pasture, the largest being the 114 acres of Green Hall, situated near Highley Wood. Highley's origins as a forest-fringe parish, and the nature of its soil, affected the nature of its pre-enclosure agrarian system to the end.

The only truly common pasture land seems to have been Highley Wood in the north of the parish, where all tenants had rights of pasture according to the number of acres in their holding. Sixteenth-century leases give the extent of this wood as 40 acres, but the more detailed survey of 1603 gives 137½ acres, a much more plausible figure. In the south of the parish a tongue of Earnwood Park, property of the lord of the manor of Kinlet, extended into Highley, and legally did not concern Highley villagers at all, although there had been cases of poaching in the park in the fifteenth century, and the same temptation obviously remained.

Highley also differed from the classic three-field system regions in the distribution of its meadows. Usually the common meadows would be divided up in much the same manner as the arable land, though with less permanent divisions, and frequently lots would be drawn to decide which 'doles' a tenant received. There is no indication of this happening in Highley. In the 1570s and 1580s we find several mentions of 'little meadows', obviously enclosed, and only two larger meadows – Coltam Meadow and Held Meadow – which could conceivably have been sub-divided. The 1603 survey is silent here, merely grouping together meadow and orchard, and listing each tenant as having an amount varying between a quarter of an acre and 11 acres, with an average holding of about four acres.

Pre-enclosure Highley can never have presented the open, almost treeless aspect of the true 'champion' country. Besides the Wood and Park and the hedges of the arable fields, the tenants' holdings, presumably their pasture closes, were all well-wooded. Highley Wood, although described in a rental of 1601 as having mostly 'dotted and firewood trees . . . and some underwood and bushes'[12] was found in 1603 to contain 3,200 oak trees. William

[12] P.R.O. LR2/185 ff. 144–6v.: Survey of Highley, 1601.

Pountney's large pasture tenement of Green Hall alone had 920 oaks and 20 ashes. Altogether the 16 holdings mentioned had growing on them 2,900 oaks and 60 ashes. To this of course must be added the unspecified amount of orchard, and any trees in the gardens and home closes attached to the houses.

With all this timber available (at a price) it is not surprising that the majority of houses in Highley were of timber-frame construction. In the typical Midland open-field village, farmsteads were clustered together in the centre, perhaps round a green or along a village street. In Wigston they were 'never out in the fields', but 'either faced the street . . . or lay at right angles to it.'[13] Although Highley was basically a nucleated settlement, centred on the church and manor house, there were in the sixteenth century houses out, if not in the open fields, at least on the edges of them, and in the pasture lands on the margins of the parish. In addition, the settlement of Netherton, half a mile or so west of the centre, was made up of six or seven houses.

All arable lands were not roughly equidistant from all farm-houses, and although Highley is not a large parish, the possession of strips in Rea Field, for instance, was a serious inconvenience to the man living in Netherton. This factor should not be under-estimated in any consideration of the enclosure activities of the seventeenth century.

This, then, is the physical context in which pre-enclosure society in Highley existed, and it is important to have some idea of this background before attempting any study of that society, for in the day-to-day life of the sixteenth-century peasant farmer, the lay-out of the land he worked loomed larger than almost any other factor.

The operation of the system is best illustrated by looking in detail at one peasant holding in this open-field lay-out. Only one such detailed extent survives, in the lease granted to Nicholas Bradley in 1569.[14] Bradley came to Highley from Northfield in Worcestershire as a young married man with an infant son, and settled in the hamlet of Netherton. His lease was for 1,000 years, so to all intents and purposes he was as secure in his tenure as a freeholder, although he paid a rent of 9s 4d per annum rather than the nominal chief rent of a freeholder.

The lease specifies pasture and arable land, but makes no

[13] Hoskins, *The Midland Peasant*, p. 148.
[14] S.P.L. Misc. Deeds 1919: Lease from J. Littleton to N. Bradley, 1569.

mention of meadow as a separate category. However, one item in the list of pasture closes has the addition 'and one little meadow adjoining, about two acres', suggesting that there may be no distinction between meadow and pasture in other entries. In only one case is the pasture specifically called a 'close' – but other pastures all have separate (and often identifiable) names, and it is clear that they too were enclosed. There were seven of these pasture closes, varying in size from two to eight acres. The total acreage is 31.

Bradley's arable land was entirely comprised of strips in the open fields. In Cockshutt Field he held 49 'rudges' of land, grouped in 11 parcels. At least 40 of these can be positively identified as lying in the south of the field, nearest to his pasture and house. In Netherton Little Field he held 35 strips in 10 groups. The largest number of strips, 57, was in South Field, of which all but 10 lay in the west of the field, nearest Netherton. In the most distant field, Rea Field, Bradley had only six strips.

Thus there was a total of 147 strips of arable land. If a strip was indeed something between a fifth and a quarter of an acre, Bradley's arable acreage would be between 29 and 37, comparable with his pasture total. In order to be at all viable as a unit, such small strips would need to be amalgamated to some extent, as indeed they were. Only one strip stood alone, and although one block had 12 strips together, the mean group was four, or about one acre.

Unfortunately Bradley died intestate in 1607, and so we have no will or inventory to supply further information about the stock he kept on his farm, or any of the crops grown. Court rolls tell us only that he kept pigs, which in 1575 he had failed to ring.[15]

The Court Leet of the manor of Highley was held twice a year during Littleton's ownership, and a good series of rolls survives from the period 1570–93, with a later sequence from 1609 to 1617.[16] The rolls throw considerable light on the communal aspects of pre-enclosure farming in the village. Rules were necessary to ensure that everyone ringed and yoked his pigs by Christmas, for instance, or maintained his stretch of hedge once the arable fields were sown until after harvest. It also fell to the court to allocate the number of beasts each tenant could graze on the commons, to

[15] B.R.L. Hagley Hall MSS. 377991 f. 55r: Highley Court Roll 14 Oct 17 Eliz. I.
[16] B.R.L. Hagley Hall MSS 377989–94: Highley Court Rolls, 1570–1617.

decide what heriot was due to the lord on the death of a tenant, and to admit his or her successor to the holding after establishing right of title.

Besides these communal decisions, the court settled disputes between tenants and fixed fines for offenders. By far the most frequent disputes were over hedges; often a tenant was negligent of repairing a gap in his hedge, presumably allowing beasts to stray and cause damage, as George Pearson's black goat did in 1571. Sometimes tenants, or their servants, had cut firewood from a neighbour's hedge. Most frequent of all were cases of hedges not being 'on their right course' – attempts to increase one's holding at someone else's expense. Thomas Lowe of Borle Mill was presented at each court throughout the 1570s because he had not moved one of his hedges; in his case, since he apparently preferred to pay the fines rather than lose the land, there seems little the court could do about it. But in the main the court seems to have been successful in ensuring the relatively smooth operation of a communal system of agriculture, and imposing its discipline at all levels of village society.

We can divide the sixteenth-century population of Highley into four broad social groups, if we bear in mind certain riders. First, we are not dealing with a community dominated by a distinct peasant elite: some families were better off than the majority, but there is no very great disparity, and thus the division between, for instance, yeomen and husbandmen is to some extent an arbitrary one. There is the natural bias of our information towards the wealthier classes, who are more frequently mentioned in wills, leases and so on. It is much more difficult to make any accurate assessment of the numbers and condition of day labourers and servants. Finally there is the overlapping of categories – the cottagers who supplemented their income by wage labour, for example. Nevertheless, it is useful to make this division, into yeomen or greater farmers; husbandmen or lesser farmers; artisans and smallholders; and day labourers and servants.

The 1543 lay subsidy return for Highley was the most comprehensive of the century.[17] It lists 27 men, and is a useful starting point for a consideration of the distribution of wealth in Highley, highlighting as it does the situation at the very beginning of our period. The list shows no dominating yeoman or gentry

[17] P.R.O. E179 166/159: Lay Subsidy Roll, 35 Henry VIII.

family at the top, but rather a steady gradation from more prosperous to less. There were four men taxed on £7 or £8, one of them the miller and one the tenant of the demesne lands. Below them is a larger group, assessed on £3–£5: eight relatively comfortably-off families with an income above subsistence level, and consequently with the potential to benefit from the inflation of the later sixteenth century. Between them, these two groups (44 per cent of the number taxed) paid 75 per cent of the sum levied, 38 per cent by the first group and 37 per cent by the second.

They are followed by a small group taxed on £2, contributing 10 per cent of the total levied. Finally there is the largest group of all, 11 men taxed on 20s or 26s 8d, who among them contribute only 15 per cent of the wealth of the community. In both these groups we find men whom we know to have been artisans and servants. At the very bottom of the list are two young men paying on 20s whose inclusion here is interesting, for both William Holloway and Thomas Lowe were sons of relatively prosperous families, and the probability is that they were earning a wage as live-in servants on another farm until such time as they could enter the family holding – a practice which we know was common in the seventeenth century.

The accompanying table 1.1 includes surnames of the tax-payers, for two reasons. Firstly this illustrates the problem of identification which we encounter in subsequent documents: there are six men named Lowe, for example. Secondly, it shows how the proliferation of well-established village families, with downward as well as upward social mobility, had led to branches of the same family occupying considerably disparate socioeconomic positions.

Table 1.1   1543 lay subsidy return

£7–£8	Holloway, Lowe, Palmer, Oseland
£3–£5	Haykorne, Pountney, Pountney, Rowley, Nichols, Holloway, Palmer, Lowe
£2	Dale, Mynsterley, Lowe, Goodman
£1–26s 8d	Lowe, Lowe, Nayless, Byshoppe, Pountney, Pountney, Charnocke, Hancorne, no surname, Holloway, Lowe.

A rental of 1587 names 21 tenants, and echoes closely the financial hierarchy indicated by the 1543 Subsidy.[18] Rentals from

[18] B.R.L. Hagly Hall MSS. 351963: Rental of Highley, 1587.

the turn of the century are less useful, for a few tenants, like the Peirsons, had already bought their holdings; and other sources indicate growing numbers of landless labourers in at least temporary residence on the manor.

Finally, it is important to ask how complete any reconstruction of the village population in the later sixteenth century is likely to be. Manorial rentals and wills cover freehold and copyhold tenants. Sub-letting undoubtedly went on: yet unless these sub-tenants were largely members of established families (and the evidence suggests that this may well have been the case) it is hard to imagine them being resident for any length of time without figuring in parish registers or appearing before the manor or church courts. Those most likely to be missing from existing records are the landless labourers and, especially, the servants. The latter, when mentioned in court records, are rarely even given a surname. There were undoubtedly servants in Highley of whom we have no knowledge. Labourers can often be identified from parish registers, court records or wills, although of course those whose stay in the parish was very short might have escaped record.

The wealthiest section of the community was the group of principal landholders. As well as those families named in the 1543 subsidy, we must add to the group the Harrises, freehold tenants of one and a half virgates of land who were in Highley by 1568, and the Peirsons, who came in 1558 to take over the manor house and demesne lands. Nevertheless, this most prosperous group remained small. In 1587, four tenants of the manor together paid 48 per cent of the total rent due: in 1603 four tenants (though not the same four) paid 47 per cent of the total.

Thus with the addition of principal freeholders we find perhaps six or seven families consistently forming what we shall call Group I, the substantial yeomanry of the village. It is instructive to look more closely at one or two of these families, to see by what means they achieved and maintained their position.

In 1543, John Oseland was assessed on a personal estate of £7. He had been granted a 21-year lease of the demesne lands of the manor in 1521, at an annual rent of 34s.[19] In fact Oseland was still in possession of the manor farm on his death in 1558, and his widow Margery took over, still paying the same rent. Margery was not long to enjoy the chief holding of the manor, for on 7th

[19] *Letters and Papers, Foreign and Domestic* Henry VIII, 3 Part 1, No. 1379.

February 1558–59 George Peirson 'entered the premises with the permission of Sir John Littleton'. Margery brought a bill of complaint against Littleton and his protege which reached the Court of Requests in 1560, alleging that Peirson had 'beat poor beasts and cattle steading and pasturing on the premises . . . and contrary to all equity and good conscience daily . . . threatens vexation and trouble to a poor widow to expel her out of the premises . . . which she is not able because of impotency to resist.'[20]

Margery was not as friendless as this would have us believe, for the Oselands were still influential in the area. There were six middle-aged sons of John and Margery still living at this date, one or two of whom may have still shared the family home until Peirson's intrusion. One son, Richard, settled at Sutton, a hamlet two miles away in the parish of Chelmarsh. Another, Robert, was nominally tenant of a cottage and six acres of land in Highley, but would have spent much time away from the village in his capacity as a Yeoman of the Guard. On his death in 1577 his brother Edward, who seems the least prosperous of the brothers, was admitted tenant of this small holding. A fourth brother, John, appears to have left Highley as a young man, and may have settled in neighbouring Arley. A fifth, George, is not recorded as buried at Highley, but lived there at least until 1579. He probably never married, was sole executor of his mother's will in 1566, and was clearly quite prosperous as his considerable loans to other villagers show. Finally, there was Thomas Oseland, the parish priest since 1554. He was born about 1511 and educated at school (probably the Grammar School at Bridgnorth) but not university.[21] He remained vicar until his death in 1588.

Only one of these sons left a descendant in Highley – John, son of Edward. Somewhat surprisingly, in view of Edward's relative poverty, his son was able in 1587 to take over a holding of 70 acres at an annual rent of 28s. This may well have been with the assistance of his uncle the priest, for Thomas Oseland's will shows that he was in the habit of lending quite large sums to family and parishioners.

John Oseland and his wife, apparently childless, still occupied the same farm in 1603, after which we lose sight of them

20 P.R.O. Req 2 248/45: Case between J. Littleton and M. Oseland, 1560.
21 A. J. Knapton, 'Another Elizabethan clergy list', *T.S.A.S.*, XLVI (1), (1931).

completely. By 1618 the farm belonged to Oliver Harris, and one of the chief families of sixteenth-century Highley was no longer represented in the village. The Oselands had been squeezed out of the demesne farm by pressure from the lord of the manor (for Margery was unsuccessful in her suit, and Peirson stayed and prospered); some sons left the village to make a living elsewhere; those who remained failed to produce heirs; and ultimately their lands were acquired by a rising new generation of freeholders.

Upward mobility, too was possible: with luck and judgement a man could advance his position from the ranks of the 'middling sort' to become one of the most prosperous men of the community. In 1585, John Pountney of the Rea farm died, and his son William was admitted as tenant. John had paid tax on £4 in 1543. In 1564 William had married Ann daughter of Thurstan Holloway of Green Hall (whose father was one of the wealthiest men in the village in 1543, when he paid tax on £8). It would be useful to know where and how William and Ann lived for the first 20 years of their married life – but beyond the fact that they remained in Highley the existing evidence is insufficient to tell us. After 1585, their fortunes improved. In 1587, William was paying £1 13s 6d per annum rent for the Rea farm and a meadow that had been acquired to add to it, one of the highest rents in the village. Then in the same year his father-in-law Thurstan Holloway died, and William became tenant of the Holloway holdings too. He moved into Green Hall, leaving his son Thomas at the Rea. By 1603, father and son between them paid £3 9s annual rent, or 32 per cent of the whole village total. They held altogether over 212 acres, the largest family holding in Highley.

Unfortunately, no will or inventory survives for William Pountney, so we have no idea of the wealth generated by this extensive farm or of the range of stock maintained. It was largely a pastoral farm, having only six acres of arable out of its total of 157 acres, so obviously this was not peasant farming, but a commercial enterprise, raising sheep and cattle for profit. A fortunate, or prudent, marriage to a woman without brothers was the foundation for Pountney's success: but he also contributed energy and acumen (and patience) in the acquiring and successful running of such a large farm.

Consistently throughout this pre-enclosure period, then, we find a group of about six families in a markedly favourable financial situation. They represent perhaps one sixth of the total population. The composition of the class fluctuated, but its overall numbers remained stable. In the inflation experienced throughout this period, and especially after 1590, only the man with a surplus of production could hope to prosper. The subsistence farmer and the artisan could with luck and good harvests (or by increasing the price of their services and goods) only maintain their standard of living.

We must not assume, however, that it was only this most prosperous section of the community who were able to benefit from rising prices by selling surplus produce. Our division into 'greater' and 'lesser' farmers is in many ways an arbitrary one, and there is a danger of over-emphasising the differences between the position of a man paying tax on £7 in 1543, and one paying on £4 or £5. Highley's economic hierarchy was a matter of gradations rather than of clear-out domination by a peasant elite.

The second group, consisting at the start of our period of men with land or goods to the value of £3–£5, could in times of reasonable harvests (and with stable rents) produce a surplus to sell in a rising market and accumulate profits. That this had been the case in the 1580s and 1590s is demonstrated by the ability of so many men in this group to buy their farms when they came onto the market in the early seventeenth century.

Most farms in Highley were not large. The earliest date for which we can estimate a mean farm size is 1603, when the average farm was 38.8 acres – although this excludes the demesne among others. Similarly small farms have certainly been identified in broadly comparable areas at this date.[22] The families in our second group were generally in possession of farms of between average and twice-average size, and similarly in the 1543 Subsidy were taxed on amounts varying from average to twice the average. Bowden calculates that an arable farm of 30 acres might provide £14–£15 profit in the early seventeenth century, or a margin of £3–£5 over subsistence.[23] Thus, except in bad harvests, the men in this group might expect a reasonably comfortable living from their holdings.

[22] V. H. T. Skipp, 'Economic and social change in the Forest of Arden, 1530–1649', in J. Thirsk (ed), *Land, Church and People: Essays presented to Professor H. P. R. Finberg*, Agric. Hist. Rev., Supplement (1970), pp. 84–111.
[23] P. J. Bowden, 'Agricultural prices, farm profits, and rents', in J. Thrisk (ed), *The Agrarian History of England and Wales, IV, 1500–1640* (Cambridge, 1967), pp. 593–694.

They seem consistently to have made up about a third of the settled population of the village, and the composition of the group to be more stable than any other. Only one of the surnames of the 1543 Group II is not found in the rentals of 1601–03. These were the chief husbandmen of the parish, who whether their land was copyhold or leasehold held for terms of at least three lives. The frequency of the three-life tenure was a major factor in the continuity of the group.

These husbandmen also kept servants, and they and their widows often left quite substantial personal estates in their wills.

A typical husbandman family was that of Rowley of Netherton. William Rowley was assessed on £3 in 1543, only fractionally above average. He died in 1569, and the copy-hold farm passed to his son Thomas, who paid the relatively low rent of 9s 4d per annum for the rest of the century. The holding consisted of two houses, 25 acres of arable land, 12 of pasture and 6 of meadow: a total of 43 acres. The Rowleys prospered: in the early seventeenth century the farm was purchased, and by the time of Richard Rowley's death in 1651 he could style himself 'yeoman' and affix his seal to his will, in which he left bequests of £125 in cash to relatives, and gifts of corn to poor neighbours.

The holdings of these 'above-subsistence' farmers consisted of both arable and pasture, usually with more arable. The typical farmer in this group would hold about 20 acres of arable land in the common fields; some 12–15 acres of pasture; and perhaps five acres of meadow, as well as common rights. For this he would pay around 13s a year in rent. Importantly, this rent was stable: all these holdings were copyhold or leasehold for term of lives, or held on very long leases, and it was difficult to increase their rents. Gilbert Littleton, lord of the manor from 1590, came to an agreement with tenants which restricted rises in entry fines. Not only did rents not rise: during the economic crisis of 1596–97, a Littleton family dispute meant that some tenants paid no rent at all.[24]

Grain prices rose spectacularly in the 1590s, although they had been on the increase since 1570.[25] The area around Highley was affected by this inflation: the vicar of neighbouring Chelmarsh felt

[24] J. Tonks, 'The Littleton family and their estates, 1540–1640' (unpublished M. Litt. thesis, University of Oxford, 1978).

[25] J. Burnett, A History of the Cost of Living (Harmondsworth, 1969), p. 62.

it worth recording in his parish register 'And then was rye sould in Brudgnorth for xvjs. the Stryke'.[26] In the absence of rack-renting or vastly increased entry fines, therefore, the opportunity existed for the accumulation of wealth that could lay the basis for the land purchases, house building, and ultimately enclosure, of the early seventeenth century.

The third group, artisans and cottagers, should properly include both the four '£2 men' of 1543, and some of those taxed on 20s. It is difficult to assess the total population in this group, but an estimate of one quarter based on the 1587 rental appears reasonable. They contribute around 10 per cent to the total rent of the village in those cases where it can be computed.

The average cottage holding was just under five acres – nowhere near the size required to support and feed a family, although above the figure of four acres required by law from 1589. These cottagers in many cases paid a disproportionately high rent for their land: Thomas Charnock paid 13s 4d a year for a mere 15 acres, for instance, and Anne Nichols 6s 8d for three and a quarter acres. Cottagers also had common rights: beasts could be pastured in Highley Wood in proportion to the amount of land held.

Nevertheless, the income from these holdings must have been supplemented by other earnings, either from wage labour or from a craft. It is here that the distinction between these men and the labourers of Group IV (themselves presumably sub-tenants of cottages) becomes blurred. Of four men convicted in the manor court of 1609 of selling ale in unsealed measures, three were cottagers and one a labourer; and there must have been several other cottagers practising as shoemakers, tailors, carpenters and so on. Wills are rarely found from this group, and there are no surviving inventories for the period to reveal the presence of tools of a trade amongst a man's belongings. We know that there were at various times during this period several tailors, a weaver, a mason and a blacksmith at work in the village. Beyond that we can only surmise how most cottagers managed to live. Work would be available on larger farms at harvest, and the barge traffic which was heavy on the Severn between the market towns of Bridgnorth and Bewdley very probably provided some employment.

Certainly the artisans and cottagers were not favourably placed

---

[26] *Parish Registers of Chelmarsh, Neenton and Billingsley*, Shropshire Parish Register Society: Hereford Diocese, Vol. III, Part 2 (1903), first pagination, p. 18.

to benefit from rising prices: not only did they have no crops to sell, but they were forced to buy to live. To survive the inflation artisans would have to raise their own prices, creating further problems for those below substantial husbandman level. There was less continuity here than in Groups I and II. Cottagers were more likely to leave the village, less likely to be succeeded by sons in the same holding.

One family who did stay throughout our period and well into the seventeenth century were the Charnocks. In 1543 Richard Charnock was one of the group assessed on 20s, the lowest figure taxed. On his death in 1569 his widow was admitted as tenant of the messuage and five acres of land, copyhold tenure, at an annual rent of 3s 4d. Heriot was claimed in goods 'because there is no stock', so the five acres were used exclusively for crops.

In 1571, when Margery died, her son Thomas came into possession of the tenement 'for his own life only'. There were still no farm animals to provide a heriot. Thomas was already 40 years old, a married man with five children, and the wording of Richard's will suggests that all three generations shared the family cottage.

Sometime before 1587, Thomas Charnock seems to have acquired more land, for in that year he paid the same rent (13s 4d) that he was still paying in 1603 for 15 leasehold acres. The family was still regarded as poor, however, for in 1598 Thomas's eldest son William received a charitable bequest as a 'poor neighbour' in the will of Thomas Palmer.

We are in a position to know more about how the Charnocks made a living because they, uniquely among Highley families, appear in the Recusant Rolls of the 1590s.[27] Financial penalties for adhering to the Catholic faith were severe: fines of £80 and £140 were imposed on each of the three Charnocks. These can never have been paid, for such sums were well beyond the means of the family. Occupations are given here, and their discrepancies are interesting. In 1595, three family members were listed: Anne, wife of Thomas Charnock, tailor; Richard Charnock, tailor; and George Charnock, also a tailor. In 1592, however, George and Richard had been optimistically styled 'yeoman'; and in 1596 Thomas appears as a husbandman. Apparently then the family were tailors who also combined to farm the 15 acre holding.

[27] Catholic Records Society, *Records Series*, 18 (1916) and 61 (1970).

The eldest son, William, is not mentioned in the Recusant Rolls. It is possible that he worked for a time on the farm of John Pountney at Woodend in Highley, for by the latter's will of 1585 he is to choose the sheep which form one of the bequests, although receiving nothing himself. Richard and William Charnock were two of the four erring ale sellers of 1609. Thus the family was involved in three, if not four, different occupations in order to eke out a living. This must have been a familiar pattern for the smallholders of Highley, for at 15 acres the Charnock holding was the largest in this group.

Some cottagers, unlike the Charnocks, did keep stock. Humfrey Clare, a cottager who paid 3s 8d p.a. rent until his death in 1577, was fined in the court of May 1575 for failing to ring his pigs, for instance. In the pre-enclosure agrarian system, cottagers at least had some rights of commons in Highley Wood, which facilitated the keeping of stock. Whatever crops and stock were produced, however, were for home consumption, for these smallholders were farming for subsistence and not for profit.

The fourth group, day-labourers and servants, is the most difficult to identify. Rentals and surveys are silent here, and the chief sources are parish registers and court records. The situation with servants, especially women, is complicated by the failure to record their surnames. Manor and church courts mention such individuals as Sybil, servant of John Pountney, who cut wood in a neighbour's hedge in 1572. Only three sixteenth-century testators specify bequests to named individuals actually described as 'my servant', though in several other cases small bequests were made to men and women who seem to have been either house-servants or farm labourers. Of the seven named servants, five are recorded in Highley parish registers. The other two, both women, seem by their surnames to have come from neighbouring parishes. We know from retrospective evidence given later in the seventeenth century that several young people of both sexes had come from nearby villages to work as resident servants on Highley farms from about 1620, and it seems reasonable to assume that this had also been the case in the pre-enclosure period.

Wage labourers are somewhat more historically visible, and for the present purpose of determining the financial hierarchy of households, more relevant. They did not live-in on farms as servants did, and were usually married men with families of their own. In only one case is a man actually described in the registers as a 'day labourer'. This was John Potter, who came to Highley with his wife and at least one child shortly before 1592. They had previously lived in Alveley, across the Severn, and remained in Highley until both John and his wife died in 1630. The family lived in a cottage on the north side of the open Cockshutt Field, and Potter at one stage worked for the widow Palmer at Netherton, from whom he received a one-shilling bequest in 1603.

Potter's length of residence makes his career easier to trace than that of other more peripatetic labourers. Parish registers do suggest that others also moved into and through the village, particularly in the 1580s and 1590s. Baptisms during these two decades include 10 surnames not previously encountered: these are all families who do not feature in manorial rentals, and who mostly left Highley again before their deaths. They were almost certainly the families of day labourers, moving from village to village in search of work. Some can indeed be traced in other nearby parishes before and after their stay in Highley.

It is no coincidence that this increased movement of labourers (which is considered more fully in chapter 3) came with the rapid inflation of the 1580s and 1590s. It was, of course, a widespread phenomenon, and one which late-sixteenth-century legislation attempted to regulate.[28] With wages lagging behind prices, the labourer's position became increasingly perilous. Enclosure had not yet begun in Highley, but was under way in several other parishes of the area. This must have contributed to the pool of landless wage-labourers on the market. The yeomen and substantial husbandmen of Highley, exploiting the buoyant market for surplus produce, were moving beyond peasant farming towards farming for profit, and consequently able to employ more wage labourers. The tradition of the live-in, unmarried 'servant in husbandry' was to continue well into the nineteenth century, but by the 1580s it existed side-by-side with the 'farm labourer', a family man who lived in a cottage not even necessarily near to the farmhouse.

These were undoubtedly the poorest families of the village: we have few details of their income in this period, and no wills from servants or farm labourers to give an idea of their standard of

---

[28] P. Corrigan and D. Sayer, *The Great Arch: English State Formation as Cultural Revolution* (Oxford, 1985), pp. 67–8.

living. What we do have, significantly, is a contemporary indication of who was regarded as 'poor' within the community. Several testators of this period left money to 'the poor of the parish of Highley'; but some three or four actually specify whom they regarded as deserving of charity. In several cases these were widows of cottagers or labourers, and their children. In two other instances, the beneficiaries were men from our list of 'new arrivals' of the period 1580–1600. The other men mentioned were cottagers or servants.

There is only one family about whom we can assemble enough information to use as an illustration of this class, and it is in some respects untypical. The Dales were servants who progressed to become cottagers: and in his will of 1636 Thurstan Dale could call himself a yeoman, though not with strict accuracy. Unlike many other families in this class, they lived in Highley throughout our present period.

In 1543 Richard Dale was taxed on 40s. He was almost certainly the father of Humfrey, who was servant to the vicar, Thomas Oseland. In the latter's will he was described as 'my old servant' – and a trusted one at that, for his master had lent him 40s, which was still owing at that time. Humfrey's son Thurstan followed him into the vicar's household. In 1579 Thurstan married Joan Bishoppe, whose father Humfrey had been taxed on 20s in 1543, and who was herself a servant of the vicar. The couple received bequests of household goods, including a bed, in their master's will. Oseland died in 1587, and we do not know what happened to the couple in the next three years.

However, in 1590 Humfrey Bishoppe died, and Thurstan and Joan came into possession of his 'tenement and two parcels of land' which in 1603 amounted to four and three-quarter acres at an annual rent of the 4s 8d. They were nevertheless still regarded as poor, for Thurstan was one of the 'poor neighbours' of a 1598 will. Only one child, a daughter, survived, and she and her husband appear to have shared the family home after their marriage in 1601. Thurstan supplemented their income by selling ale, and probably by day-labouring too. In fact it would seem that the family's improving fortunes in the seventeenth century were the result of brewing and, probably, inn-keeping rather than agriculture, for in his will Thurstan listed a brewing cauldron and 'treenen barrels'; and his grandson was certainly a 'victualler' 30 years later.

This will shows that Thurstan had during his long life achieved a relatively comfortable material standard. His house seems to have consisted of at least four rooms plus a kitchen, and was amply if plainly furnished. Farm stock included sheep, pigs and poultry.

For most servants and labourers, and even cottagers, such relative prosperity was unattainable. Thurstan Dale had only one child, assistance from his employer when starting married life, and a son-in-law who worked with him to build up family fortunes. Others without these advantages faced a difficult life and a destitute old age. Throughout the period, the inhabitants of Highley were aware of the problems of the poor of the community; problems which increased as the sixteenth century progressed, but which were largely left to individual philanthropy to alleviate.

Although Wrightson and Levine in their study of Terling found a greater diversity of wealth than we find in Highley (their first category, gentry and large farmers, is comprised entirely of men wealthier than any in Highley) the overall proportions of the four categories into which they divide the village population are strikingly similar.[29] Hoskins in his analysis of the 1524 Lay Subsidy for Wigston finds a picture even more similar to that in Highley, for there too was an absence of the dominating wealthy class present in the Essex village.[30]

We have examined the distribution of wealth in Highley, and its associated hierarchy, in considerable detail, both for its intrinsic importance to the social structure of the village, and because of its relative accessibility to modern research. We must not, however, assume that it overlaps completely with other possible hierarchies (notably of power and status) within the community. That the link between wealth and status was strong is generally accepted: Wrightson shows how, for contemporary writers, wealth was seen as 'an important determinant of social status'.[31]

While this is broadly true of Highley, there are nevertheless indications that status could depend not only on wealth: other possible factors include length of residence in the village; literacy; family reputation; personal character, and so on. These 'status

[29] K. Wrightson and D. Levine, *Poverty and Piety in an English Village: Terling, 1525–1700* (New York, San Francisco and London, 1979), p. 34.

[30] Hoskins, *The Midland Peasant*, pp. 142–4.

[31] K. Wrightson, *English Society 1580–1680* (London, 1982), p. 35.

hierarchies' are naturally difficult to assess: much of our evidence is inferential rather than direct, as contemporary records are rarely explicit about an indivdual's standing in the eyes of his fellows.

One possible indication is to be found in the names of witnesses to wills: it appears to have been the practice to use reliable neighbours who were not beneficiaries as witnesses. As well as the parish priest who almost invariably witnessed (and probably wrote) the wills, we find principal tenants like George Peirson or Oliver Harris appearing more frequently than others. However, another wealthy freeholder – the miller Thomas Lowe – was never called upon to witness a will. It is probably no coincidence that he was a persistent offender in the manor court, with an average of four or five indictments against him per court, far more than any other villager.

Wealthier men could very quickly be absorbed into the community: Nicholas Bradley began to witness wills in the same year that he arrived in Highley as a 'middling' leasehold tenant. By no means all witnesses were principal tenants, however. Humfrey Dale, servant, witnessed the will of Margery Oseland in 1566, and William Charnock, labourer and tailor, that of John Pountney in 1585. These men were both probably in the employ of the testator's family.

Witnesses of course represent the choice of an individual testator, who might have personal regard (or antipathy) not shared by the rest of the community at large. Some names occur so frequently, however, that these men may be assumed to have enjoyed considerable status within the community. They are often – but by no means always – the more prosperous.

Juries at the manor court were supposedly elected by all those attending, and therefore should represent a less personal choice than witnesses to wills. By no means all tenants were elected: throughout the 1570s, for example, only 16 different men were chosen as jurors. Although as in wills we find some correlation with personal prosperity, the regular jurors were not simply the largest farmers in the community. Three men were cottagers (one later described as 'poor') and one an artisan. There are notable omissions from the list, including not only Thomas Lowe the miller, whose absence is hardly surprising in view of his record in the courts, but at least three Group II farmers. Clearly some criterion other than wealth or size of farm was being applied, and it seems reasonable to suppose that, in view of the nature of the jurors' task, a reputation for personal integrity formed part of it.

The elected officers of the court – constables, affeerers and tithingmen – are not without interest, for while affeerers and tithingmen were always drawn from the ranks of jurors, constables usually were not. The latter post was traditionally a lowly and unpopular one, and here it is given to those who were not considered suitable as jurors, although in some cases their financial position was superior to that of several of the jurors.

The only other chosen representatives of whom we have any knowledge in this period are the churchwardens. Unfortunately the parish registers at this date hardly ever record churchwardens, and so we are left with only occasional mentions in diocesan records. From these it is apparent that low financial status was no bar, as at least one servant and two cottagers acted as church-warden.[32] For the years 1608–11, eight wardens are named in parish registers, and include four cottagers as well as two yeomen.

Furthermore it would seem that changes in status occurred more slowly than those in finances to which they were linked. In examining the distribution of wealth in Highley we have noted families rising and falling in the financial scale, and the possibilities for fluidity in the social structure of the community must not be overlooked. We have charted the decline in the fortunes of the Oseland family: yet Edward and George Oseland feature pro-minently in wills and court rolls long after this decline was under way. Just as there are indications that status could linger after wealth was largely gone, so with William Pountney we find that it could lag behind financial advancement. Pountney married in 1564; he came into possession of his father's lands in 1585 and his father-in-law's in 1588: yet he witnessed no will during our period, and only begins to appear in lists of jurors in the court rolls of the 1590s.

The one group of men which was excluded from participation in village administration was not the whole category of 'labourers and poorer craftsmen' of Wrightson's national picture, but a more narrowly-defined one of immigrant and peripatetic poor.[33] As we have seen, some relatively poor men could and did participate in village affairs: but they are without exception long-term residents,

[32] H.R.O. Archdeacon's Visitation, 1582.
[33] Wrightson, *English Society*, p. 36.

usually born in Highley of established local families. Wealthier men, like George Peirson and Nicholas Bradley, could rapidly establish themselves, but this was not the case with newly-arrived cottagers and labourers.

One factor which was important in determining the social structure of the village (and, as in Pountney's case, advancement within it) was marriage. Endogamous marriages did not to any significant extent cut across class divisions. Figure 1.1, which represents all marriages between native partners in the period 1551–1619, illustrates the web of marriage ties within the community. It shows how the half-dozen or so most prosperous families were all linked by marriage.

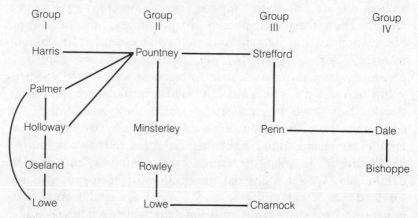

Figure 1.1   Endogamous marriages 1550–1620 (by socioeconomic groups)

Members of Groups III and IV largely married within these groups too, and are connected to the main 'marriage network' by gentle gradations. Thurstan Dale and Joan Bishoppe, who married in 1579, were both servants at that time; their daughter married into the Penn family, who were cottagers and inn-keepers. A Penn married a Strefford (blacksmiths) who were related by marriage to a less well-off branch of the Pountney family.

Inter-marriage between the principal tenant families of the village had been common at a period before the commencement of parish registers, for wills of the early years of this period indicate other alliances between, for instance, the families of Pountney and Holloway; Pountney and Dallowe; Holloway and Lowe and others among the generation marrying in the 1530s and 1540s.

The full range of kinship ties thus engendered, and the decline in endogamous marriage within some groups, will concern us later: here it is sufficient to note the absence of any real discrepancy between the financial positions of bride and groom in endogamous marriages. The divisions in society suggested by the distribution of wealth seem to have had empirical purchase at least in the area of marriage.

Thus it seems that while a division into economic groups is only one possible way of viewing the social structure of Highley in this pre-enclosure period, it is nevertheless a way which carried significance for the members of the community themselves. Yet it would be a gross over-simplification to assert that an individual's status within the community was invariably in direct proportion to his personal wealth.

Financial advancement was dependent on the acquisition of land – by marriage and inheritance as in the case of William Pountney, or by purchase in the later part of the period. Since yeoman and husbandman families tended to inter-marry, and were more able to amass cash profits, it is hardly surprising that the acquisition of land was largely confined to these groups. But by the late sixteenth century there was little or no marginal land left to be brought into cultivation, and most holdings were on long leases or by copyhold for three lives. In general if advancement was sought it had to be sought elsewhere. Downward social mobility also occurred, of course. This could easily be brought about by the premature death of the head of the household; though its effects seem to have been felt most at husbandman and cottager level. Those sons who did not enter the family holding could find themselves cottagers rather than yeomen, as Edward Oseland did. Families living on the margins of self-sufficiency on smallholdings were naturally most vulnerable to the harsh economic climate of the last years of the sixteenth century, as they would be to the enclosure of common land in the seventeenth.

Such movement as did take place seems to have been between our socioeconomic groups I and II on the one hand, and III and IV on the other. This would appear to bear out Wrightson's contention that, although social stratification was well-defined, the gaps between groups were not uniform.[34] In Highley the most discernible gulf was between those who could live from their land,

---

[34] K. Wrightson, 'The social order of early modern England', in L. Bonfield, R. Smith and K. Wrightson (eds), *The World We Have Gained* (Oxford, 1986).

with a little over for profit (by whatever tenure that land was held, and whether the individuals thought of themselves as yeomen or husbandmen); and those for whom husbandry was of necessity combined with some other activity.

A total of 23 wills made by inhabitants of Highley between 1544 and 1620 survives. Only four of these were proved in the Prerogative Court of Canterbury: the remainder were proved in local diocesan courts. Unfortunately almost no probate inventories survive for Hereford diocese from before 1660. Only one remains for Highley, and that a rather uninformative inventory of 1560. However, the wills themselves are a very valuable source for any examination of the community during this period. Our immediate concern is with wills as economic indicators, but they also supply information about family life and social contacts in a way that no other single sixteenth-century source can.

Virtually all wills of this period were made by individuals in our first two socioeconomic categories, yeomen and husbandmen. Only one will belongs to an artisan/smallholder – that of Richard Charnock made in 1569. Indeed, among men in Groups I and II will-making was so prevalent that a list of adult male burials from the parish register with no associated will becomes instructive: certain families, like Bishoppe, Dallow, Nashe, Nicholls and Clare, are revealed as consistently below will-making class, which corresponds with information from other sources about the financial status of these families. Five of the extant wills were made by women, in all cases the widows of men of yeoman or substantial husbandman status.

In all, almost a third of adult males buried in Highley during the period (as well as the widows of some of them) left wills, a much higher percentage than is found in succeeding periods. Although there are, therefore, enough wills to enable us to draw a picture of some aspects of life for almost half the population of the village, the class-bias of the data must be constantly remembered.

In general, these wills display the preoccupations of a peasant economy. Property is rarely bequeathed, and although cash bequests are made in 15 of the 23 wills, they usually represent a minor part of the bequests, especially in the first half of the period. Crops and farm animals are mentioned, though perhaps with less frequency than one might expect. The majority of the bequests involve household items – furniture, clothing, utensils – that were at the disposal of the testator. In one respect, however, a cash economy based on farming for profit rather than subsistence does seem to have been evolving, for several of the debts due to testators represent payments outstanding for goods or services provided.

Before 1580, cash bequests in wills form a minor part of the provisions made: only seven testators (out of 14) left specific sums of money; and in all cases but one these are very small sums. Furthermore in two cases the option is left that the legacy be paid 'in money or money worth'; and three other wills mention money only once each. This makes it very difficult to assess an individual's wealth from his will, as totalling the trivial sums bequeathed would mean little.

Probate acts recorded in the consistory court at Hereford sometimes give totals of the estate of the deceased. There are eleven such totals for inhabitants of Highley in surviving Act Books for the period. In view of the sums mentioned in debts – and even in bequests – these seem suspiciously low. The most valuable estate, at £41 15s 6d, was that of Richard Lowe who died in 1579. Next is a group, including other members of the prosperous Lowe family as well as John Oseland of the demesne farm, all valued at around £20. Then there is a gap to the third group of the less well-off (such as Thurstan Pountney the blacksmith) with estates of about two pounds.

However, these probate acts all date from before 1582, and there is evidence of an increasing amount of cash in circulation in the village in the second half of our period, from 1580–1620. Sums of money are more frequently mentioned, though still side-by-side with items of clothing and small personal effects; and the sums are larger. Skipp cites a six-fold increase in numbers of wills specifying debts due to the testator in Warwickshire villages of the sixteenth century as evidence of increased peasant wealth during the period.[35] Table 1.2 shows a similar increase in Highley in debts both due to and owed by testators.

In all, over half the Highley wills list sums of money due to the testator from creditors, usually local people and often members of his family. These lists are both more frequent and more extensive (and the sums of money larger) in the second half of the period. In some cases the reason for the debt is specified: Thomas Lowe the

[35] Skipp, 'Economic and social change in the Forest of Arden'.

Table 1.2 Debts in wills, 1544–1620

	1544–80	1581–1620
Wills with cash bequests	7	9
Wills with debts due	6	7
Wills with debts owing	5	4
Total of wills	14	9

miller was owed 5s 8d 'for malte' in 1580; and in 1603 Anne Palmer's brother owed her £5 13s 4d 'for two kine'.

Where the origin of the debt is not specified, it can sometimes be deduced. One of the longest lists of debts for the pre-1580 period is that in the will of Thomas Low, 1565, who lists 18 creditors and a total of £15 10s outstanding. Low describes himself as a 'waterman', and we may assume that these debts represent payments for carriage of goods on the Severn. They must also have constituted the great majority of Low's capital, for the total bequests in his will are 10 pounds to his two daughers, four pounds to his two sons, and 'an old heiffer'.

Another long list of creditors is the total of 29 in the will of Thomas Holloway made in 1558. Holloway was owed money for, among many unspecified causes, a gelding and a mare, and for 'a quarter of beef' as well as twice 'for meate'. Apparently he combined horse-dealing and butchery with his farming activities. John Pountney in 1585 was careful also to list goods paid for but not received: 'I paid for seven trees to the old John Foxall . . . but I have as yet one a way and six trees do yet remain.'

Some of the debts do represent straightforward cash loans rather than outstanding payments. The same John Pountney records a debt due from Sir John Littleton of five pounds 'which I paid to his man to his use'. Towards the end of the period there are mentions of more formal debts 'as I have specialty to show' – careful business transactions, like that between John Holloway (1611 will) and George Pountney, 'who oweth me at this instant £44 by bond of four score for payment thereof'. But for most of the period, loans were small and apparently informal. Some were essentially charitable in origin, like the £15 6s 4d due to the vicar Thomas Oseland from 16 people, many of whom were poor villagers owing a few shillings each.

Probably both loans and outstanding payments are involved in longer lists like that of Thurstan Holloway, a yeoman who died in 1588. He records 26 debts due, with a total of over £71. Similarly, Richard Palmer in 1597 was owed £60 5s. Since Holloway and Palmer paid annual rents of 32s 4d and 13s 4d respectively, these sums can be seen in some sort of perspective. Whether or not they represent cash gains from the sale of surplus produce, they show the extent to which cash could be amassed by the successful farmer.

Lists of sums owed by the testator are usually less extensive. Only a third of testators list debts they owed, and these are usually of quite small sums. Some individuals, of course, could have been more scrupulous than others about what constituted a debt: probably Thomas Pountney was unusually careful when in his will of 1544 he recorded debts to several in-laws and even to his wife. However, in general the yeoman and substantial husbandman of Highley was more likely to be owed money than to owe it. By the end of the sixteenth century he was part of a cash economy, with quite considerable sums of money changing hands in return for goods or services, or in the form of loans. Several men were at specific times owed sums that would pay the rent of their farms for 50 years or more. It was the presence of this kind of ready money in the village economy that made possible the buying of freeholds, enclosing of land and rebuilding of farmhouses that characterized Jacobean Highley.

However for most of this period cash was only one concern of the yeomen and husbandmen of the village. It is only at the very end of the period that we find mention of leases of property. Prior to this, the major preoccupation of testators was with the disposal of furniture and household goods, often including what would seem to modern eyes to be very trivial items. Even Thurstan Holloway, the wealthy yeoman with £71 owed to him, specified the destination of, among much else, his 'two meatcloths'. It is this concern with the smallest domestic items, and with articles of clothing, which above all else distinguishes the sixteenth-century will from its later counterparts.

Not only does this reveal much about the economy in which men had grown up, and whose terms of reference they still used; it is also a useful substitute for the missing inventories of the period. From the household items mentioned in wills we can deduce much about the standard of living in the more prosperous homes of Highley. Although we lack the completeness offered by inventories, this is in part compensated for by our ability to discern what the testator himself regarded as being his most important possessions. Thus we find itemized in sixteenth-century wills utensils which by the later seventeenth century had become sufficiently commonplace to be subsumed under a general description. Everitt has shown how even the labouring population increased the proportion of their wealth which was invested in household goods during the second half of the sixteenth century.[36] For the yeomen and husbandmen of Highley, household goods were the outward sign of their prosperity: although household goods were still strictly utilitarian (there are no purely luxury items), it seems to have been a matter of pride to have more of them, and to use superior materials.

Certain items of furniture are regularly mentioned in wills, and none more frequently than beds and bedding. A careful distinction is made between feather and flock beds, and between flaxen and hempen sheets. Margery Oseland (1566) possessed at least four feather beds, several 'bolsters and canvasses', and flaxen sheets. At the other end of the social scale (for will-making) Richard Charnock (1569) lists only three hempen sheets. Several references are made to a bed 'with its appurtenances'. According to the will of Thomas Oseland in 1577, usual 'appurtenances' comprised 'a bolster, canvas, blanket, pair of sheets and a green bed hillinge', or coverlet.

Storage seems to have been the second concern in furnishing. The typical family in this will-making group possessed three 'coffers', the most usual furniture for storing clothes and linen. Even the relatively poor Richard Charnock had three coffers, a cupboard and a press. Tables are rarely mentioned and chairs never. Neither, more surprisingly, are stools or forms. It is tempting to see in this the reflection of a life-style in which there

[36] A. M. Everitt, 'Farm labourers', in Thirsk, *Agrarian History*, pp. 396-454.

was little leisure time, and where the majority of time spent indoors was for sleeping. However, some seating must have been provided, and there may well be other reasons why it does not figure as prominently as bedding in wills. Wrightson and Levine find no mention of joined (i.e. professionally made) furniture before 1600 in the wills of Terling in prosperous Essex.[37] Similarly in Highley, all furniture listed seems to have been capable of rough and easy construction.

Utensils for cooking and eating are itemized with surprising frequency and minuteness. Thirteen of the 23 wills of this period mention utensils, ranging from quite large and valuable cauldrons to small basins. The lists are so detailed, and repetition from list to list so common, that we can arrive at an accurate picture of the utensils owned by the average yeoman/husbandman family of the sixteenth century. There would be two or three brass pots and two or three brass pans; some pewter dishes and some wooden ones; a cauldron for cooking; several small brass dishes and basins; and probably some candlesticks – the latter implying the use, at least occasionally, of expensive wax candles rather than the rushlights of the poor.

There are few signs of any other luxuries, however, such as appear in the later seventeenth century, even in the wealthiest households – no carpets, cushions, timepieces; and only the vicar mentioned books. It appears that what money was spent on the home went on providing comfortable bedding and eating. Some of the increased cash in the village economy must have been spent on improvements to the standard of home comforts. Hoskins finds that 'the material standard of living [in Wigston] . . . doubled between the middle of the sixteenth century and the end.'[38] There is no evidence in the wills of Highley for this kind of spectacular improvement. The pewter vessels and feather beds that elsewhere mark a rise in the standard of living towards the end of the sixteenth century are already found in Highley, at least among the better-off, by mid century. If anything, it was quantity (which we have no satisfactory way of measuring in the absence of inventories) rather than quality of household goods which improved; and we have to wait for the seventeenth century for any appreciable change in material standards.

[37] Wrightson and Levine, *Poverty and Piety*, p. 38.
[38] Hoskins, *The Midland Peasant*, p. 296.

The third concern of testators was with clothing. The usual practice was to specify the 'best' coat or gown, the other or others being presumably not worth bequeathing; although occasionally a 'second' best garment is listed. The men who mention clothes describe between them what was probably a complete wardrobe for a sixteenth-century farmer, with the exception of shoes or boots: a coat, or perhaps two; a doublet (on one occasion also 'my letherne dublett'); hose; a cloak and a hat. Women's clothing is less often mentioned, but consisted at least of a couple of gowns, petticoats, aprons, kerchiefs and, in one case, a 'reband of silke'. Curiously, no female outdoor clothes are listed. The very appearance of articles of clothing in wills, right down to hose and kerchiefs, is indicative of their relative value. After 1600, clothes ceased to be mentioned separately in Highley wills, although their collective value was estimated by appraisors for inventories.

The only surviving sixteenth-century inventory for Highley is that of the goods of Margery Pountney, taken in 1560. This is a short and uninformative document compared to the detailed inventories of the seventeenth and eighteenth centuries, but is nevertheless interesting. Margery was a widow, and apparently had been left half of her husband's possessions (a common practice), for each item in the short list is prefaced by the words 'half of' – her brass, pewter, etc. Clothes were estimated as being worth 8s out of a total of £7 2s 8d. The percentage devoted to household goods, valued at 24s or 16 per cent of the total, corresponds with the 10–15 per cent which Hoskins found to be the norm in Wigston at the same period.[39] These household categories are bedding at 10 shillings, brass and pewter (6s 8d), vessels (3s 4d) and 'half of one loom' (4s). The rest is made up of farm stock, and represents one of our few guides to the values of farm animals in Highley at this period.

The stock of Margery Pountney's farm in 1560 consisted of five cows, two 'year-old beasts', one heifer, three weaned calves, four oxen, and an unspecified number of pigs. No sheep or poultry are mentioned. Easily the most valuable item, at £3, is 'half of four oxen'. This, the minimum size of a plough-team, indicates that some arable as well as dairy farming must have been pursued on the holding, in spite of the lack of any grain crops in the inventory. Possibly the estimated values in this inventory are too low, for

[39] *Ibid.*, p. 295.

although the price of cattle more than doubled between 1560 and the end of the century, Margery Pountney's cows at the former date were valued at 12s 8d each, while in 1603 Anne Palmer was owed £2 16s 8d for each cow. However suspect the values, though, this is the only complete account which has come down to us of the range of stock on one of the farms of the manor.

Otherwise wills provide only a known minimum. Eight wills in fact mention farm stock, and although none can be regarded as a complete list they do indicate that a mixed husbandry using cattle, sheep and pigs was practised. Heriots paid to the lord of the manor during the second half of the century show that usually a farmer's most valuable beast was an ox, and that although some cooperation between neighbours may have been necessary to muster a full plough-team, most farmers were engaged to a greater or lesser extent in arable farming.

These heriots, and items in wills like the 'old heifer' belonging to Thomas Low, waterman, support the view that even those primarily engaged in a craft or trade also kept some animals and cultivated some land. There is also support for Everitt's finding that the staple of the labourer's or smallholder's stock-farming was the cow, and not the pig as it was to be in the nineteenth century.[40]

Only two wills mention crops or produce. In 1558 Richard Pountney left 20 strike of rye to his wife, and in 1585 John Pountney was owed 10 strike of barley and one of oats, three hops of wheat, a stone of tallow and a stone of wool, which may represent purchases rather than produce, for his farm consisted almost entirely of pasture land, with less than two acres of arable. If this is the case, it marks another departure from subsistence farming for family consumption, even if an exchange in kind rather than a cash transaction is indicated.

The end of the sixteenth century marks a change in the tone and type of wills. Although there would still be the occasional testator who bequeathed brass basins and towels, increasingly provisions were for sums of money and leases of property. The three wills of the period 1605–20 illustrate this change: none of them mentions personal or household possessions at all, for they are exclusively concerned with cash bequests and, in one case, with a farm lease for 1,000 years recently purchased by the testator. The farmers of Highley were moving away from a true peasant economy, where

[40] Everitt, 'Farm labourers', p. 414.

household goods were the most important items at their disposal. Succession to a farm could no longer be left to the manor court to ratify, but became the responsibility of the freeholder or fixed-term leaseholder. Increasing amounts of cash in the village economy meant a corresponding rise in the number of wills dealing exclusively in bequests of money.

We must not lose sight of the fact that such guidance as wills can provide to economic conditions within the community applies only to its more prosperous members. It is doubtful if there was much brass or pewter in the homes of poorer artisans and cottagers, or many feather beds – or that the head of the household was involved in cash transactions where large sums of money changed hands. We can say, however, that quite a large proportion of the population – up to 40 per cent – lived in relative comfort. While minor gradations in the type and range of possessions between Group I and II households may be discerned – and were doubtless more readily visible to contemporaries – there seems no very great difference in life-style between the more and less prosperous farmers in this will-making group. The difference is one of the quantity of possessions, rather than their quality.

The major economic division in Highley would seem to have been not, as in some contemporary communities of the area, between one or two families of dominant wealth and position and the rest; but between those holding a farm of 30 acres or so (and thus above subsistence level), making wills, and forming between a third and a half of the village population, and the less historically visible group struggling to support themselves from a combination of farming and labouring activities.

The rural economy that underpinned society and the distribution of wealth within it form a necessary background to the examination of other forces within the community. The beginnings of the polarization of wealth that accelerated with enclosure can be seen in the 1580s and 1590s. Although we have called this the 'pre-enclosure period' in order to contrast life-styles under two different economic systems, we should not make the mistake of viewing the years 1550–1620 as static in themselves. The final era of Highley's ancient common-field system of agriculture was in itself a period of change: and it is not too much to argue that without that change, enclosure could not have come about when it did. In fact in many ways certain developments of the late sixteenth century – the increase in numbers of peripatetic landless labourers and the growth of a cash economy which enabled tenants to buy their holdings – may be seen as part of a cumulative and protracted procedure which we can for convenience subsume under the term 'enclosure'.

2

Life and Death

In this short early period it is not possible to apply precise statistical measures to data derived from the parish registers: total population was small, the time span under consideration relatively short, and the quality of registration in its early years open to question. Nevertheless, it is useful to determine as far as possible – even if rather impressionistically – the basic demographic patterns in the community.

In the absence of 1563 ecclesiastical census returns for the diocese, there is no very exact indication of the total population of Highley in the sixteenth century. The 1543 Lay Subsidy Return, by far the fullest of the century, names 27 men.[1] A list of tenants of the manor in 1578 names 28 individuals, and rentals of 1601 and 1603 produce a similar total.[2] None of these sources, however, can be regarded as providing a complete list of householders: on the one hand they exclude some, such as the parish priest and at least two men who did not hold land of the lord of the manor; while on the other hand some individuals, like the two young men in 1543 who were not yet householders, should properly be excluded.

Nevertheless, we can arrive at a rough estimate of total population based on a figure of 27 households. If we adopt the mean household size of 4.75 suggested by Laslett, this gives a population of 128.[3] A lower mean size of 4.3 has also been suggested for places other than London,[4] giving a population of 116. The actual total, allowing for some omissions in the listings particularly in the later years of the period, probably varied

[1] P.R.O. E 179 166/159: Lay Subsidy Roll, 35 Hen VIII.

[2] B.R.L. Hagley Hall MSS 377991 and 357347; P.R.O. LR 2/185.

[3] P. Laslett and R. Wall (eds), *Household and Family in Past Time* (Cambridge, 1972), pp. 132–4.

[4] T. Arkell, 'Multiplying factors for estimating total populations from the Hearth Tax', *Local Population Studies* 28 (1982), p. 53.

between 120 and 150, but in the absence of more illuminating information this must remain a 'best guess'.

The village population during this pre-enclosure period seems to have remained fairly constant, growing only with the addition of increased numbers of peripatetic labourers in the later years, and with considerable emigration to off-set natural growth.

For natural growth was the overall trend in the community. Figure 2.1 shows baptisms and burials in five-year moving totals, and demonstrates how for most of the period the former outnumbered the latter. This was not the case, however, in the early years: it was not until the mid 1560s that baptisms regularly outstripped burials. Real growth would appear to have begun in the 1560s after a period of stagnation or even decline. The absence of pre-1550 parish registers prevents us from ascertaining the length of this period, and the possible defects in registration in its early years mean that conclusions about this decade must be cautious. But Dyer's study of Worcester and certain Worcestershire parishes does show a similar pattern in this neighbouring county, in which he demonstrates a mid-century 'crisis' which reached a peak in the later 1550s, and only really passed around 1570.[5]

The situation in Highley at this period seems in considerable measure due to an increase in burials, which reached a peak in the late 1550s not reached again until after 1600. There is no evidence, however, of the sudden and disastrous epidemics noted elsewhere at this time: rather there was a steady rise in deaths of the more vulnerable in the community – the elderly (as shown by wills) and the very young.

Baptisms, too, were fewer in number than they would ever be again. This may in part be attributed to under-registration in the earliest years of the registers: nevertheless, baptisms in the later 1550s were as low as 50 per cent of burials.

After the mid 1560s, growth was sustained until the late 1590s. Baptisms were regularly 150 per cent of burials, and in the early 1590s exceptionally low burial totals gave rise to a brief period where births outnumbered deaths by 4 to 1. In the later 1590s – a period of poor harvests and high inflation – burials increased again, though without reaching their 1550s level, and baptisms decreased until for a few years rough parity prevailed. After 1600, although deaths continued to increase, they did so at a less marked rate than

[5] A. Dyer, *The City of Worcester in the Sixteenth Century* (Leicester, 1973), pp. 44–7.

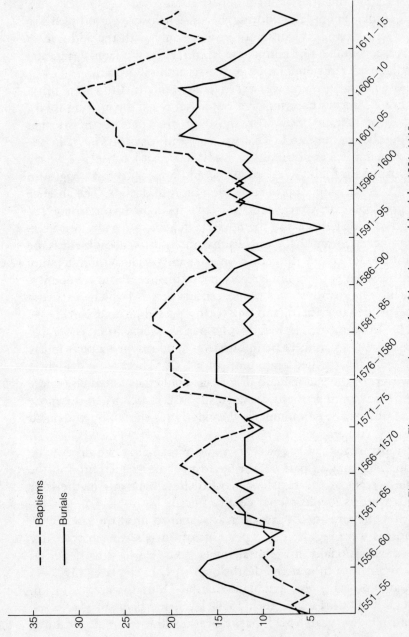

Figure 2.1 Five-year moving totals of baptisms and burials, 1551–1619

did births, and at the end of our period gowth was once more considerable.

The small population of the village in this period means that not too much reliance can be placed on short-term fluctuations. However, the overall pattern of demographic trends in Highley, as indicated by crude aggregative figures, does mirror that found in many English communities.[6] We can, however, look a little more closely at the demographic realities behind these trends by examining individual experience.

We cannot of course compute age at death for those born before the beginning of the parish registers in 1551, some of whom might indeed have lived throughout this period. We must look elsewhere for any information on adult mortality. Wills of the period give the overall impression of testators of fairly advanced years: half of the testators mention married children, and nearly half mention grandchildren. In one case at least, even the grandchildren were themselves married. Age at death can be ascertained or closely estimated in 30 per cent of these wills, and gives an approximate average of 58 years.

A synthesis of information from wills with that from parish registers is even more revealing. In only 1 case of 23 were the parents of a testator still alive. In only 4 cases were there apparently children under 16 left orphaned – and in all instances one parent still remained. Several testators mention children who were themselves middle-aged: Margery Oseland who died in 1566 left a son of 52; Margery Holloway died in 1564, when her granddaughter had already been married for 10 years. These are not isolated instances: 7 of the 23 testators are known to have had children aged over 40 at the time of their death, and are unlikely themselves to have been much less than 70. In fact, only 6 can reasonably be estimated to be under 50 years old: one of them we know to have been 36, almost certainly the youngest.

Although there is a natural bias in wills towards the better-off, and towards those who did not die suddenly, enough wills survive for this period to suggest that, having reached adulthood, it was usual to survive into one's fifties, and that an age at death in the late seventies was by no means rare. A couple having children could

[6] E. A. Wrigley, *An Introduction to English Historical Demography from the Sixteenth to the Nineteenth Century* (London, 1966).

reasonably expect to see those children to maturity, and indeed to live to see grandchildren.

Table 2.1 Juvenile mortality rates 1551–1619

	% of those baptised buried as infants	% of those baptised buried as children	infants as % all burials	children as % all burials
1551–84	7.9	4.5	9.0	5.1
1585–1619	11.4	6.8	17.2	11.5

By no means everyone, however, did survive to adulthood. Table 2.1 details juvenile mortality, making a distinction between infants of less than one year, and children aged 1 to 15. Mortality is also shown in two ways: the percentage of those baptised who actually died in infancy or childhood is shown; and also; since some children born in the parish almost certainly left before reaching the age of 16, juvenile burials are shown as a proportion of all burials to try to offset the effects of emigration on mortality rates. In general, the first year of life was the most dangerous one, for deaths in the first year regularly outnumber those in the next 15. Although levels of juvenile mortality seem to have been somewhat higher in the second half of the period, at no time can they be regarded as high by the standards of the sixteenth century.

Child mortality, in particular, would appear to have been lower in Highley at this period than the norm. It is difficult to arrive at any assessment of national figures, of course, but the findings of Wrigley and Schofield for the period 1550–1649 suggest that mortality even for those aged 1–10 was more likely to be nearer to 25 per cent of all baptisms.[7] The moderate levels of juvenile mortality found in Highley mean that only a minority of families lost more than one child, and in many cases all children baptised survived to maturity. We certainly do not, after 1560, encounter a situation where parents routinely anticipated the loss of several children.

We can only guess at the causes of death, both among children and among adults. The relatively low levels of child mortality

[7] R. Schofield and E. A. Wrigley, 'Infant and child mortality in England in the late Tudor and early Stuart period', in *Health, Medicine and Mortality in the Sixteenth Century*, ed C. Webster (Cambridge, 1979), pp. 61–95.

suggest a reasonable standard of health and nutrition in the community. Child deaths were presumably the result largely of infectious rather than degenerative diseases, and the children of Highley seem quite well-equipped to overcome them, after the first few dangerous months of life. We have even less idea of the causes of adult death. The usual preamble to wills – 'being sick and weak in body but of perfect mind and remembrance' – is not much help. However, several such wills were made years before death, suggesting either a temporary illness from which a recovery was made, or a long-term degeneration. Accidents occasionally proved fatal. In 1598 Thomas Palmer was 'slaine with his plowe'; and in 1607 a boat returning from Bewdley Fair on St. Andrew's Eve (29th November) sank and at least two people were drowned in the Severn.

It is similarly possible to make only a very tentative estimate of the death rate in Highley during this period, because our knowledge of the total population is imperfect. If we assume it to have been 125 for most of the period, we find a death rate overall of 20 per 1,000 per annum. Wrigley and Schofield suggest a national norm of about 25 per 1,000 for the pre–1640 period.[8] The potential for growth in sixteenth-century Highley, then, with only moderate levels of juvenile mortality, with what appears to be a somewhat lower than average death rate, and with a good chance of those beginning a family surviving to complete it, was considerable.

Yet the birth rate in pre-enclosure Highley was not particularly high. With the same caveat that applies to the death rate, we can postulate an annual birth rate for the period of about 27 per 1,000. This is on the lower limits suggested by Wrigley and Schofield of 28 to 40 per 1,000.[9] If the total population was in fact less than 125, the birth and death rates would naturally be somewhat higher. But these low rates also suggest that Highley's population is unlikely to have been significantly larger than our estimate, unless there was considerable and consistent under-registration of vital events throughout the period.

An important factor governing marital fertility is the age at marriage of couples in the community. Unfortunately, we are only occasionally able to determine with exactitude the age of marriage

---

[8] E. A. Wrigley and R. Schofield, *The Population History of England, 1541–1841* (Cambridge, 1982), pp. 182–3.
[9] *Ibid.*, p. 174.

partners, many of whom in this period were born before the commencement of registration. All examples thereafter come from the second half of the period, and the group of brides is only 12 (at a mean age at first marriage of 25.8 years), and of grooms even less – too few to do more than lend tentative support to the supposition that age at marriage was in the mid to late twenties.

Where duration of marriage can be assessed, we find a mean duration of 35 years. This is a minimum figure, as in some cases (about 30 per cent) the marriage date itself is not known and the duration of the marriage has been reckoned from the baptism of the first child to the death of the first partner to die. Some marriages lasted over 50 years – one as long as 58 years.

This is a surprisingly long average duration. It supports the impression of relative longevity in Tudor Highley, at least among the settled population, and has several effects. Few marriages were broken by death during potentially fertile years, thus removing one possible check on marital fertility. In fact the mean fertility span for the period, that is the interval between first and last births in the family, was 12 years 10 months. Thus couples were likely, on average, to live together for 20–25 years after the birth of their last child: long enough, as we have seen, to see all children to adulthood. This had an effect on inheritance practices and on migration: children could not expect to come into any inheritance much before they were 30, and many sons, presumably recognising this, left the village in early manhood; set themselves up elsewhere via apprenticeships or with parental help; and never permanently returned.

There is little evidence of marriage specifically delayed until the death of a parent brought inheritance of a farm. Twenty-six marriages of Highley men were examined with this in mind. In 10 cases, the information was not possible to determine. Of the remaining 16, only in 3 cases was the father already dead when the son married; and in none of these is there a direct causal relationship discernible – in one instance the father had been dead for 25 years. In the 13 cases where the father was still alive at the son's marriage, the mean number of years which would elapse before the father eventually did die was 16.4 years. Thus it seems to have been acknowledged that awaiting paternal death, and thus inheritance, before marriage was not a practical proposition. A man was likely to have adult children of his own before his father died.

The view that inheritance expectations militated against early marriage would appear not to hold good for pre-enclosure Highley. This does not of course mean that marriage necessarily was early – such evidence as there is suggests that it was relatively late. What it does suggest is some measure of dual tenancy, with father and married son both supporting families from the same holding. Hilton suggests that this family structure was characteristic of western European peasant societies from the thirteenth century.[10]

When marriages were eventually broken by death, it was the wife who was more likely to survive. Thirty-five marriages of this period yielded suitable information, and in 20 of them it was the husband who died first. Remarriage was, on the whole, not common. Only four marriages taking place at Highley itself seem to have been second marriages for one or both parties – two between widow and widower, and two between widower and spinster.

Although instances of remarriage are few, it does appear that Highley men were more likely to marry a second time than were women. The mean time elapsed between bereavement and re-marriage for men was two and a half years. None of the 20 widows of the sample remarried, though three left the village and may have married elsewhere – less than probable in the case of Ann Nichols who was over 70 when she left. The average length of widowhood, without remarriage, was 13.2 years for women and 7.6 years for men.

Widows, then, did not feel compelled to marry for a second time. Either their social and economic position remained quite satisfactory as widows; or men felt no pressure to marry widows for economic reasons. The careful provision for widows made in wills appears to support the former view. Neither do the terms of wills show any disapproval of, or obstacles to, a widow's remarriage. Thomas Palmer (died 1605) is explicit: 'My will is that Isobel my wife shall hold and enjoy my house and living during the term of her natural life . . . And if my said wife do happen to marry again then my will is that she shall pay to my three daughters . . . five pounds apiece towards their preferment.' In addition, Isobel received all her husband's goods and chattels.

That widows of landholders took a keen and knowledgeable interest in their holdings is shown by their own wills and by court

[10] R. J. Hilton, *Bondmen Made Free* (London, 1973), p. 27.

rolls. They certainly appear to have been more than nominal heads of household, a situation recognized by the very terms of tenure, which was commonly for the lives of a man, his wife, and son – or occasionally daughter. This applies to the widows of cottagers as well as of yeomen and husbandmen. It is interesting that when Ann Nichols referred to above sold her cottage in 1609, the court roll states that Ann Nichols and her son John transferred their right and title . . . whence falls to the lord one cupboard and one table being the best of her goods. Ann had been widowed for 12 years, and her son John was a married man of 49: yet the goods are her goods. In the view of the court, she was the head of the household, and responsible for selling the cottage without permission.

The circumstances of landless widows were presumably less favourable. Two wills of the late 1590s list among 'poor neighbours' the same three widows, one of whom was Ann Nichols. The other two were probably in even poorer circumstances, as must have been the widows of peripatetic labouring men. A majority of village widows, however, continued to exercise a real measure of influence over the family holding, whatever its size.

It was rare for a marriage to be broken early by death in childbirth: only one female death in the whole period can be directly linked to a baptism, which is a remarkably low figure. In our sample group of 35 marriages, only two appear to have been ended by the death of a partner during productive years, leaving two widowers, one with one child and the other with none. (Both remarried, after intervals of four and three years respectively, and had children by their second wives).

Death, then, rarely acted as a brake on marital fertility in the pre-enclosure period. In fact the mean completed family size in this period was 5.7 children, or 5.2 if we include the two childless marriages. Given an average marriage duration of 35 years, this is not a high figure, though it is within the parameters established by large-scale studies.[11]

Late marriage may well have been a factor in limiting family size – though in some cases this seems unlikely to be the only explanation for a relatively short fertility span. One couple, for example, was married for 55 years, yet produced children only

[11] Wrigley and Schofield, 'English population history from family reconstitution: summary results 1600–1799', *Population Studies* 37 (1983), p. 176.

during the first 14 years; another couple had children for only three and a half years of a 40-year marriage. Conversely, in some cases fertility spans are so long that the women must have been very young when marriage took place: Alice Harris for instance gave birth to her last child 28 years after the first.

In general, though, fertility was concentrated into the early years of marriage. In 16 completed families where exact date of marriage is known, two-thirds of children were born within the first 10 years; and 7 of the couples had ceased to have children by this time. Others continued to produce children at ever-shorter intervals. William and Anne Pountney had 7 children in the first 20 years of marriage – and another 5 after that.

Those who had more children were generally those with larger land holdings. If opportunities for wage labour were limited in this pre-enclosure society – partly limited indeed by the very size of families of larger farmers – the smallholder whose children were more likely to become a strain on limited resources than valuable contributors to family income had a greater incentive to limit their family. The average number of children per family among small tenants and cottagers was below five, while for freeholders and the wealthiest tenants it was more than eight. The largest families were those of Oliver Harris, freehold tenant of Woodend, and William Pountney of Green Hall, both of whom had 12 children. Other large families, of 8 to 10 children, were those of Peirson, Palmer, Holloway and Henry Pountney – all yeomen. Families of two to five children, on the other hand, belonged to those like the Dales, Streffords and Charnocks who were cottagers and artisans.

There is some evidence that breast-feeding may have been used to prolong post-natal amenorrhoea, and thus act as a contraceptive measure. Certainly birth intervals were shorter following the death of an infant in the first few weeks of life.

Only one case of wet-nursing is mentioned during the period. The burial is recorded in December 1599 of 'Katherine daugher of Edward Bridgeman, a child whom Bennett Dallow nursed'. Bennett Dallow's own child had been buried in March of that year, shortly after baptism. The practice may, of course, have been more widespread than surviving records indicate.

Illegitimacy remained low throughout the period. Only five illegitimate baptisms are recorded, three of those after 1610 – which represents a ratio of 2.2 per cent. However, where the interval between marriage and baptism of the first child can be determined, we find a high incidence of bridal pregnancy. Over half of these brides were pregnant at the time of their marriage. Pre-marital sexual activity seems to have been quite usual at all levels of village society, for these pregnant brides came from (and married into) the families of yeomen as well as their poorer neighbours. Richard Palmer of Potters married Elizabeth Lowe in June 1577: their first child was baptised a scant three months later. Several of these protogenesic intervals are of the order of two or three months, so these pregnancies were hardly the result of betrothal/marriage procedures taking a few weeks all told. Marriage, however, did usually follow conception; and the high levels of bridal pregnancy together with low illegitimacy rates argue for community mores where sexual licence could anticipate, but not be independent of, marriage.

The evidence for this early period does not allow a detailed examination of household size and structure in the community. All it does indicate is that the households of the wealthier families must have been considerably larger than those of smallholders and labourers. Yeomen and better-off husbandmen had more children; they were perhaps more likely to be able to keep those children at home in adolescence; and they were the families who kept resident servants.

To gain some idea of the realities of life and death in the period, we can look in detail at the experience of three families. Oliver Harris was a well-off freehold tenant of the manor. He married his wife Alice – not at Highley – sometime before May 1568 when their first child was baptised. The couple baptised 12 children in all, 7 boys and 5 girls, between 1568 and 1595. All of these children survived infancy. Oliver died in 1626 and Alice in 1627/8: both must have been approaching 80 years old. Six of their seven sons were also buried at Highley; two died in their thirties, at 36 and 31; one at 54, and the remaining three in their early sixties. Only one of the daughters remained in the parish after marriage, and was buried there at the age of 70.

Thomas Rowley, as we saw in the previous chapter, was less wealthy. He and his wife Elizabeth married in 1562. Their ages at the time, of course, are not known, but they survived to 1615 and 1619 respectively and so must have lived somewhere near 80 years. They had seven children between 1563 and 1574, and then ceased child-bearing presumably well before Elizabeth's biological clock had run down. One child died in infancy and was followed by another at a shorter-than-usual interval. The two surviving boys were both eventually buried at Highley, one age 76 and the other 81. Two of the daughters married, both in their early thirties, and left the village; nothing more is known of the other two.

The family of Thurstan Dale has also been discussed. He and his wife were both servants when they married in 1579, and both had probably been born before 1551. They had only two children, one of whom died in infancy. Their surviving daughter married at the unusually early age of 19 (and lived to the age of 85). Thurstan was unlikely to have been less than 80 when he died in 1635. His wife had died in 1619.

These three families illustrate many of the general demographic trends of the community in this period. Although of course there were exceptions, the features shown are widespread: the better-off had more children; infant mortality was not high; marriage age was generally late; and considerable longevity was by no means unusual at all levels of society. Three, possibly four, of the Harris sons, and two of the Rowleys, never married. Indeed, the evidence from the parish as a whole would seem to support the view that high numbers never marrying, as well as late age at first marriage, characterized the early modern English marriage pattern.[12]

To sum up the demographic picture in pre-enclosure Highley, then: the population, after a period of stagnation before 1560, was growing, with a surplus of births over deaths. This was aided by a relatively low rate of juvenile mortality – indeed as far as we can determine by a reasonably low rate of mortality altogether. Fertility was steady but not particularly high, due to a (probably) late first marriage, and to intervals of on average two and a half years between successive births. Wealthier families tended to have more children than did poorer ones, but otherwise there is little discernible difference between the demographic experience of yeomen and cottagers.

It is the comparative healthiness of the community as a whole which is perhaps the most striking feature of the period. It was unusual for a marriage to be broken by death in its fertile years; couples could reasonably expect to live to see all their children become adults; and most children, far from being orphaned at an

---

[12] A. Macfarlane, *Marriage and Love in England* (Oxford, 1986), pp. 23–6.

early age, grew up with not only parents but also at least some grandparents still alive. The valid comparisons, however, are with subsequent phases of pre-industrial development and with the early years of industrialization, not with modern conditions. Although no epidemics affected the village during this period, there is some evidence to suggest that the population lived sufficiently close to the margins of subsistence that poor harvests and the rise in grain prices could have a noticeable effect on both mortality and fertility. Yet the underlying trend throughout the period was still one of growth. This feature in particular, and the demographic profile of the community in general, forms a necessary backdrop to the study of village social relations.

3
Neighbours

It would be wrong to regard pre-enclosure Highley as a closed community with little movement in or out. In fact, although a nucleus of settled families continued to be represented throughout the period, there was a considerable degree of mobility amongst certain groups or categories of people. Short-term movements of servants both into and out of the village are almost impossible to quantify: we can say only that they were constant and considerable. Permanent immigration and emigration of both individuals and whole families is somewhat more historically visible, and shows interesting age- and class-specific variations.

Movement of whole families is easiest to identify, but was least likely to occur. Those whom we might call the 'settled' population, tenants of the manor with several years' residence in Highley, were unlikely to leave. Figure 3.1 illustrates how only a small number of those surnames found towards the beginning of our period had vanished by its end. In most cases this can be shown to be the result of families dying out, or continuing to be represented only in the female line. In only two cases do families appear to have sold their interest in land in Highley in order to move elsewhere. This in turn, under the prevalent manorial system, left little scope for families of this class to move in. We have seen how the arrival of George Peirson to take over the demesne lands, even with the support of the lord of the manor, was resisted. Figure 3.1 also shows an increase in the numbers of immigrant families in the second and third decades of the seventeenth century, when the breakdown of the manorial system gave greater scope for this kind of immigration.

In addition to those settled families, however, the records indicate a substratum of families who are represented by a single entry in the parish registers, and are only rarely mentioned in other

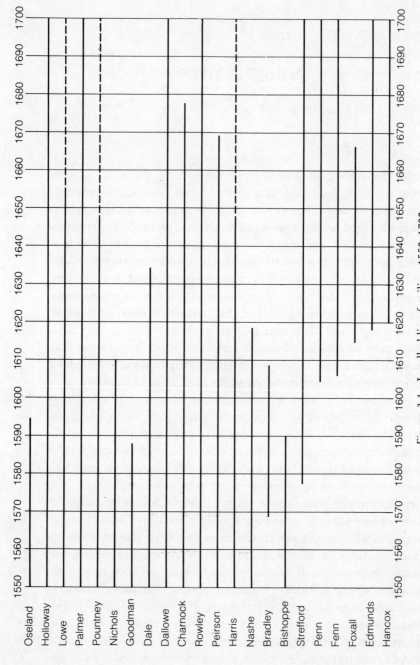

Figure 3.1 Landholding families, 1550–1700

Note: broken lines indicate periods when principal branch of family lived elsewhere

documentation. In most cases the single entry is a baptism, suggesting a period of residence of less than five years, and perhaps only a couple of months. These 'transient' families first appear in significant numbers in the 1570s, and form about one eighth of all baptisms during the period 1550–1620. Sometimes their stay was very short, and they did not qualify as residents at all – as in the baptism in 1591 of 'Ann daughter of Richard Massie, a traveller'. In other cases, though, the stay was less transitory, and the man must have followed some occupation in Highley. In most instances, this must have been agricultural wage labour.

By the 1580s, then, 30 years before the break-up of the common field system of agriculture, there are indications of a landless proletariat, of married men with children rather than living-in servants, engaged in a series of frequent short-distance moves around the south Shropshire countryside in search of work. Occasionally we can trace the steps of these moves. Richard Sheyles married at Chelmarsh in 1572, and the couple's first child was baptised there in 1574. A move to another neighbouring parish may then have followed: by 1580 the couple were in Highley, where another child was baptised. Subsequently the family was living in Earnwood in the parish of Kinlet.[1]

Also occasionally, we learn that these transient families were recognized as poor by their contemporaries. Thomas Jennyns, for example, whose son John was baptised at Highley in 1595, was bequeated a shilling by Thomas Palmer in 1598 as a 'poor neighbour'.

Table 3.1 goes some way towards illustrating this mobility of families. It examines the mobility of all fathers baptising children at Highley by the decade in which they first appear, and makes a distinction between 'transient' fathers (i.e. 'one-entry' in the baptism register) and those who baptised a number of children in the parish. The table shows how relatively stable were the latter families. Until the decade 1600–09, a period of incipient change in village affairs, it was very unusual for a man in this 'settled' group to leave the parish before his own death.

Thus there would appear to be two distinct types of life experience in the pre-enclosure community. Those who could obtain some land in Highley, even just the four or five acres that went with a cottage, tended to remain there all their married lives.

[1] S.R.O. Childe MSS. 56/16: Court roll of Cleobury Mortimer Liberties, 1600.

Table 3.1   Mobility of fathers of children baptised 1560–1619

	'new' fathers	one-entry fathers	buried at Highley	two + entries	buried at Highley
1560–69	9	1	0	8	8
1570–79	8	4	0	4	4
1580–89	10	4	0	6	5
1590–99	10	7	1	3	3
1600–09	14	3	0	11	7
1610–19	11	5	0	6	3
Total	62	24	1	38	30

Those who could not would seem to have been engaged in a series of moves every three or four years, or perhaps less, from village to village.

Because landholding families at all levels were unlikely to leave, the opportunities for immigrating families to become established were limited. Thus we find that most of the 'settled' fathers had themselves been born in Highley. Of the nine settled new fathers of the period 1580–99, seven had themselves been baptised in the parish. Again, there was more movement in the early seventeenth century – only nine of the 17 settled new fathers of 1600–19 were native to Highley. It is of course not possible to carry out the same exercise for fathers before 1581, since baptisms are only available from 1551. But the surnames of the settled families in this earlier period show them to have been well established at the time of the 1543 Lay Subsidy, and often before.

This continuity of residence of landholding families would seem to suggest that there was little emigration from Highley during the period. In fact, as we have seen, emigration was greater on balance than immigration: although no absolute population figures are available for this period, it is clear that Highley grew at a much slower rate than its demographic situation would allow. Most of this emigration was not undertaken by families, but by individuals.

A consistently large proportion of those baptised at Highley are not mentioned again in any form of parish registration, manorial record, or court case. Table 3.2 makes a distinction between these individuals and those who are last recorded as adult residents of the village, perhaps at marriage or when appearing before church or manor court. The most striking thing about these figures is the very high rate of emigration by young people that they demonstrate. Large numbers of young people left Highley before they reached marriageable age. Some may have gone a considerable distance to take up a career. The Bristol Apprentice Book for 1542–52 records two young men from Highley; William Palmer, who became an apprentice hooper in 1546, and John Clare apprenticed as a joiner in 1550.[2] Certainly other towns, smaller but nearer, must have been the target of the young men of Highley. Hey shows that the woodland parishes of north Shropshire, some 30 or 40 miles away, experienced net immigration at this period, as land was cleared and brought into cultivation.[3] It is probable that many immigrants came from the more extensively farmed south-east of the county. In other cases it was likely that the moves were over shorter distances to spend a few years as farm servants in neighbouring parishes. In either case, these young people married and settled in their new homes, and did not return to live in their native parish.

Table 3.2 Emigration of those baptised 1551–99

Birth cohort	Total surviving infancy	No. last recorded at baptism	No. last recorded as adult	Buried at Highley
1551–59	12	10	2	0
1560–69	23	11	4	8
1570–79	26	15	3	8
1580–89	34	21	7	6
1590–99	25	17	3	5

Unfortunately, it is rarely known just where they had settled. Testators frequently make plain in their wills that they have adult children living elsewhere, but rarely mention the place by name. One example will suffice. The children of Richard Palmer, one of the most prosperous copyhold tenants of the manor, were born in the 1570s and 1580s. When Richard himself made his will in 1632, he gave some indications of the subsequent careers of these children, of whom we should otherwise know little beyond their baptism.

One son had married, not at Highley, but was living there with

[2] E. Ralph and N. M. Hardwick, *Calendar of the Bristol Apprentice Book 1532–1565: Part II 1542–1552*, Bristol Record Society Publications XXXIII (1980).
[3] D. Hey, *An English Rural Community: Myddle under the Tudors and Stuarts* (Leicester, 1974), p. 170.

his wife and children. He was the only child to remain in Highley. Two other sons had married and settled elsewhere – we are not told where – and had several children of their own. One daughter had married a man from Alveley, across the Severn, although this marriage is not recorded at Highley, and was living there. Another daughter had married at Highley, and had gone to live in Bewdley, 10 miles away, where she remained with her children in spite of the death of her husband. One son is not mentioned in the will, and must be presumed to have died somewhere other than Highley, though he can be traced there at the age of 22. Finally, another daughter is not mentioned, and had probably died some time after 1598, when she is known to have been alive, aged 17. She is not recorded as buried at Highley.

Thus, of the seven children of Richard Palmer, only one settled in Highley and was in turn buried there. The other six all survived childhood, and left the village – four of them certainly to settle and raise children elsewhere. Palmer's family is by no means untypical: rather the number of children settling elsewhere would appear to be the norm.

The majority of those leaving after marriage were, as one would expect, women. The fact of their marrying at Highley does not of course preclude their having also spent some time outside the village. Marriage was in fact a prime cause of mobility in the community. Since couples tended to settle in the man's home parish, women were even less likely than men to end their lives in their native parish. In a sample of 23 reconstituted families, a total of 66 boys survived infancy, of whom 29 were buried in their birthplace. Of the 58 surviving girls, only eight were actually buried at Highley. Similarly, only 15 per cent of those mothers appearing in the baptism register over the period 1581–1620 had themselves been baptised at Highley. This 'turnover' of women at marriage constituted a major source of migration.

The geographical limits of the marriage market at this date are only partially recoverable. Recording of the parish of origin at marriage in the parish register is incomplete and apparently haphazard. In only eight marriages is a specific parish, other than Highley, mentioned, although scrutiny of the surnames involved reveals a much larger number of marriage partners whose names are not encountered elsewhere in any Highley records.

There are 50 marriages recorded in the period 1550–1620. In 12 of these, both partners were either baptised at Highley or came from known resident families. In a further 12, neither partner appears to be local, while in the remaining 26 one of the partners was apparently a resident. In 23 of this last group, a woman from Highley married exogamously; and the fact that in only two cases were children of the marriage subsequently baptised in the parish supports the conclusion that settlement in the husband's parish was the norm.

Of the eight instances of a specific home parish of a marriage partner, two are of the neighbouring parish of Kinlet. A further three – Rock, Belbroughton and Ribbesford – are 10–15 miles away, in Worcestershire. The remaining three, Ludlow, Clee Downtown and Onibury, are in west Shropshire, at a distance of 15–20 miles. Thus we can at least say that the choice of marriage partner was not restricted to a limited circle of nearby parishes: though further evidence, particularly from wills, shows that several Highley women had indeed married partners from, and settled in, neighbouring villages.

It also seems that the upper stratum of the yeomanry – those like the Lowes and Peirsons who in the first half of the seventeenth century would be aspiring to the gentry – began after the turn of the century to withdraw from the local marriage community and to seek their partners further afield. Men like Thomas Lowe and William Pountney who had themselves married endogamously (or very locally) found their sons and daughters drawing on a much wider geographical area.

The personal ties built up by migration between inhabitants of Highley and other communities were not the only points of contact. Lists of debtors and creditors appended to the majority of wills of this period frequently name the home village or town of the individuals listed. These places represent a minimum range of 'business' contacts for, as with the marriage records, we find several individuals mentioned with no indication of place even though they are not apparently Highley residents. Figure 3.2 shows the places that are specified, and their relative distances from Highley. The majority are located in the immediate neighbour-hood; villages within a ten-miles radius like Alveley, Billingsley, Chorley and so on. The two links with Frankley arise out of transactions specified to be with the Littleton family. Those places at a greater distance from Highley, like Worcester and Tewkesbury, each mentioned twice, are also on the River Severn, and may represent some degree of involvement in river traffic. Dyer in his study of sixteenth-century Worcester points out that most of the city's firewood came down the Severn from the Wyre Forest area, of which Highley marked the northern extent.[4] At least one Highley man was involved in this type of transaction, for in his will of 1598 Thomas Palmer records a debt of 46s for 'carrying wood out of Higleys wood to Severn'. Mentions of creditors in the riverside ports of Bewdley and Tewkesbury are found, not unexpectedly, in the will of Thomas Low, waterman.

The nature and significance of these financial transactions concerns us elsewhere: here it is the delineation of the social area of the community that is of interest. Financial links appear to have been quite common between Highley and surrounding rural areas of south Shropshire and north Worcestershire (most of the villages on the sketch map, figure 3.2, are mentioned several times each), and not uncommon with towns downriver on the Severn. There is no evidence of links outside the West Midlands. Not all names of creditors are accompanied by a place of residence: but several can be traced to nearby parishes, and it seems probable that they too would fit the general pattern of a social area dominated by the towns of the Severn and the villages of its rural hinterland.

Some further evidence of links with a wider community than the village itself may be gleaned from the names of witnesses to wills. Here, however, inhabitants showed a marked preference for local residents, not only in cases of urgency when availability was the obvious criterion. Of 64 named witnesses of the period, 43 were known inhabitants of Highley and only 21 are 'outside' names – and some of the latter may indeed have been temporary residents like farm servants. In only two cases are the parishes of witnesses recorded: they were Cleobury Mortimer, nine miles away, and 'Elmley', probably Elmley Lovett, a village situated between Kidderminster and Droitwich.

Contacts with the surrounding area, then, were frequent: but, as has been found elsewhere, they were largely contained within a radius of 10 miles or so, with only occasional contacts at a greater distance.[5] Certainly the surviving evidence shows that Highley was

[4] A. Dyer, *The City of Worcester in the Sixteenth Century* (Leicester, 1973), p. 54.
[5] K. Wrightson and D. Levine, *Poverty and Piety in an English Village: Terling 1525–1700* (London, New York, San Francisco, 1979), p. 76.

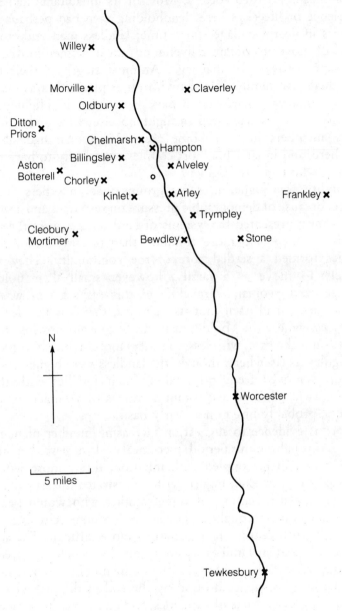

Figure 3.2 Home parishes of debtors and creditors of Highley testators
1544–1620

by no means a closed society. Most of its inhabitants had some experience of life elsewhere: landholding men had perhaps been servants in nearby villages for a time; landless men undertook a round of moves to obtain a livelihood; most women moved as a necessary corollary of marriage. At most stages of their lives, individuals had family contacts with other places. It was unusual for both marriage partners to have been born in Highley: the majority of wives had been brought up elsewhere and still had family members in their home areas. Most men had siblings elsewhere, and in later life most couples were likely to have adult children who had left Highley.

Mobility was higher in some groups than in others. Young people, because of demographic pressure on resources and a lack of opportunity presented by systems of land tenure, were the most mobile: to leave was more common than to stay. Landholding families formed a settled core of the community. They were unlikely to move as a family, however small their holding. Cottager and yeoman were alike in this respect – it was the possession of land itself, not its quantity, that was the deciding factor. Elsewhere (in Myddle in north Shropshire for instance[6]), this was not the case, with lesser farmers more stable than greater. In Highley as elsewhere, though, the landless were highly mobile. Labourers moved frequently, taking their families with them. There was in addition a constant turnover of younger living-in servants, probably hired on a yearly basis.[7]

There is evidence to suggest an increasing number of migrant families throughout this period: piecemeal enclosure was beginning in the area which, coupled with inflation, threw more workers onto the labour market. Figure 3.1 has illustrated the arrival in the early seventeenth century of some families who would become settled and remain throughout the century: economic circumstances in the sixteenth century had made this more difficult. The actual number of resident families was not, initially, much increased by these new arrivals, because of the dwindling number of branches of older families. What we do find by the end of the pre-enclosure period is a greater range of surnames, and consequently somewhat less involved kinship networks within the community.

The high levels of mobility in sixteenth-century Highley would

---

[6] Hey, *An English Rural Community*.

[7] A. Kussmaul, *Servants in Husbandry in Early Modern England* (Cambridge, 1981).

appear at first sight to be incompatible with a society of dense kinship networks. Terling, for example, exhibited high mobility and loose kinship links, while Myddle did have more complex interrelationships but lower migration levels.[8] In Highley, both appear side by side. We have seen that a settled core of families remained in spite of the considerable degree of migration in the community as a whole. Although many adolescents apparently left the village, a number consistently remained (or returned) to marry and settle. In spite of the frequency of exogamous marriages, a sufficient number of endogamous marriages also took place to assist the build-up of complex kinship networks.

The system of holding land for three lives led to continuity of family if not of individual. Unlike the short leases of the seventeenth and eighteenth centuries, tenancies in the pre-enclosure period could be inherited, whether they were copyhold or leasehold. Continuity of family had been a feature of the community in the first half of the sixteenth century, too. All the surnames from the 1524 lay subsidy were still represented in the village in 1600, and already by the early years of the century there were several branches of the same surname – three Pountneys, two Lowes and two Palmers.[9] The subsidy of 1543 names more individuals, but we find the same kind of duplication of surnames – six Lowes, four Pountneys, three Holloways, and so on.[10] The involved kinship networks which we find at the beginning of our period had been evolved and built up over two three generations, if not more. There had been Pountneys and Palmers, for instance, in Highley since at least the middle of the fifteenth century.

Marriages which took place within the period 1550–1620 between these already interrelated families produced networks so dense as to defy diagrammatic representation. One illustration of the result is that of the 17 tenants of the manor named in the rental of 1601, only four were not related to any of the others. These include two men who had arrived in the village with their families during our period. The remainder were linked by ties of blood and of marriage several times over. Indeed, as a further example, Thomas Pountney was related, with varying degrees of remoteness, to all the other 12.

[8] Wrightson and Levine, *Poverty and Piety*, pp. 81–91. Hey, *An English Rural Community*, pp. 207–9.

[9] P.R.O. E 179 166/131: Lay Subsidy Roll, 16 Henry VIII.

[10] P.R.O. E 179 166/159: Lay Subsidy Roll, 35 Henry VIII.

These tenants of the manor were, however, more likely to be interrelated than the remainder of the population of the village. In the absence of a listing of inhabitants of Highley anywhere near this date, an attempt was made to synthesize information from parish registers, wills, manorial records and court cases to produce a list of known householders for the year 1600. Almost certainly, this fails to include some of the peripatetic labouring families, who were less likely than others to be part of the kinship networks of the community. On the other hand, it is probable that some relationships existed that are undetected. The list produces 29 householders, of whom 21 were related to at least one other. Significantly, of the eight who were not related, four were landless labourers or servants. The settled core which made up the majority of the village population, at any rate, was closely interrelated.

The fact that these relationships existed, of course, does not tell us how far they were recognized: indeed the modern researcher may well be aware of relationships that were only vaguely – if at all – known to those involved. The degree of recognition of kin is difficult to assess from the available sources. It has become almost a truism of historical sociology that kin recognition in preindustrial England was both narrow and genealogically shallow.[11] However, the prevailing economic and social structure of the community (as well as varying personal experience) would appear capable of influencing the range of kin recognized. In preenclosure Highley, with its tight kinship networks among landholding families, one would expect at least a recognition of some kin beyond the primary links of the nuclear family. Certainly kin recognition would appear to be wider during this period than it was subsequently to be. This is not of course to deny the overwhelming importance of the nuclear family: all testators, for instance, thought first of their spouses and children, where any existed, and made careful provision for them before considering any less closely related kin.

That a network wider than that of the nuclear family was recognized, and could be important, is shown in the actual succession of holdings on the manor. Where there was no son or daughter to take over on the death of a tenant, a more distant relative was admitted instead. In the case of the childless Thomas

[11] A. Macfarlane, *The Origins of English Individualism* (Oxford, 1978).

and Ann Palmer, it was the wife's brother who took over: the unmarried Richard Palmer's holding went to his nephew.

Table 3.3 Relationships other than spouse and child acknowledged in wills, 1544–1620

								Number of wills								
1	2	3	4	5	6	7	8	9
sister-in-law	stepson	sister	son-in-law	brother-in-law	nephew	brother		godchild
father-in-law	great-	2nd cousin		niece				
stepdaughter	nephew			cousin				
illegit. son								
spouse's niece								
spouse's nephew								
'kinsman'								
step-grandson								

Table 3.3 shows the range of non-nuclear relationships acknowledged in wills: the figures represent the number of wills in which the relationships occur – some wills mention several cousins, nephews etc. It can be seen that quite distant relations received bequests, including cousins and their children, great-nephews, and so on. Obligation (or affection) towards this wider family was more often expressed by childless testators, as one might expect: but this was by no means always the case. The strength of ties of affinity is shown by the number of testators mentioning relatives by marriage. Brothers-in-law, for instance, are named as beneficiaries in five wills.

Clearly, although the nuclear family was of prime importance to testators, they also thought of themselves as part of a wider network of kinship, at least when they came to make their wills. There are some indications that it was not only in wills that this extended family was recognized: there are for example several mentions of money or goods which have at some time in the past been lent to nephews, brothers-in-law, and so on. The will of George Harris, 1607, states 'I lent 40s in gold to my brother in law Thomas Pountney . . . which is to be repaid to my sister Judith'. Ann Palmer in 1603 gave 'to Richard Holloway my brother's son 8s 4d being parcel of the sum of £5 13s 4d which he oweth me for two kine.' In 1585, John Pountney recorded that 'My brother-in-law Thomas Mellichop oweth me 20s'.

There was quite clearly considerable contact between extended family members, even when, like Thomas Mellichop, these family members lived outside Highley. For the most part, however, those secondary kin recognized lived in Highley itself. Links were certainly maintained with adult children living elsewhere, but contact with less close relatives was more likely to be confined to those living near at hand. Furthermore, although wills do display some awareness of the extended family, we must not lose sight of the predominance of the nuclear family. Of the 23 wills analyzed in table 3.3, 13 mentioned spouses and 17 mentioned children.

The kind of mutual support (lending money, supplying stock etc.) which could be found among members of the extended family was also a characteristic of social relations with neighbours within the community. Indeed, given the degree of interrelationship in pre-enclosure Highley, neighbours frequently were kin.

Close contact with neighbours was unavoidable. The agricultural organization itself called for a certain co-operation between neighbours: open field farming was only possible with a degree of communal effort, or at the least some synchronization of activities. The small size of the community meant that the same men were constantly serving together as manorial and parochial officers; and also presumably that everyone was well known to everyone else. The extensive network of small loans, and the incidence of charitable bequests, adds to this picture of a close-knit, mutually supportive community. Certainly, the lists of debtors and creditors which we have already discussed points to a situation in which the lending of money and goods between neighbours was widespread. The sums involved, at least until the turn of the century, were generally small: the majority of 'neighbourly' debts were of the order of 5 or 10 shillings.

Many inhabitants appear on lists of both debtors and creditors. There is no clear distinction between a 'lending group' and a 'borrowing group'. Although those owed money tended by and large to come from the yeoman and husbandman classes, a cottager like William Charnock also appears on the list. The list of those owing money is longer, and does include more servants and cottagers: but it also contains the names of most of the yeomen of the village. The extent of this system of loans is indicated by the fact that 70 per cent of all wills of this period detail debts, and that all these include some debts between neighbours.

A high level of lending and borrowing within the community would seem not to have been unusual at this period. Those villages examined by Spufford[12] and by Skipp[13] showed a similar frequency of small loans. Table 3.4 differentiates between types of persons involved in transactions recorded in Highley wills. The high figure for transactions with non-kin resident outside Highley is somewhat distorted by long lists of extra-parochial debts in the wills of two individuals. Nevertheless, nearly a third of the loans were between villagers who were not closely related.

Table 3.4 Persons involved in Debt transactions, 1550–1619

Transactions	Kin	Non-kin Highley	Non-kin elsewhere	Total
Number	21	56	110	187
Percentage	11%	30%	59%	100%

Although some of these debts reflect what seem to be relations of patronage (like the debts of 24s and 40s respectively owed to the vicar by Thurstan Dale 'my servant' and Humfrey Dale 'my olde servant'), the majority were financial arrangements between equals, presumably for mutual convenience. There is rarely any mention of bonds or any similar official record of these debts. Not only was money lending between neighbours very common: it was also highly informal.

Sometimes, as a gesture of goodwill, part of a debt could be written off in a will – thus Anne Palmer in 1603: 'I give to Anne Richard Dallowes daughter a lambe, and also I do forgeve to the said Richard Dallowe 8s which he oweth me.'

The more prosperous inhabitants showed a sense of obligation towards the poor of their community. Private charity, as indicated by charitable bequests in wills, could take an individual or a collective form. Sometimes the bequest was a sum of money to 'the poor of the parish of Highley', which was administered by the clergy and churchwardens. The most substantial of this type of

---

[12] M. Spufford, *Contrasting Communities: English Villagers in the Sixteenth and Seventeenth Centuries* (Cambridge, 1979), pp. 212–3.
[13] V. H. T. Skipp, 'Economic and social change in the Forest of Arden, 1530–1649' in *Land, Church and People: Essays Presented to Professor H. P. R. Finberg*, ed J. Thirsk (Supplement to Agricultural History Review, 18, 1970), p. 105.

bequest was that of Richard Lowe, who left £10 of his total estate of £41 15s 6d to the poor of the parish. The burial entry for George Harris in the parish register of 1609 records that 'The said George Harris at the tyme of his deceasse gave to the said Parish of Higley the summe of twenty six shillings and eight pence to continewe in stocke to the use of the same parish'. The capital from the bequests of Lowe, Harris and others was retained (and the interest presumably distributed as we know it was later) until the building of a poor-house in the mid-eighteenth century.

Other testators preferred to make specific bequests to individuals. Where it was made clear that the beneficiaries were 'my poor neighbour' or 'my old servant' the charitable nature of the bequest is obvious. In other cases, we must presume charitable intent where the recipient is not a relative and is known to have been considerably less well-off than the testator. The latter, however, are only a small minority of cases.

The majority of charitable bequests come after 1580, and are basically of two kinds: those to servants and ex-servants, who stood in some kind of personal relationship to the testator; and those to others whose only claim would seem to be that they lived in the same village, and were poor. The latter clearly exhibit a wider sense of social obligation.

Those leaving money to the poor, whether severally or collectively, were naturally enough from social groups I and II. They also tended to be those with few dependants to provide for: the group of those who left money specifically and unambiguously to the poor comprised four unmarried men, one childless man and one childless widow. The sense of obligation towards the immediate family outweighed that towards the wider community, although there is further evidence of a sense of belonging both to parish and diocese in the numbers of bequests to the church of Highley and the cathedral of Hereford.

However, not all relations between villagers were of a supportive or philanthropic nature. There is another side to the picture – the long-running disputes over hedges and the fights between neighbours; the cases of 'malicious rimes' and those based on 'common fame' and gossip. Richard Palmer in his will of 1597 left a charitable bequest to his 'poor neighbour' Richard Dallow. A quarter of a century earlier the two men had appeared before the manor court after they had fought to the point of drawing blood with a sickle.[14] This is an apt illustration of the range of neighbourly relations in pre-enclosure Highley.

Records of Quarter Sessions at Shrewsbury do not survive before 1638, unfortunately. The county courts, however, were only part of an involved system of judiciary affecting the pre-enclosure society. Ecclesiastical courts dealt with such matters as church attendance and sexual transgressions. In addition, Highley was subject to two manor courts: that of the manor of Highley itself; and the Court Baron of the Borough of Cleobury Mortimer and its liberties, which included Highley and several of its neighbours. Records of the latter court exist from 1600–26, although with some gaps.[15] Both courts dealt with disputes over land, boundaries and stock; with brewing offences, fights between neighbours, and so on.

Their records show the kind of tensions which existed between neighbours in the pre-enclosure period. The most frequently recorded disputes in the Highley manor court rolls are over land, and in particular the position of hedges. In virtually every roll of the sixteenth century (of which 26 survive), orders are made for individuals to move a hedge onto its 'right course', and for jurors to investigate the boundaries between certain tenants. Another common offence was the taking of firewood from the woods and hedges of neighbours.

Frequently, disputes between neighbours flared into violence: there are numerous cases of 'affray' recorded. These seem not to have been regarded as very serious misdemeanours, meriting a lower fine than chopping a neighbour's hedge, although one imagines that when Dallow and Palmer came to blows with the sickle, or when Thomas Rowley assaulted Richard Goodman with a pitchfork – 'striking him on the head and drawing blood' – the consequences could have been quite serious. With one exception, these fights were always between two men only, and seem to have been sudden and unpremeditated. Where weapons are mentioned, they are always such agricultural implements as could be expected to be readily at hand.

The one exception in surviving records is what appears to have been a full-scale fight which broke out between two groups during a village celebration in 1606. The Cleobury Mortimer court was

[14] B.R.L. Hagley Hall MSS. 377991 fol. 5r.
[15] S.R.O. Childe MSS 56/15–26; Court rolls of Cleobury Mortimer Liberties, 1598–1626.

ordered to investigate 'qui pugnavit apud Higley apud le Wake'.[16] They found that two groups, of five and six men, had fought, and practically everyone had drawn blood on everyone else. The groups seem to have formed partially along family lines, with two Pountney brothers heavily involved on one side, and Richard Palmer and two of his sons on the other. There is nothing to suggest, however, that this fight was part of a family feud. At all levels of village society, men were quick to resort to blows over day-to-day disputes, but there is no sign of long-standing animosity.

The Act Books of the consistory court at Hereford give us some additional insight into social relations and mores in pre-enclosure Highley. After decisions about probate, the most frequent cases brought to court involving Highley inhabitants were sexual offences. These were either illegitimate pregnancies, or allegations of extra- or pre-marital sexual relations.

As we have noted, parish registers show a very low illegitimacy rate during this period. However, a few cases are recorded in the Act Books which did not result in baptisms of illegitimate children at Highley. This is probably because the mothers were only temporarily resident in Highley, and went home for their confinements – almost certainly the case where the women were described as servants. Of the six illegitimate pregnancies reported to the court during this period, two were of servants, and two others of women whose surnames are not found elsewhere in Highley and who were probably also servants. The cases are worth treating individually for the light they throw on sexual activity in the parish at this date.

One man, John Pountney of the Woodend, was judged responsible for two pregnancies in 1570 – one of Anne Heycocke and the other of Joyce (no surname), his servant. Neither baptism is recorded at Highley, although presumably one of the children is the 'base son' for whom Pountney made provision in his will of 1585. In 1570, Pountney was already married, and his wife had given birth to a son in the previous year.

Pountney's near neighbour, the freeholder Oliver Harris, was not married in 1566 when he came before the court for 'impregnating' Anne Lewys, who may well also have been a servant. The baptism of their son Humphrey is registered in

November 1566, 18 months before the baptism of another Humphrey, first of the large family of Oliver and Alice Harris. Humphrey Lewis later appears in the parish registers of Chelmarsh. Harris had not married Humphrey's mother, although presumably free to do so.

Apparently, the circumstances afforded by the presence of living-in female servants, away from their families, provided an opportunity for sexual activity, whether between master and servant or fellow servants. Several of the relationships which led to court action smack of master/servant exploitation. Thomas Lowe was found guilty of adultery with his servant Matilda Harryes in 1566; Joan Malpas, who was charged together with (married) John Peirson in 1600, was almost certainly his servant too.

These cases seem to reflect short-term relationships. The case of Anne Nashe and John Potter, however, was different. They were charged with immorality at several courts from 1596 to 1600. In their final appearance, Anne's name is given as Nashe alias Potter, although John Potter was certainly married in 1594, and there is no sign of his wife having died in the interim. Indeed, she is probably the Joan Potter who, with Eleanor her daughter, received a charitable bequest in a will of 1603. It looks rather as if John Potter, a day labourer, had abandoned one woman in favour of another; and that this had become accepted in the community, for although no subsequent marriage is recorded, John Potter and 'Anne his wife' were both buried in 1630.

Cases of pre-marital pregnancy where the couple married before the child's birth did not often come to court. We have seen how Highley's brides were often pregnant at the time of their marriage, which argues a degree of sexual freedom where marriage was already in view. It also points to a village-wide morality, where such pre-marital sexuality was tolerated at all levels of society. Pregnant brides were frequent in yeoman as well as cottager families. Yet only one case of 'ante nuptial fornication' was reported to the ecclesiastical authorities.

Those convicted of moral offences were made to do penance three times in specified churches, and sometimes had to travel quite considerable distances to do so. We can only speculate about attitudes towards illegitimacy. In the absence of secular court records for this period, we do not know what arrangements were made for the maintenance of illegitimate children. That some men acknowledged their obligations is shown by the substantial bequests of John Pountney to his sixteen year old bastard son.

The consequences could undoubtedly be unpleasant: William Charnock was brought before the court in 1615 for 'receiving' his pregnant daughter, so even basic shelter might be hard to come by for the single mother. The same Alice Charnock tried to conceal the birth of the child, but there was a 'common fame' that it had been secretly buried in a garden. Given the size and nature of the community, it must have been difficult to hide this or any other misdemeanour. Since, however, it was up to local officers to report offences to the courts, all cases passed through a filter of village (male) opinion.

Social relations between villagers, then, were regulated by a number of authorities. As we have noted when discussing status in the community, the main criterion for elected office, whether manorial or parochial, would seem to have been settled residence in Highley rather than a simple measure of personal wealth. Indeed, the number of offices was so considerable, given the small population, that men of all classes could expect to serve regularly. The nature of the office frequently imposed some degree of communal activity on villagers. The 12 jurors of the court leet, for instance, were charged at each court to 'take a view' of disputed hedges and report to the next court together.

We cannot know what proportion of offences were dealt with by the local officer as arbitrator, or which he chose not to report to a higher authority. Since constables and so on were drawn from all classes save perhaps the very poorest of peripatetic labourers, this meant that no wealth-based oligarchy of prosperous residents existed to exercise authority over the rest. All men, even freeholders, were tenants of the manor, and theoretically at least subject to the same laws and conditions.

The relative egalitarianism of social relations in this pre-enclosure period is epitomized in the relationship between parish and clergyman. Two men between them span most of the period: Thomas Oseland, vicar from 1554 to 1588/9, and Robert Barrett c.1590 to 1626. Oseland was a local man with family ties in the village, and apparently held in high regard. He is mentioned in virtually every will during his incumbency as a witness or overseer. In 1557 John Holloway left £10 to 'Sir Oseland my ghostly father'. Oseland certainly lent money to poor parishioners, and probably taught some village boys to read and write – he left books to a local boy 'if they be for his learning'.

Neither Oseland nor his successor Barrett was university educated. Both men farmed lands in the parish as their parishioners did: indeed Barrett was in the forefront of the move to enclose open field holdings. Earlier, he had appeared before the manor court in a dispute over land exactly as did other tenants. Both vicars lived next to the church in the centre of the village, in a modest vicarage, and Oseland's will suggests that financially he was of the 'middling sort' of village society. Certainly the social distance between vicar and people was much less marked than it was to become in succeeding periods.

The open-field system did much to foster this relative egalitarianism. Involvement in agriculture was universal, and farming in common demanded a certain degree of contact and co-operation between individuals. The key division in society on the manor was between those who held land and those who did not: this resulted in a lack of real social distance among greater and lesser tenants,

Plate 1 Church House, home of the parish priest until the early seventeenth century. It stands only a few yards from the church.

and in a status hierarchy which was determined by factors such as long residence and personal reputation as well as by wealth. Only the small numbers of landless labourers were excluded, for they fulfilled neither the landholding nor length of residence criteria.

There was geographical mobility and social contact with a wider area, yet this still took place within the framework of a stable society, where most families resident in 1550 were still represented 70 years later. There was a high level of participation and integration in what was still a relatively homogeneous society. The core of the community was settled, densely inter-related and to a considerable degree self-regulatory. Those on its margins – the landless – were a small proportion but one which was growing from the late sixteenth century. This polarization was to be a chief feature of the post-enclosure community.

PART II

The Parish
1620–1780

4

Tenants and Labourers

The enclosure of Highley's common fields was achieved, apparently by mutual agreement of the landholders, in the second and third decades of the seventeenth century. It seems to have been a relatively peaceful and gradual process, and no deeds recording enclosure were enrolled in Chancery.

A number of factors stimulated the urge to enclose. John Littleton, the lord of the manor, had died in prison in 1601, leaving his widow Meriel heavily in debt. It was suggested in a Chancery court case of 1604 that some of the estate should be sold to meet these debts, assessed at £10,000.[1] The 1603 survey of the manor of Highley may well have been the result of the need to estimate the value of parts of the estate prior to sale.

This survey records in its margins amounts 'agreed with' tenants of each holding. The marginal additions are not dated: however, two leases have survived, both dated 1607, where tenants paid Meriel Littleton the exact sums noted beside their names on the survey.[2] It seems probable that the additions were made in or shortly before 1607. They were not in fact, as has understandably been assumed,[3] sums agreed for the purchase of the freehold, but for 2,000-year leases. In practice, this gave tenure almost as secure as freehold, but there were certain differences: rent continued to be paid, apparently at the same rate as under the previous tenure; heriots and suit of court were still due from leaseholders.

Leases could, however, be sold; and as early as 1610 Richard Holloway sold his newly-acquired lease to Thomas Lowe for a

[1] P.R.O. C/30/15: Case in Chancery.
[2] S.R.O. 1671/: Lease from M. Littleton to R. Rowley, 1607; Lease from M. Littleton to I. Palmer, 1607.
[3] J. Tonks, *The Littleton Family and their Estates, 1540–1640* (unpublished thesis, University of Oxford, 1978).

considerable profit.[4] In 1609, Anne Nichols sold her title to a cottage and smallholding – presumably a similar lease, as the sum of £6 13s 4d had earlier been agreed for this holding.

In all, the sale of long leases raised over £680, in amounts varying from £6 13s 4d to £100.[5] We have seen when examining wills of the later part of the sixteenth century that there were increased amounts of cash in circulation in the village economy which enabled tenants to purchase these leases. It would also seem, from prices paid subsequently for the same properties, that Meriel Littleton's straitened circumstances enabled tenants to agree terms favourable to themselves.

In 1618, Meriel Littleton finally sold the last of her interests in the manor of Highley.[6] Some deeds have survived which record the final sale of the freehold of properties leased earlier, all dated 1618.[7] The sums paid for the actual freehold were considerably smaller than those agreed for the long leases: Richard Rowley, for instance, paid £86 13s 4d for his 2,000-year lease in 1607, and only £13 7s for the freehold of the same farm in 1618.[8] Thus a glebe terrier of 1625 was able to note that the parishioners were 'all freeholders'.[9]

The evidence of these leases and sales suggests that some exchange and engrossing of arable lands had been going on throughout the period. In 1607, some lands were excluded from Oliver Harris's tenement, being then in the occupation of Richard Palmer. It looks as if the two men had exchanged these lands prior to this date. Furthermore, some of the strips appear to have been enclosed already: 'one parcel of land about eight ridges . . . lying in a close of the said Richard Palmer'.[10]

By 1618, Highley Wood, the common pasture in the north of the parish, had been divided up and apportioned to landholders in lieu of their rights of common according to the amount of land they held. These shares, as mentioned in later transfers of property, varied between one and a half and 15 acres: in fact the nine shares

[4] S.P.L. Misc. Deeds 1922: Sale from R. Holloway to T. Lowe, 1610.

[5] B.R.L. Hagley Hall MSS. 357347: Survey of Highley, 1603.

[6] T. F. Duke, *The Antiquities of Shropshire* (1844).

[7] S.R.O. 1080/: Sale from M. Littleton to F. Holloway, 1618. S.R.O. 247/1: Grant from M. Littleton to O. Harris, 1618.

[8] S.R.O. 1671/: Lease from M. Littleton to R. Rowley, 1607; Sale from M. Littleton to R. Rowley, 1618.

[9] H.R.O. Highley glebe terrier, 1625.

[10] S.R.O. 1277/Box 6: Lease from M. Littleton to O. Harris, 1609.

which can subsequently be traced account for over half the available 137 acres. Thus if the remaining principal landholders received comparable shares, there was little or no land left for cottagers with smallholdings, although they too would have lost their rights of common.

Our principal source for the actual process of enclosure is the glebe terrier of 1625, in which the vicar, Robert Barrett, outlines the moves he had made to consolidate and enclose his glebeland. The glebe share of Highley Wood was 10 acres, in 'one leasowe or pasture lately enclosed out of the common called Higleyes Wood which was limited and measured out in lieu of the common of pasture to the said vicarage'. The parishioners 'did exchange and enclose their comon field lande for theyr more comodious use thereof.' Barrett goes on to specify the exchanges he had agreed to in order to enclose his 'dispersed glebe lands.' Nine landholers had exchanged with Barrett, so they were also engaged in consolidating and, presumably, enclosing their lands.

Quality of land appears to have been taken into consideration when these exchanges were made, for they were not always measure for measure. Barrett gave Thomas Lowe all 26 of his strips in Cockshoote Field, which were in dispersed parcels, and Lowe in return gave 'two foot for one in measure' of his land situated nearer to the vicarage. The trading in land could be even more involved, as when Barrett made another exchange with Lowe, receiving four strips which he then promptly swapped for a little meadow belonging to John Peirson.

Barrett's chief aim was to gather his glebelands into closes in the vicinity of his new vicarage: he was not entirely successful, for some land remained enclosed, but at an inconvenient distance – and was still situated where Barrett's efforts had left it at the time of the tithe award of 1841. In the process of enclosure, some arable land was converted to pasture. In 1618, for instance, Oliver Harris owned 'one pasture . . . about eight rudges' and 'one acre in Rea Field in a pasture enclosed out of Rea Field.' It seems, however, that the immediate aim of the complicated manoeuvres detailed in the glebe terrier was, for most landholders, the same as Barrett's – the creation of closes of arable grouped as nearly as possible together and centring on the farmhouse.

The 10 men involved in exchanges of glebe land cannot have been the only ones in the village undertaking similar transactions.

Plate 2 The Old Vicarage was built c.1620, and remained the vicarage until the 1950s. Gothic windows and weather boarding were added during the incumbency of Samuel Burrows, 1790–1843.

All the chief landholders must have been involved, for we know that large areas of the common fields were being enclosed by these men. It is doubtful if any strips at all were left. The glebe terrier mentions only four ridges 'which do lie open and unenclosed.' A deed of 1656 mentions 'nineteen ridges or selions in Higley Field', so it may be that some vestigial open field was left, although it is equally possible that this represents only a customary form of wording.[11]

Thus the period 1607–25 brought many changes. The tenants of the manor had become first holders of exceptionally long leases, and then freeholders; and had had to find considerable cash sums in order to do so. In 1618 came the sale of the manor itself. There is no evidence that Thomas Lowe, the new lord of the manor, exercised the same sort of control that the Littletons had done, or even that manor courts were still continued. The division of the common pasture of Highley Wood was a major factor in the process of enclosure, and would have had profound effects, particularly on those who lost rights of common within it without gaining a viable share of land. The actual exchange and enclosure of arable strips appears to have gone on in a piecemeal fashion over several years, and to have been achieved relatively equably.

As a result, the typical farmer of the community was no longer a copyhold tenant of scattered strips of arable with associated rights of pasturage: from the 1620s he was the freeholder of a more-or-less compact farm, where he could change land usage and farming methods at will. One of the most significant developments of the next century was the way in which this typical farmer became again the tenant of an absentee landlord.

Some cottagers and smallholders had become freeholders, too, while others were now the tenants of local landlords. The process by which land passed out of the ownership of local residents was a gradual one, and was brought about by families dying out, or property passing to a distant branch, as well as by direct sale. By 1671, for example, the 'Mrs Harris' who had inherited Haselwells Farm lived 'above fourscore miles away', and the farmhouse and lands were rented out.[12] Some families sold up in order to move elsewhere: George Pountney sold Green Hall, purchased by his father only 20 years before, as early as 1639, and left Highley.[13]

[11] S.P.L. Misc. Deeds 428: Release from T. Lowe to H. Grove, 1656.
[12] P.R.O. E 134 21 & 22 Chas II Hil. 29.
[13] S.P.L. Misc. Deeds 650: Sale from G. Pountney to S. Edmonds, 1639.

Other men sold their freeholds, but remained as tenants of the property, like William Rowley who sold his 'messuage, meese place and lands' in 1683, but whose family continued as tenants for generations.[14]

Some points of financial crisis can be identified. The large ex-demesne farm of the Peirsons was being eroded from 1660, when its share of Highley Wood was sold and Churchyard House, the second house of the estate, and almost half the farm lands were first mortgaged and then sold.[15] Sometimes the decline in fortunes could be dramatic: Thomas Lowe had acquired the manor in 1618 and steadily accumulated holdings as they became available; at his death in 1630 he owned at least five houses and associated lands. He became lay appropriator of the great tithes; built himself a seat on the north side of the chancel of the church; and was granted a coat of arms by 1623.[16] His son was educated at the Inns of Court. His career typified the 'rise of the gentry', the creation of a class of minor gentry and squirearchy from the ranks of the more prosperous peasant strata which was a feature of the period.

Yet Lowe's sons died young, and he was succeeded by his grandson, also Thomas, who began selling off parts of the estate by 1648, mortgaged the rest in 1653, and was apparently forced to sell altogether three years later.

Thus the two principal landowning families of the village experienced great financial difficulties at more or less the same time. Cottagers similarly found that they could not continue as owner-occupiers: John Penn bought his cottage in 1655 during the sale of Lowe property, but was forced to sell again in 1682. The situation was strikingly similar to that at Sherington in Bucking-hamshire, where 'modest freeholders gained ground . . . when manorial lords sold out their interests, and continued to flourish until the 1660s [when they] were driven out by indebtedness.'[17] The same trends were followed elsewhere, when low grain prices encouraged conversion to large-scale pasture farming.

In Highley's case, the new landlords were unable or unwilling to

---

[14] S.R.O. 1671/: Sale from R. Rowley to J. Windle, 1683.
[15] G.R.O. G/6 D2153/531-4: Sales and quitclaims, 1661-62.
[16] Harleian Society, *The Visitation of Shropshire, I* (London, 1889), p. 340.
[17] A. C. Chibnall, *Sherington: Fiefs and Fields of a Buckinghamshire Village* (1965), cited in J. Thirsk, 'Seventeenth century agriculture and social change', in *Land, Church and People: Essays Presented to Professor H. P. R. Finberg*. ed. J. Thirsk (Supplement to Agricultural History Review, 18, 1970), p. 156.

create large pastoral farms, and mixed farming in small units remained the norm. The absentee owners were in the main local gentry and clergy from the surrounding south Shropshire area centred on Bridgnorth. From 1656 the lord of the manor was Richard Cresswell of Sidbury, five or six miles away. He seems never to have lived in the new house which he had built in Highley: in the 1670s and 1680s his stewards were in residence there and in charge of farming operations. Other absentee landlords were content to lease their property without, apparently, taking much personal interest in it.

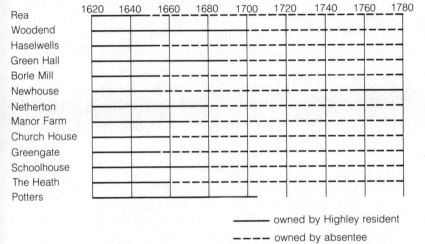

                    owned by Highley resident

                    owned by absentee

Figure 4.1   Ownership of principal farms, 1620–1780

Figure 4.1 illustrates the way in which the principal farms of the parish passed out of the hands of owner-occupiers, until at the end of our period virtually all were in the possession of absentee owners. A deed of 1760 itemizes the farms from which tithes were due, with their occupiers. Ten of the 14 farms were in the occupation of tenants or under-tenants.[18] A mass of documentation survives from the late seventeenth century onwards detailing the descent of property and its leasing. However, for the tenant farmer, the details of the inheritance of title from, for example, Mr Bell of Bridgnorth via Mrs Weaver to the Reverend Amphlett of Enville in Staffordshire probably had little significance, provided that his rent stayed the same.

The way in which farms in Highley were let, often field by field

[18] S.R.O. 1671/: Sale from T. Rogers to J. Amphlett, 1760.

and for short periods of time, is well illustrated by the details of two farms, Haselwells and The Rea, in the mid-seventeenth century. Tithes of these farms, among others, were the subject of a dispute between vicar and parishioners which can be traced through the church courts and central Exchequer records during the period 1667–77.[19] Witnesses who had rented all or part of the farms gave evidence, and although the dates may not be strictly accurate, a sufficient timetable can be reconstructed to show the way in which available farm land was rented out.

Rea Farm

c.1656	Robert Dorsett rented the farm for one year.
pre-1669	John Dallow rented the farm.
1661–71	Thomas Penn rented half the farm.
1668–9	John Matthews rented part of the farm.
1670–1	Ursula Bowen rented the farm (or part).
1672	Richard James occupied the farmhouse.
1677	Richard James and Henry Longmore rented the farm.

Haselwells

pre–1653	Francis Perkes rented the farm.
c.1653–63	Robert Martin rented the farm.
1664	Thomas Dallow rented one meadow.
pre-1669	William Rowley rented one meadow.
1670–1	Richard Wilkes rented the farm.
1672	Robert Dorsett occupied the farmhouse.

One of the chief characteristics of pre-enclosure Highley, the continuity of occupation of a farm by the same family – prompted largely by the system of tenure – had clearly been lost. Leases could be as short as one year, giving rise to the same kind of mobility among landholding families as had previously been confined to landless labourers. A series of leases of Churchyard House survives and names six different tenants during the first half of the eighteenth century.[20] In addition, separate fields were, as in the case of Haselwells farm, sublet from time to time.

The information about rent that can be recovered indicates that

[19] P.R.O. E 126/158; E 126/406; E 134 21 & 22 Chas II Hil. 29 and 22 Chas II Mich. 7; H.R.O. Depositions Box 2 vol. 4.

[20] G.R.O. G/6 D2153/572–3, 594–7, 604, 626–7, 643, 648–9: Leases, 1701–52.

there were very considerable increases over those rates paid by tenants of the manor in the early seventeenth century. The highest rent on the manor in 1603 had been less than 50 shillings per annum, with the majority at less than a pound. By the middle of the seventeenth century, John Fenn was paying £12 a year for a much smaller farm. In 1660, Haselwells cost £20 per annum to rent, and individual meadows elsewhere in the parish cost between £2 and £6 10s a year. The series of leases of Churchyard House shows how its rent rose from £15 a year in 1701 to £19 in 1715, £21 in 1721 and £23 in 1729. It also shows that undertenants could expect to pay more than the main tenant, for in 1714 the farm was sublet for £27 a year.

Property in the village would never again be sold at the advantageous rates achieved by tenants who bought their freeholds in the early years of the seventeenth century. Even if we add together the sums paid for the initial long leases in 1607 and those smaller amounts paid for the freeholds a decade or so later, we still find that property prices had been exceptionally low. In 1639, Green Hall and its lands were sold for £600: unfortunately, this is the only farm on the 1603 survey where no sum 'agreed for' has been entered. However, no other property commanded more than £100 for the long lease, and probably another £20 for the freehold. Green Hall seems even at a conservative estimate to have trebled its value in 20 years.

Plate 3 Green Hall, photographed shortly before its demolition about 1920. Its design was clearly very similar to that of the vicarage.

Smaller estates, too, could show a profit. John Penn's cottage and small enclosure cost him £45 in 1655: he sold it in 1682 for £60. A single acre of pasture was sold in 1667 for £14 10s. The profit available was obviously an incentive to the local man to sell: but against this must be offset the greatly increased rents which he then would have to pay. Since most sales were preceded by mortgages or other indications of financial hardship, it would appear that freeholders sold more out of necessity than out of deliberate policy.

Thus the cost of land, now enclosed and therefore more valuable, rose beyond the reach of local residents. The new owners were the rising squirearchy of the wider neighbourhood: in Highley no single landowner emerged to dominate the property market. The demesne lands were broken up into two or three separate farms with different owners. The Lowe family's bid to become village squires failed during the Parliamentary era, and there was also some division of their properties. Richard Cresswell, who bought the bulk of the Lowe estates, was the nearest that Highley had to a squire during this period: but his main residence was always elsewhere, and in the early eighteenth century the estate was further divided, some land going to Bridgnorth Corporation as a charitable trust, and the rest to another absentee landlord who rented out both house and land.[21]

Highley remained significantly more 'open' than other nearby villages with resident gentry. The edges of social stratification within the community are blurred by the rise of the tenant farmer. In the main, occupiers of the largest farms in the village were tenants: the few owner-occupiers were mostly artisans and husbandmen. Nevertheless, a village oligarchy of chief tenant farmers did emerge during the late seventeenth century. Economic changes attendant upon enclosure helped to form this group, but it was also given cohesion by the developments in the administrative machinery begun by the Elizabethan Poor Law and reinforced by later seventeenth-century legislation like the 1662 Act of Settlement. These men constituted the parish vestry; they provided the churchwardens and overseers of the poor, and certainly had more power over their neighbours than had their pre-enclosure counterparts. More villagers now looked to them for employment on a long-term basis. They controlled the poor relief payments; were

[21] S.R.O. 1080/: Sale from R. Cresswell to Bridgnorth Corporation, 1709.

responsible for reporting misdemeanours to the courts; collected rates; administered private charities. For most of this period of enclosed agriculture, the characteristic division of village society was between tenant farmer and landless labourer.

Throughout this period, farming remained the hub of the village economy. It was clearly well known that coal and building stone lay underground, for several leases from as early as 1618 specifically reserve mining rights: yet there was apparently very little exploitation of mineral wealth during the period. Most men worked on the land at some time of the year or for part of their working day, including blacksmiths, tailors and innkeepers. In the absence of resident gentry for most of the period, even the most prosperous men were working farmers. In the absence of organized industry, even artisans and craftsmen continued to have some experience of husbandry either as labourers or smallholders.

The nature of this farming, and the wealth that it engendered, is partly revealed by a series of probate inventories which survive from 1666–1740. Inventories list both household goods and farm stock and crops, and estates itemized vary in value between £357 and £4 17s (both in the 1720s). Table 4.1 shows the value of those estates where reliable totals are given.

Table 4.1 Probate Inventories 1666–1740

Value	Number of inventories	Farm equipment, crops and stock as % of value
£200+	6	55%
£100–£199	1	78%
£50–£99	5	47%
£25–£49	2 ⎫	
£10–£24	2 ⎬	19%
£1–£9	1 ⎭	

The wealthiest men had, on average, well over half of their wealth invested in farm equipment, crops and stock. The exception was the vicar, John Burton, of whose goods only 34 per cent were tied up in farming, while the mean for the others was 60 per cent. Smaller estates, those between £50 and £100 in total, were slightly less dependent on farm stock; and those men whose goods were worth less than £50 had only 19 per cent invested in farming or trade equipment. Since basic necessities like furnishing took up an irreducible minimum, poorer men had less money to invest in their means of livelihood – and got a correspondingly smaller return.

Most farmers practised mixed husbandry. Richard Palmer, whose inventory was taken in March 1666/7, was probably typical of the larger farmer. His crops, growing and stored, were more or less equal in value to his stock. His crops, and the eight oxen of his plough team, were valued at £66, while his 21 cattle, 94 sheep and unspecified number of pigs and poultry were worth £69.

Yelling finds a movement towards pastoral farming among newly-enclosed parishes of north Worcestershire in the sixteenth century, and a return to arable from mid seventeenth century.[22] Highley may well have followed the same pattern: some enclosed arable was converted to pasture early in the seventeenth century; by the time of the first inventories arable was equally as important as pastoral husbandry; by 1730 there are indications that arable production was beginning to predominate in some cases (in December 1729 John Pountney had only five cows and four sheep, but had 236 bushels of grains and pulse in store and 10 acres of sown winter corn); and in 1752 the terms of a lease had to be specifically worded to prevent the tenant ploughing up pasture land.[23]

Although farmers kept a range of livestock – cattle, sheep, pigs and poultry appear on every farmer's inventory – dairying seems to have been most important. Several farms possessed a dairy with cheese presses and vats, and more cheese than would be needed for home consumption – as many as 200 cheeses in one case. Cattle are often specified as milch cows. A usual herd consisted of 10 or 12 cows and calves and a bull. In addition, teams of oxen were still kept for ploughing: farmers had two, four, six or even eight oxen, valued at about £4 each. This, together with ploughs, harrows and chains, represents a considerable capital investment, often the largest sum in the inventory. The market at Bridgnorth specialized in oxen, but also provided an outlet for old dairy animals fattened for slaughter.[24] Highley farmers appear to have bred their own dairy cattle.

Numbers of pigs kept are rarely specified, though most farmers

[22] J. A. Yelling, *Common Field and Enclosure in England 1450–1850* (London and Basingstoke, 1977), pp. 183–6.

[23] G.R.O. G/6 D2153/648: Lease from T. Weaver to R. Adams, 1752.

[24] P. R. Edwards, 'The cattle trade of Shropshire in the late sixteenth and seventeenth centuries', *Midland History*, VI (1981).

and some poorer men had at least some. Not all farmers in the group kept sheep, although the majority had small flocks. Wool was stored in only 4 of the 17 houses surveyed, and all in very small domestic quantities.

Hemp and flax were more important yarns. Enclosed, consolidated farms gave greater opportunity for the cultivation of hemp and flax, which was often undertaken as a sideline by dairy farmers in the West Midlands.[25] From the late seventeenth century the field name 'the Hempyard' begins to occur quite frequently. Several inventories list 'hemp and flax already dressed' (1692), 'hemp and hurden yarn and flax' (1700), and so on.

Another new crop was clover. In 1668 John Matthews mowed 10 loads of clover grass at Rea Farm.[26] By 1700, clover seed and clover riddles were commonly found in farmhouses.

In spite of the introduction of new crops, however, wheat, barley and oats continued to be the main crops grown, and most farmers grew all three, with the addition of peas, beans and vetches. In September 1700, Robert Dorsett's newly-harvested crops of 'graine of all sorts', barley, oats and peas were worth £88 10s of his total estate of £248. Records of the seventeenth century tithe dispute tell us that all farmers also made considerable quantities of hay: one witness remembered that in the 1620s Richard Palmer had regularly mowed 'upwards of thirty loads of hay each year.'[27]

Few inventories survive of craftsmen and tradesmen: only four men in the group were not principally farmers, and even they were also involved in agriculture. Samuel Jones, a blacksmith who died in 1712, left six sheep worth one pound as well as the equipment in his shop. The miller who died in 1740 also kept pigs. The poorest man for whom an inventory survives was Richard Hancox, described as a pauper, who was apparently an artisan of some sort, for 'tools in the shop' were worth eight shillings. His only livestock were poultry, valued at a shilling out of his total estate of £4 17s.

The combination of agriculture with some other livelihood was quite common even among men with sizeable farms. Clearly this was the case with the Reverend John Burton: it also applied to

[25] Thirsk, 'Seventeenth century agriculture', p. 171.
[26] P.R.O. E 134 21 & 22 Chas II Hil. 29.
[27] P.R.O. E 134 22 Chas II Mich. 7.

John Pountney who died in 1700 owning considerable farm stock
and crops, as well as coffin boards, tools, 52 lb of iron and other
goods 'in the shop' and more 'at his shop down at is mothers.'
[sic]

   Information on occupations other than farming or farm labouring
is scarce throughout the period. The community always supported
at least one blacksmith and one miller. At several times, too, a
tailor is mentioned. Other occupations specified at various times
are victualler, sawyer and wheelwright. These men seem to have
been providing a purely local service. The 'potfounder' (1660–75)
and brickmaker (1725) may have been involved in supplying a
somewhat wider area. Yet no real industry had developed.

   The nearest to 'real' industry was the quarrying which went on
intermittently for most of the period. In 1623, Thomas Palmer 'of
Hyggley' was paid for 15 tons of stone for the repair of Bewdley
bridge, and for their carriage to the Severn.[28] From 1720 to about
1740 the quarry at 'Severnside' was on land owned by the vicar,
who entered his personal quarrying accounts in the back of the
parish Easter Book.[29] The works were not extensive. In 1729 Higgs
recorded 'Now got this year at Highley Quarry two hearths and
some small stone and 15 or 16 flagstones.' Hearths were taken up
the Severn to furnaces at Willey, Leighton and Coalbrookdale in
the expanding industrial area of the middle Severn valley. Highley
men were paid for drawing the stone to the river (a short distance
only), and for making and mending 'carrs' and 'rolls' to carry it.
There is no record, however, of who actually quarried the stone, or
whether or not they were Highley residents. Similar small-scale
quarrying may have gone on at other periods too.

   River traffic continued to play a part in the village economy:
farm produce probably followed stone up-river to the increasing
markets of the area around Coalbrookdale. From at least 1740 to
his death in 1764, Edward Wilcox owned barges which plied the
river. His last was a trow, the largest type of vessel on the river, up
to 90 tons and worth in 1758 about £300,[30] which was called 'The
Charming Molly'. Wilcox was probably the only man of even
moderate wealth in Highley throughout the period who did not
derive the greater part of his income from agriculture.

[28] J. R. Burton, *A History of Bewdley* (London, 1883).
[29] S.R.O. 4123/Ti/1: Highley Easter Book.
[30] S. Davies 'Bewdley and the Severn Trow' (Bewdley Museum information sheet, ND).

The village economy between 1620 and 1780 was thus almost exclusively agrarian: it relied on the mixed husbandry of relatively small farms, supported by a few tradesmen and craftsmen supplying local needs, and by growing numbers of landless labourers and living-in servants.

The categories which we used when defining the socioeconomic groups in the pre-enclosure community retain their validity in this period. Groups I and II still represent the greater and lesser farmers, again regardless of whether they were freeholders or tenants. The craftsmen and cottagers (with very few exceptions) may still be regarded as Group III, although the number of smallholders able to support their families from cottage plots with only occasional recourse to other occupations declined after enclosure. Group IV, labourers, was greatly increased. Live-in farm service represented rather a stage in life than socioeconomic status, at least in the first half of the period, and perhaps we should properly consider young resident 'servants in husbandry' as a separate category.

In the 1620s, wealthy yeomen like Thomas Lowe, George Peirson and Thomas Pountney had acquired considerable property, and were styling themselves 'gentlemen'. They, together with Richard Palmer and Oliver Harris (who now owned both Woodend and Haselwells farms), and the current vicar, constituted a group of six or seven substantial families. They were freeholders, and had all gained a sizeable piece of pasture from the division of Highley Wood, which they often rented out as it stood or with the addition of a cottage or two, to add to their newly-consolidated farms.

The lay subsidy return of 1628 names only eight individuals[31]: that for 1664 similarly lists seven.[32] The indications are of a fairly constant number of families in this class, comprising some 15–20 per cent of the total population.

As we have seen, the fortunes of most of these families declined after mid century, and they were replaced by substantial tenant farmers. Since the number and size of farms remained more or less constant, however, the size of the elite group did not change very much even if the men who formed it were no longer 'gentlemen' and freeholders. The Poll Book of 1714 lists seven Highley

[31] P.R.O. E 179 167/201: Lay Subsidy return, 4 Chas I.
[32] P.R.O. E 179 255/32: Lay Subsidy return, 15 Chas II.

residents with the necessary qualifications to vote.[33] A single
surviving Land Tax return of 1767 shows nine principal rate-
payers.[34] Wills and inventories of the eighteenth century show that
these families enjoyed a level of material culture at least comparable
to the yeomen of the earlier part of our period, in spite of their
nominally lower status. The eighteenth-century elite were by and
large men who had come to Highley from elsewhere, and whose
families rarely remained for more than a generation, and often
much less.

The best guide to social and economic structure at any time
during this period is provided by the Hearth Tax returns of the
third quarter of the seventeenth century, for it seems reasonable to
infer some correlation between size of house and personal wealth
and position. Table 4.2 uses the 1672 Hearth Tax (which includes
exemptions) to demonstrate the size of respective groups at that
date.

Table 4.2   Distribution of socioeconomic groups in the Hearth Tax 1672

Groups	I	II	III	IV
Number of Hearths	4–7	2–3	1	exempt
Number of households	7	10	12	8

The number of households in the wealthiest group corresponds
very well with our estimates from other sources. These men were
those whose inventories totalled over £200. Their wills mention
considerable sums in cash or bonds and, in the early years,
property. Typical is the will of Francis Holloway, which was
proved in 1651. Besides his farm stock of 4 oxen, 15 cows, 68 sheep
and 40 pigs, he left legacies of £291 in cash or in bonds for debts
due to him. George Peirson, who died in 1654, left to his sons two
houses and extensive associated lands, and to his two daughters
£200 each. Property was usually, but not invariably, in Highley.
By the time of his death in 1632 Richard Palmer owned not only
his farm in Highley, but also a 'house, tenement, tanhouse . . . mill,
stable . . . closes, gardens . . . pools, places for lying of hides and
drying of leather' in Bewdley.

[33] *Pole Book for the County of Shropshire* (Shrewsbury, 1714).
[34] W.R.O. Bearcroft papers 705/95: Land Tax return, 1767.

By the end of our period, cash sums bequeathed by tenant farmers could be considerable. Joseph Cook's will, proved in 1771, mentions a total of £886 in cash bequests alone, beside the unspecified value of farm and household goods and the sums previously given to two of his children who, he tells us, have been 'provided for in my lifetime'.

There is a discernible qualitative difference between the households of these elite families and others in the community, whereas in the pre-enclosure period the difference was rather one of quantity. Prosperous families in the sixteenth century tended to own more of the same goods; while by the mid-seventeenth century the wealthiest homes had cushions, carpets, clocks, books, which were rarely if ever found in the homes of the less prosperous. By the second and third decades of the eighteenth century we find items like 'delf plates', looking glasses, warming pans, watches, jewellery, flaxen napkins and silver cups, as well as more utilitarian items in the houses of principal farmers.

The houses of men in this group were in fact larger than might be suggested by the four to seven hearths on which they paid tax. In 1672 the vicarage was assessed on seven hearths: in 1720 it had in fact 19 rooms, if one includes the cellar, wash house and brew house. Similarly the Palmer family farm, called Potters, was taxed on five hearths, when an inventory of 1667 lists a total of 15 rooms. It seems from these and other examples that only one in three rooms, approximately, could be expected to have fireplaces.

Palmer's inventory gives much information about the daily life of this group. Part of the house was used for storing grain, including the main upstairs room which, being over the hall, was reliably dry. Five rooms, including the parlour downstairs, were used for sleeping. The hall and lower parlour were eating and sitting rooms: the remaining rooms were used as one would expect – the kitchen for cooking, pantry for storing provisions and cellar for drink. The distinguishing feature of these large farmhouses (besides the greater comfort in their furnishings) was the separation of functions such as storage, cooking and sleeping into their own areas rather than in the multiple-usage rooms of poorer families.

The principal farmers of the village were better able to achieve this greater degree of comfort because many of them had taken the opportunity afforded by the purchase of the freeholds to their property to rebuild or at least enlarge their houses. Surviving

Plate 4 The Peirson's manor house. The left half is of sixteenth century date; the right was added by Thomas Peirson in 1629.

architectural evidence points to a general rebuilding in the first half of the seventeenth century, and occasionally a more precise date can be assigned to the improvements. Thomas Peirson, for instance, dated and initialled the new wing which he built on the family farmhouse in 1629.

Group II, smaller farmers, are represented by those who paid Hearth Tax on two or three hearths. In the inventories there is a noticeable gap between those valued at over £200 and the rest, all below £100. The husbandman's estate was usually worth some £60–80. The Hearth Tax suggests that there were 10 men in this group in 1672, or about 15–30 per cent of the population – a proportion which probably remained quite steady, although in the early eighteenth century there are signs of a few craftsmen joining this group. In the absence of their wills or inventories we cannot be sure of relative wealth, but the blacksmith and brickmaker who employed living-in servants in the 1720s should probably be included in this category.

A typical inventory of this group is that of William Rowley taken in 1730. His house was assessed on two hearths in 1672: in fact it had two ground-floor rooms with chambers over, plus a buttery and a brewhouse. There was certainly less specialization of usage here than in the homes of the more prosperous: in the absence of a kitchen or pantry, the hall served for cooking and storage of provisions as well as sitting and eating. The main bedroom also provided storage for cheese vats, a saddle and pillion, and so on. Both yeomen and husbandmen (as we may for convenience call Groups I and II) show a considerable degree of self-sufficiency well into the eighteenth century. They made cider, beer and cheese at home, and stored home-reared bacon and beef. Flax and wool could be spun at home. There is noticeably less luxury, though, in the homes of men like Rowley, although his inventory is 50 years later than that of Palmer. Even as late as 1730, Rowley had no non-functional items at all – no books, no cushions or carpets – and the house had no 'best' rooms.

Wills of husbandmen in the first half of the period, up to about 1700, show a greater concern with household goods than do those of their wealthier neighbours. Property, and even cash, are rarely mentioned. Thurstan Dale's will, made in 1636, is typical of a husbandman's will of the seventeenth century, where household items like brass pans, bolsters and treen barrels are separately bequeathed as they had been by all classes in the pre-enclosure period. Prosperous yeomen had largely ceased to specify such items by this date. Nearly a century later John Ellis, also a husbandman, similarly has only £7 in cash listed among his bequests: but he does not itemize his 'household goods and implements of husbandry' individually.

Together, the farmers and a few successful craftsmen made up some 40–50 per cent of the total village population for most of this period. This is further reflected in the poor rate payments. Let us take by way of example the overseers' accounts for 1754.[35] Twenty-three individual heads of household contributed to the poor rate, probably comprising by this date a little under half of the total. Nine principal landholders paid £1 or more, at what appears to be 11d in the pound, and may be equated with our Group I. The remaining 14 represent this second group. The indications are consistent that at least a relative degree of financial security was enjoyed during this period by just under half the total population of the community.

The remainder were, in varying degrees, poor. Francis Lowe, a tailor, was by his own admission 'but a poor man', as he reported having told the vicar during the tithe dispute of 1668.[36] Yet with his trade and the 'little piece of upland ground' which he rented and from which he made hay, he was well off compared with many of the community. With his ability to supplement his income by at least some husbandry, Lowe was in an increasingly unusual position. The nature of Group III, artisans and cottagers, changed after enclosure.

The five and six acre holdings, plus rights of common, which had given cottagers at least a measure of self-sufficiency, shrank. First they became less viable with the loss of opportunities for grazing on common pasture or arable. Then the new owners were often reluctant to spare much land to accompany a cottage. In 1653, Thomas Lowe owned five cottages: all had a garden; two also had an orchard; one had 'a little meadow' and one a 'hemplack'.[37] No-one was going to obtain a family living off that. Three of these five cottagers were in fact among the 'poor of the parish' left charitable bequests in a will of 1651. Some of the

[35] S.R.O. 4123/P/1: Highley overseers' accounts, 1724–61.
[36] P.R.O. E 134 21 & 22 Chas II Hil. 29.
[37] S.R.O. 1671/: Mortgage by T. Lowe, 1653.

cottages were newly built on land enclosed out of Highley Wood, and seem not to have had the statutory four acres of land.

Thus some families who had previously combined a smallholding with some other occupation were now virtually landless. Allen Fenn, aged 66, described himself as a labourer in 1670, and recounted his memories of the family holding 'which is now called Fenn's tenement' and in the occupation of Richard Holloway – that is, part of a larger farm.[38] The two and three-quarter acres of 'Charnockes tenement' became part of the Rowley's farm by the end of the century. As more cottages were built in the eighteenth century, the trend continued.

For much of this period, one half of the community virtually employed the other half. The 12 families in one-hearth houses in 1672, together with the eight who were exempted from payment altogether, must have relied on trade or day-labour for their livelihood. Some men combined the two: John Penn paid tax on one hearth, in a house which is elsewhere described as a cottage.[39] In 1670 he called himself a 'victualler', but told how two years previously he had worked as a labourer at haymaking.[40] This must have been a common occurrence among men in Group III.

One artisan from this group was Samuel Jones, blacksmith, who died in 1712/13. His possessions were valued at £16 8s 6d. His sparse household goods totalled only £5 9s 6d, and consisted of a bed and bedlinen, table and chairs, a cupboard and chests for storage, a pot and two kettles for cooking, and some pewter utensils. Only one room is mentioned, besides the shop. There the hammer, anvil, bellows and other tools of his trade were worth £6 2s 6d. There appears to have been no cash in the house, for the usual 'money in pocket' is not included, although there is mention of 'money due in the shop book'. Jones and his wife eked a living from his trade (and their six sheep), but it was clearly not a very prosperous one.

The group of wage-labourers, which we have seen was already in existence in the late sixteenth century, increased during this period. This was partly, though not entirely, due to enclosure. We have seen some of the difficulties facing cottagers or smallholders as a result of enclosure: undoubtedly, those who lost rights which they

[38] P.R.O. E 134 22 Chas II Mich. 7.
[39] S.R.O. 1080/: Sale from T. Lowe to J. Penne, 1655.
[40] P.R.O. E 134 22 Chas II Mich. 7.

had held under the common-field system were forced into increasing reliance on wage labour. Yet other factors, too, encouraged this trend. In the first 30 or more years after enclosure in Highley, wages were low and new freeholders could afford to employ the labour needed for the initial hedging and fencing of enclosed fields. More labour-intensive crops began to be grown. The way in which land remained in the hands of several owners, either resident or absentee, resulted in the kind of open society where the movement of labourers was more possible; and the division of Highley Wood and the enclosure of the arable fields provided more potential building land for cottages. Thus the demand for wage-labourers was stimulated at a time when more men were being forced into the labour market.

Even labourers in full-time employment were poor: seasonal lay-offs and the stagnation in real wages kept them so. Not all – or even most – of those exempt from Hearth Tax payments were elderly or widowed: the majority were family men in employment. By the closing decades of our period, the employed (or unemployed) considerably outnumbered the employers. No new farms could be created – there was not the land – and no industries had yet become really established.

Numbers of labourers in the parish are hard to assess, especially as the distinction between cottagers and labourers became blurred, and migration of labourers and their families became even more frequent. There could sometimes, however, be considerable continuity of employment for labourers. William Jefferies, one of the exempt group of 1672, reported two years earlier that he was a 52–year-old labourer, who had worked for the same farmer for 18 consecutive years.[41]

This group, the poorest in the village, comprised 21.6 per cent of all heads of household in 1672, very close to the figure of 23 per cent exempt in the whole of Shropshire quoted by Wrightson.[42] Most of these men, and some of the one-hearth group too, were or had been labourers.

In the 1720s, no less than 70 per cent of all adult burials are recorded as 'pauper'. This of course exaggerates the proportion of the very poor in the community, for many had fallen into poverty only when prevented by age from working. It does, however,

[41] *Ibid.*
[42] K. Wrightson, *English Society 1580–1680* (London, 1982), p. 148.

demonstrate how widespread poverty in later life had become.

One of these 'paupers' buried during the decade was Richard Hancox, for whom a probate inventory survives. Hancox appears to have been one of those who had struggled on the margins of poverty for most of his life, and only became destitute towards its end. He was 74 when he died, and seems to have been no longer working. He had paid tax on one hearth in 1672, probably for the same 'cottage, garden and orchard' rented by his mother in 1653. This was basically a two-up, two-down house with a single-storey buttery attached, and so was probably not the most basic of village accommodation. Hancox had apparently carried on some sort of trade, for he still possessed 'tools in the shop'. Unfortunately, his household possessions are not separately itemized, though 'goods in the parlour', for instance, at five shillings cannot have been extensive. Altogether, including the largest item, wearing apparel and ready money at £1 5s, his total estate was worth £4 17s.

Servants were in some respects better off. Resident servants were of two types, domestic and servants in husbandry – although judging by the amount of butter and cheese-making, brewing and cider-making, flax spinning and so on which was carried out in larger farmhouses, the lines of distinction could be fine. What most writers in fact mean by this division is the same as that noted in eighteenth century parish books in Highley: 'men' and 'maids'. This begs the question of how much farmwork even outside the home was done by women, a question that for Highley at this period we cannot even begin to answer.

There is some evidence for live-in service in Highley at the beginning of our period, albeit given retrospectively by elderly people around 1670. Not enough instances exist for more than tentative conclusions to be drawn, but their testimonies are nevertheless interesting. The most noticeable feature of the subsequent histories of the men quoted is their rise in status: they were all 'yeomen' and all living in neighbouring villages. It does look as if service of this nature was undertaken by the sons of yeomen and husbandmen as well as by the poor. The men and women had all been in their twenties when they began their periods of service, which in most cases had not been long: where duration is mentioned it was always for two or three years, except in the case of one woman who had been for 11 years the servant of the same family. Two women servants (of the three quoted) had also married yeomen after leaving service.

The children of yeoman families appear to have gone less frequently into temporary service in the eighteenth century, and there are increasing signs of the poverty of some servants. William Harris, 'a poor servant to Mr. Lowbridge' was buried in 1726; Susannah George 'a poor apprentice servant' in 1733. By this date, the practice of apprenticing the children of the poor – in effect putting them into service – at the decision of the parish was well established.

Numbers of live-in servants show no sign of any real fall during our period. In 1756, for instance, there were still 20 resident servants in the village, of whom 11 were male. Kussmaul suggests, from a group of 63 listings of inhabitants, a national figure of 13.4 per cent of the population in service.[43] In late seventeenth century Highley, the percentage derived from the Easter Book, which excludes the vicar's household, was 12.2 per cent. It appears to have been a little over 10 per cent at the end of our period. One might expect Highley, with its lack of resident gentry, to have had somewhat fewer servants than average. In fact, although about a quarter of all households had servants in the mid-eighteenth century, numbers were not large: no-one had more than three servants, and one man and one maid was usually the maximum.

The population of Highley divides once again during this period into those with land, whatever the type of tenure, and those without, or with only a garden and orchard. Those with a sizeable farm of perhaps 50 acres or more, even if only rented, could accumulate considerable cash and live in some comfort. The 'husbandman' or smaller farmer was noticeably less well off. Richard Baxter, the Puritan theologian who lived in both Bridgnorth to the north of Highley and Kidderminster to the south, described the hardships of the small farmer in the late seventeenth century.

> If their sow pig or their hen breed chickens, they cannot afford to eat them, but must sell them to make their rent. They cannot afford to eat the eggs that their hens lay, nor the apples nor the pears that grow on their trees . . . but must make money of all. All the best of their butter and cheese they must sell . . .[44]

[43] A. Kussmaul, *Servants in Husbandry in Early Modern England* (Cambridge, 1981).
[44] Quoted in J. F. C. Harrison, *The Common People* (London, 1981), p. 137.

Certainly the husbandman or smallholder in Highley was now part of a cash economy. Usually he had to pay a cash rent; and even freeholders did not have the land to provide the full range of crops and stock needed for self-sufficiency. Thus even the smallest farmer turned to a cash-crop like hemp, and grew for profit rather than for consumption. Cash was needed for services as well as for food; the blacksmith with his 'money due in the shop book' had to be paid in cash, as did other tradesmen.

The smallest landholders were forced to turn to wage labour. This trend was exacerbated by enclosure when, as we have seen, cottagers appear to have lost access to common woodland. We must beware, however, of attributing all changes in Highley's economic structures in the seventeenth century to enclosure. The polarization of wealth, for instance, was a trend well-evidenced in villages which did not enclose at this date. Certainly the bad harvests of the 1620s and the rising cost of living throughout the first half of the century may well have forced Highley's smallest farmers off the land in any case. What enclosure did do was to accelerate trends already visible in the sixteenth century: numbers of landless labourers continued to increase; large farmers prospered at the expense of small; and the number of those living in permanent rather than cyclical poverty steadily rose.

5

Family and Household

The first indications of a possible total population size in the post-enclosure period date from the second half of the seventeenth century. Hearth tax returns and the Compton religious census of 1676 all indicate a population of about 150. These sources, and the additional parish Easter Book, are examined in more detail below: they are remarkably consistent in the estimates they provide.

Eighteenth-century sources are fewer. There are no central fiscal returns as there are for the seventeenth century; and the parochial sources on which we must rely in their absence, while unusually full, cannot be regarded as absolutely exhaustive, especially as mobility increased during the century. In fact the demographic potential for growth in the community was again severely curtailed by emigration. If we work forward from this figure of 150 in 1680, adding baptisms and subtracting burials to get some idea of the rate of natural growth, we find that without migration the total population in 1801 would have been 410, not the 274 recorded at the census. Since in fact there was substantial immigration in the 1790s, the actual net emigration in the century after 1680 must have been considerable.

In fact the indications are that the total village population did continue to grow slowly during the eighteenth century, and had probably reached 200 or a little more at the end of our period.

Figure 5.1 shows a consistent surplus of births over deaths (the figures are simple decadal aggregates). The two come closest together in the late seventeenth century, when growth was slower than at any other time. There is no mid-century deficiency in the Highley registers, as is often the case; the peaks in both baptisms and burials during the Commonwealth in fact cast some doubt on the efficiency of immediate post-Restoration registration. The most rapid growth came towards the end of our period. Baptisms

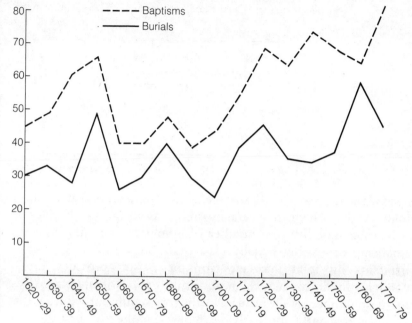

Figure 5.1   Decadal aggregates of baptisms and burials, 1620–1779

reached their peak in the 1770s, and were nearly double the number of burials. It is interesting that, immediately before industrial development in the village, Highley was an expanding community, with ever-increasing pressure upon existing resources.

The late seventeenth century – the period for which we can best estimate a birth rate based on a population of 150 – was, then, a period of stagnation. This is reflected in an annual birth rate 1670–89 of 29.3 per 1,000, with the death rate not far behind at 23.3 per 1,000. There was, however, no single decade when burials exceeded baptisms, although the 1720s and 1760s saw increased burials. Nevertheless, during the period 1760–79, with an estimated population of 200, a death rate of 26 per 1,000 per annum lagged well behind a birth rate of 37.5 per 1,000. This pattern, of growth before 1640, stagnation in the second half of the seventeenth century, and renewed and increasing growth after 1720, fits very closely what has come to be accepted as the national pattern.[1]

The pattern is also reflected in mean completed family size (see table 5.1), at least until the period 1740–79, when we find an

[1] E. A. Wrigley and R. S. Schofield, *The Population History of England 1541–1871* (London, 1981), pp. 161–2.

Table 5.1   Mean age at first marriage (years) and mean completed family size,* 1620–1779.

	Age at marriage women	Age at marriage men	Family size
1620–59	27.4	30.2	5.1
1660–99	27.4	33.7	4.4
1700–39	27.9	27.0	5.4
1740–79	23.2	27.2	4.2

* Calculated on couples in observation until the death of one of the partners

apparent anomaly. Family size seems to have decreased at a time of high fertility. There are several possible reasons for this. With ever-increasing mobility, the number of completed families becomes smaller and possibly socially biased (although a division of total baptisms by total marriages for the period provides rough confirmation in an identical mean family size). Not all fertility was marital: numbers of illegitimate births rose significantly during this period. Frequently, too, early death of one of the partners curtailed family size.

Throughout the period, families were somewhat smaller on average than they had been in the sixteenth century. In the whole group of completed families of the seventeenth century there is only one family of 10 children. In the second half of the period, although a minority of couples did produce larger families, noticeably more couples had only one or two children. Of 63 completed families, only 39 consisted of more than three children.

Yeoman farmers, who had the large families of the pre-enclosure period, gradually ceased to do so. In the first 50 years of this period, we still find members of prosperous families such as Palmers and Pountneys with nine children: but now they are joined by labourers such as William Jefferys with 10 children and Francis Horton with eight. But the wealthy farming families of the eighteenth century, like the Jordins and the Cooks, had families of four or five; while the largest families were on the whole those of men like Francis Lowe, a tailor, with 13 children, or Thomas Wall, labourer and occasional pauper, with 12. This marks a considerable change from the situation in the sixteenth century, and may suggest that with the availability of labour and the changing nature of agricultural production, farmers did not feel the same need to

provide a family workforce. The reversal of trends in family size
by both the wealthy and the poor is apparently explicable in terms
of the changes in the agrarian system. Such an explanation, which
would also see the poor responding to the replacement of a family
landholding of limited size by the opportunity of wage labour, is
attractive. But it would presuppose the deliberate exercise of
fertility control, a large assumption and one which the evidence
does not allow us adequately to test.

It is possible to calculate a mean interval between all births in
families of farmers and of labourers or poor artisans. In the first
half of the period, 1620–99, there is little difference between the
two, at 31 months for farmers and 29.5 months for the poor. In the
eighteenth century, though, there is a marked difference, with
prosperous families having children at an interval of 32.9 months
and those known to be poor at a mean interval of only 24.7
months. This does point to a socially-specific differentiation in
fertility, but would need to be tested further by the kind of analysis
of age- and duration-specific fertility rates for each group which
becomes problematic in a small parish, and by reference to a larger
sample of marriage ages so that they too could be related to
socioeconomic position.

For much of the period, an average late age at marriage
continued to be a limiting factor on marital fertility. Table 5.1 also
shows mean age at first marriage for men and women. The
relatively late marriage age which was suggested by surviving
evidence for the pre-enclosure period was continued in the
seventeenth century. The fall in marriage age apparently began
earlier for men than for women. Numbers of families in observation
in a village like Highley are not large, but it is clear that the
widespread trend towards falling marriage age in the eighteenth
century was shared in Highley.

A further limitation on family size was the frequency with
which early death interrupted the fertile span of a marriage. In the
seventeenth century alone it is possible to identify 22 cases where
death intervened in the fertile span of a couple, although in the pre-
enclosure period this was an unusual occurrence. In 12 of these 22
cases it was the husband who died, although because of men's
greater fertility span some of these husbands were by no means
young. Of the 10 wives who died in these marriages, only one
appears to have done so as a direct result of childbirth. In the

period 1700–79 there were 21 marriages interrupted in this way. In 12 instances the man died first, and of the nine women three died during or immediately after childbirth.

Widows and widowers with young children had a clear incentive to remarry. Of the 10 widowers in the seventeenth century group, seven are known to have remarried, and to have done so quite rapidly – after a mean interval of less than two years. The picture with young widows at this time is less clear. Only two of the 12 remarried at Highley, but several seem to have left the village either to remarry elsewhere or to return to their native place. Migration similarly obscures the picture in the eighteenth century: almost half the widowed did not remain in the village. Of the 10 who did, five remarried and five did not.

In fact, a considerable proportion of all marriages involved a second marriage for one or both parties. Of the 53 male partners in the completed families of the period 1620–99, 11 are known to have married more than once. As a result of late marriage and second marriage to a younger woman, some men continued to father children into old age. Henry Pountney, born in 1580, baptised the last of his 17 children by two wives in 1649, while Giles Rawlins mentioned in his will 'my child yet unborn' – a daughter baptised in 1678 after her father had died at the age of 76.

These interrupted marriages also meant that there were considerable numbers of young orphans in the community. With age at first marriage high, and fertility continuing well into middle age, especially for men, children were quite frequently deprived of one parent if not both.

Marriages were, on the whole, shorter than they had been in the pre-enclosure period, for although we still find the occasional marriage of forty years or more, the frequency of death in the earlier years of marriage clearly affected mean duration; and even when both partners survived to complete child-bearing, a duration of 25–30 years was the norm.

In the first half of the period we can arrive at a figure for duration of marriage in 52 cases, including some minimum durations where the baptism of a man and his children, and the burials of husband and wife are traceable, but the marriage itself took place elsewhere. In these cases the duration of the marriage has been reckoned from the baptism of the first child, the real figure being a year or more greater. The mean duration of 'actual' marriages during this period was 23.2 years, and of all including 'minimum' figures was 22.5 years. Thus, given reasonable longevity, some individuals – like Henry Pountney whose first marriage lasted for 25 years and second for 27 – could achieve two 'average' marriages in their lifetime. A long first marriage did not preclude remarriage by the surviving partner: Alan Fenn's first marriage lasted for 44 years, the longest in the period; yet he remarried four years before his death. Others faced a long widowhood. Richard Strefford's first marriage lasted for only two or three years, and produced one child. He remarried, and died shortly afterwards at the age of 30 in 1672. His widow, left with one child of her own and the daughter of her husband's first marriage, lived until 1706.

In the second half of the period, a total of 51 'exact' marriages had a mean duration of 23.4 years (the figure becomes 23.6 years including 'minimum' durations). There were more long marriages during this period, as one might expect with age at marriage falling. Nearly a quarter of the marriages lasted for 40 years or more. This is off-set by the numbers of marriages broken early by death – 10 in the first five years and a further eight between five and 10 years.

Throughout the post-enclosure period, then, the average marriage lasted for 23 years or so, which is considerably less than the existing evidence suggests for the pre-enclosure period. The elderly widowed showed an increased tendency to remarry. The chief difference, however, was in the numbers of widowed, and of families which contained step-brothers and sisters, and even children who were no blood relation at all to the head of the household.

We have postulated a death rate in the late seventeenth century of 23 per 1,000, rising only slightly in the eighteenth century – well within the parameters of 22 to 27 per 1,000 established by Wrigley and Schofield for the period.[2] There are no sudden peaks in burials of a sufficient magnitude to suggest epidemics of any kind. Age at death was not recorded in the parish register, and can only be arrived at by tracing back those who had been baptised in the parish. We thus have a self-selecting sample of the less mobile. Nevertheless, it is worth considering the figures. In the first half of the period, adults (over 15) died at a mean age of 55.5 years for women and 55.9 for men. More women than men reached extreme old age, but on the other hand women were more likely to die in

---

[2] Wrigley and Schofield, *Population History*, pp. 182–3.

early middle age – 21 per cent of these women died in their forties, while only 8 per cent of the men did so. In the second half of the period, men averaged 60.5 years at death, while women only achieved a mean of 52.4 years and were again at greater risk in the middle years of life.

As in the pre-enclosure period, it is rarely possible to determine the cause of death. Some families had more than their share of early deaths, possibly as a result of the spread of infectious diseases within a family. The three sons of Thomas Lowe all died between 1623 and 1629 when in their early thirties. Some deaths by accident are recorded. Francis Dovey in 1733 was 'killed with a Gunn-shot accidentally', a perennial hazard in a farming community. Drownings, in a parish bounded on three sides by waterways, were also not uncommon. Thomas Hancox 'drowned accidentally in the Borle Mill pond' at 80 years old. Coroner's inquests show drowning as a major cause of death in the parish, with four cases between 1770 and 1775 (for much of the period inquest records do not survive).[3] Barge traffic on the Severn was heavy, and three of the four men had fallen from barges. Only one violent death is recorded, that of Oliver Harris who was 'slain at Bridgnorth Fair upon St. Luke's Day'. Although no further record of the event has come to light, this does not sound like accidental death.

Nevertheless, there were some cases of considerable longevity: several men and women (especially the latter) survived to 85 and a few, like Joan Palmer who was married in 1637 and lived until 1706, were almost certainly more. Many others did not reach maturity. Table 5.2 details infant and child mortality. At the beginning of the period, juvenile mortality remained relatively high, continuing the rise from a low point in the 1570s and 1580s. A second low was reached in the second half of the seventeenth century, when only 11.4 per cent of children baptised failed to reach adulthood. Thereafter, juvenile mortality increased to something approaching its previous highest levels. Throughout, infant mortality exceeded that of children – although the possibility remains that further under-15s may have died elsewhere after leaving the village. Thus Table 5.2 also shows infant and child burials as a percentage of all burials. In the eighteenth century, one in every 10 burials was that of a child, and almost one in three that

[3] S.R.O. QR 98/3; QR 79/10; QR 82/23: Coroner's inquests 1771, 1773 and 1775.

Table 5.2 Juvenile mortality 1620–1779

	% of those baptised buried as infants	% of those baptised buried as children	infants as % all burials	children as % all burials
1620–59	14.0	3.6	16.4	10.7
1660–99	8.4	3.0	10.3	4.0
1700–39	12.2	5.1	20.0	11.7
1740–79	11.6	5.0	22.6	9.0

of a juvenile. Yet these rates are still relatively favourable compared with many of those found elsewhere.[4]

Although the small size of the parish and the difficulties presented by levels of migration limit the kind of analysis which can be undertaken, a picture does emerge of the general demographic aspects of the community which suggests that the position was in many ways less favourable than it had been in the pre-enclosure period. People tended not to live as long, and were more likely to lose a marriage partner. There were therefore more widowed and orphaned in the parish. Juvenile mortality rates were slightly higher in the eighteenth century than they had been in the sixteenth.

To assess some of the impact of these demographic factors on the community, it is useful to look in more detail at actual households. In the first part of the period, this is practically impossible. But from 1678 the vicar's Easter Book survives and, together with Hearth Tax returns, parish registers and witnesses' depositions, enables us to form a good idea of the village population size and household size in the later seventeenth century.[5]

The Easter Book does not provide a comprehensive listing of inhabitants; it does, though, list almost all heads of household by name, and the other resident adults by description – including resident servants. It continues into the nineteenth century, with varying degrees of reliability and completeness. It is somewhat complicated to use, for not everyone paid their dues every year. Because several people paid for two or even three years at once, it is necessary to consider a span of two or three years rather than one

[4] Wrigley and Schofield, *Population History*, p. 249.
[5] S.R.O. 4123/Ti/1: Highley Easter Book.

single year. Furthermore, four families known to have been resident in the 1680s, for instance, were not included, probably on the grounds of poverty, as all four were also exempt from Hearth Tax payments. It looks, then, as if the very poor may have been excluded from the Easter Book. Because of these limitations, the Easter Book is most valuable for those periods when other corroborative evidence exists.

An attempt was made to enumerate the total population of Highley in 1680, using Easter Book entries 1680–82 in conjunction with the parish register. As children under communicant age are not included in the former, all children under 15 born to couples on the listing and not buried before 1680 were added, as were the four poor families. While this method cannot claim complete accuracy, it does provide numbers in striking agreement with estimates based on the 1672 Hearth Tax return and the Compton Religious Census of 1676.[6] The latter gives a figure of 106 adults: the compilation has 105. The actual number of children in the c. 1680 compilation is 42, or 28.6 per cent of the total. Wrigley and Schofield have pointed out that many estimates of population reached by working from the Compton Census on an assumption that children made up 40 per cent of the total are too high, and find that 30 per cent is a much more realistic figure in the late seventeenth century.[7] This certainly seems to have been the case in Highley. Thus the total population derived from the 1680 head-count is 147.

The 1676 figure does not give any indication of the number of households in the parish. The 1672 Hearth Tax return, together with exemptions, lists 37 households. The compilation has 38. This would give a mean household size of just under four (3.86 on 1680–82 figures). Lastlett suggests a 'fairly constant' mean household size of 4.75, while speculating that in smaller communities it was probably somewhat higher.[8] Even if we adopt instead the lower figure of 4.3, households in late seventeenth-century Highley seem to have been somewhat smaller than the norm. A partial explanation for this is the absence of any large gentry household. The 'Squire' did not actually live in the new house

[6] P.R.O. E 179 255/35: Hearth Tax, 1672. G. D. Fletcher, 'The religious census of Shropshire in 1676', *T.S.A.S.*, 2nd Series I (1889).

[7] Wrigley and Schofield, *Population History*, p. 570.

[8] P. Laslett and R. Wall (eds), *Household and Family in Past Time*

he had built, but merely kept a steward and servant in residence.

Of the 38 households in 1680, 27 were headed by a married man. Six heads of household were widowed and five (all men) were single. The majority of households contained children under 15 – 20 of the 38 households had baptised children in the previous 14 years. The Easter Book does not mention them, but does include, as it were, adult children – who are presumed to have left home if they are not listed. Seven households listed adult sons and daughters. These were not necessarily adolescents: Thomas Dorsett aged 25 lived at home, for instance, as did Richard and Thomas Hancocks who were in their late twenties. Adult daughters, too, were sometimes in the parental household well into their twenties. The better-off were more likely to keep adult children at home: six of the seven households with adult offspring were those of principal farmers.

Not all families were strictly nuclear. In four cases elderly parents were part of their sons' households, though not the heads of them. In these cases the son was married, which appears to be a significant distinction. Where widowed parents lived with single children, whatever their age, it seems to have been the parent who was nominated head of the household. The four three-generation families are clearly defined as having a resident grandmother or grandfather (in fact two of each) who is mentioned after both the head of household and his wife.

Similarly, another four householders had resident siblings, who are listed last. Sometimes this arrangement appears to be of long standing, as with Thomas Hancocks, a single man of 52, who lived with his 60 year old brother, sister-in-law and their three adult children. In other cases it seems that the householder had only recently been elevated to that status, like Francis Holloway aged 26 and newly married, whose father and unmarried sister also lived with him.

There was a total of 18 resident servants in 12 households. Although the vicar's family is not enumerated in the Easter Book, it too may be safely assumed to have had at least one servant. Ten of these servants were female and eight male. Unfortunately, they are rarely named. Of the half-dozen who are, only two were Highley-born – a man of 21 and a woman of 29.

Four of the households apparently consisted of a single individual; all were men. Two of these single men subsequently married; the other two bachelors were Thomas Edmunds aged 25 and Thomas Peirson, 49, neither of whom seems to have done so. The adult spinster was in a less independent position, and usually had to live in the parental home unless she was in service. Margaret Matthews, though, chose to live with her married brother although both her parents were alive and living in Highley. One single woman, Elizabeth Comby, appears to have been a lodger in the house of John Smith. Otherwise, rather surprisingly, there are no indications of lodgers.

Households in 1680–82 were, then, typically mono-nuclear, although at some stage they could well contain an elderly grandparent or adult sibling. The indications are that the nuclear family was the goal, and a more extended family grouping was born of economic necessity. Where circumstances permitted, married children formed their own household. Indeed, there is no instance of two married couples living in the same household.

The age structure of the community in the 1680s is of course difficult to recover with any accuracy. The presence of the 43 children must remain conjectural; of the 105 adults, 18 were servants whose ages are generally unknown; and of course not all of the remainder were born at Highley. However, in most cases the age of a spouse, or of children, enable us to assign those whose exact birthdate is unknown with reasonable confidence to one age-band.

Figure 5.2 illustrates the results. Although with so many riders this age structure diagram must be approached with caution, it nevertheless has some interesting features – not least the relative youth of the community. The 15–19 group is very small. It appears that young people of this age were likely to be away from home, probably often working as servants elsewhere. The group would presumably be greatly increased if we could include in it the unnamed servants, who are the only individuals omitted from the diagram.

The 20–29 group is the largest. It contains those in two distinct situations; married couples, sometimes immigrants, with young children; and unmarried adults living with parents, several of whom (especially women) would leave the village upon marriage. There were very few old inhabitants, with only about seven per cent over 60. In fact Laslett finds that the percentage of over-60s in parishes examined rarely exceeded eight per cent until the

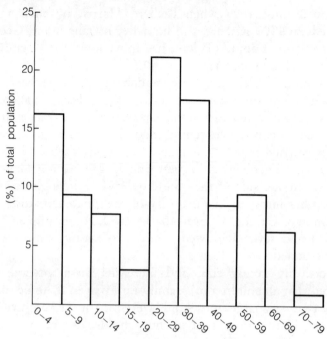

Figure 5.2   Age structure c.1680

nineteenth century.[9] Because of late marriage and prolonged fertility, some over-60s still had children at home: the youngest child of William Jefferys (born 1617) was only four years old in 1680. Children in fact made up 30 per cent of the population of late seventeenth-century Highley, and altogether over two-thirds were under 40.

The wealth of data for this period sheds some light on questions arising from the demographic background which for other periods we cannot answer. For instance, consecutive Easter Book entries show what arrangements were made for one of the groups of orphaned children. Oliver Harris of Woodend Farm was killed in October 1685. Less than two years later, in August 1687, his widow died leaving their four children, Elizabeth aged 18; Mary, 14; Richard, 11; and George aged seven. Their maternal uncle Edmund Palmer moved into Woodend Farm where he lived with three of the children. Mary moved in with her grandmother and another uncle, at the Palmer family farm. This arrangement

---

[9] P. Laslett, *Family Life and Illicit Love in Earlier Generations* (Cambridge, 1977), p. 194.

continued until 1699 when Richard Harris, by then aged 23, married. In 1700 Richard and his wife, Elizabeth and George all lived together. Edmund Palmer had moved out, presumably at the time of Richard's marriage.

This kind of help by the extended family must have been a relatively common occurrence, although the desire to keep on the Harris farm affected the particular arrangements made. It seems that such circumstances could also delay marriage – Edmund Palmer married at 48, immediately he had discharged his duties to his nieces and nephews. Elizabeth Harris, too, having taken charge of the domestic side of the household, was still single at 31 when her brother married. The majority of the inhabitants did, eventually, marry. Of the 32 over-40s in 1680, for example, 23 were married and seven widowed. Only two people, both men, had never married.

Decreasing family size, and increased birth intervals which ensured that all children of a family rarely lived at home together, meant that very large households were rare in the late seventeenth century. Three men headed households of seven, including children and servants: otherwise five was the maximum. Similarly due to levels of fertility and juvenile mortality, no family had more than four children under 15.

The compilation based on the Easter Book of 1680–82 brings out the cyclical nature of household formation, with the family shrinking and growing at various stages of its development. The Easter Book is never quite so full again during the period. However, at certain dates it can profitably be combined with other sources to give at least an impression of population growth and household size.

The Easter Book for 1696–97 can be used in conjunction with the Association Oath Roll of 1696, which lists 36 male subscribers to the Oath.[10] Not all signatories were heads of household, although the great majority – 29 out of 36 – were. A combination of the two sources gives a total of 40 households. Extended family groupings were still very much in the minority. Four households had resident widowed parents, two had adult siblings of the head, and one contained nieces and nephews. Nine families had resident servants – 14 in all. A total of 15 adult children is listed, noticeably predominating in more prosperous families.

[10] P.R.O. C 213/212: Association Oath Roll, Shropshire, 1696.

A head-count of individuals suggests a total population at the end of the seventeenth century of 145, slightly fewer than in 1680, which is compatible with the demographic stagnation identified at this period. This would give a mean household size of only 3.6. The birth rate during the 1690s, assuming a population of 145, was only 26 per 1,000 per annum, and this is reflected in the small household size and in the proportion of children in the community, which had fallen to only 27 per cent.

This, then, is the position in the late seventeenth century. The population of Highley can quite confidently be assessed at around 150, perhaps slightly lower than it had been in mid century. Households were relatively small and predominantly nuclear. The addition of servants to the household was more usual than that of members of the extended family. Not all adolescents left home, though to remain was more usual in landholding families with a farm to run. The complete absence of dual-couple households suggests that upon marriage young couples set up home separately, only later providing a home for a widowed parent.

The quality of the data in the eighteenth century is not quite so good. The number of those exempt from payment of Easter dues seems to have grown in the early years of the century. The Easter Book for the years 1706–08 yields a list of only 24 households. At least six householders known to be resident and poor were omitted, as were two others whose financial position is unknown. With the vicar's own household, this gives a minimum total of 33. This list has 82 adults: parish registers show that in 1708 they would have had 48 children under 15. This would indicate a total population of only 130, and a mean household size of almost exactly four. This total seems suspiciously low, and it may be that a few individuals who were very poor and not mentioned in parish registers have been missed. On the other hand, natural growth had, as we have seen, been very low towards the end of the seventeenth century, and net emigration had previously been high enough to offset even a considerably greater growth rate. However, growth was beginning again, if the proportion of children in the community is a guide: children on this list form 36.9 per cent of the total.

Family groups were even more exclusively nuclear in this listing. None of the 24 Easter Book householders had resident siblings, and only two shared their homes with resident parents. In one case

Henry the widowed father of Thomas Wilks, who had lived with his son's family for at least 10 years, had remarried, and his wife had joined the household. This is the only instance of two married couples living together apparent from all the listings.

Adult children are again only specified in the households of the more substantial farmers. They were mostly in their twenties, but could be considerably older – the two sons of Joan Palmer were in their sixties though their mother, in spite of her very advanced age, was the nominal head of the household.

Seven of the 24 households were headed by a widow (3) or widower (4). Five households consisted of an individual living alone, including for the first time a woman – Margery Charnock, a 56 year old spinster who had lived as a servant in the household of John and Alice Person until the death of the former in 1700. Nearly 30 years before, Margery had had an illegitimate child. She never married.

The next opportunity to compile a list with any confidence is for 1726. Firstly, the Easter Book is fuller than usual for this year, and also includes a list of individuals paying tithe eggs which includes some otherwise exempt. In addition, the earliest Poor Book to survive begins in 1724–25, and lists poor rate levies collected as well as those to whom relief was given. The compilation produces 47 households (or 44 if the four people named Edmunds, all related and assessed in the Easter Book separately did not in fact live alone but shared a home), and a total population of 165. Reference to Figure 5.1 reminds us that baptisms had increased markedly in the first quarter of the eighteenth century. In fact in the 1726 compilation children make up exactly 40 per cent of the total.

There were still virtually no extended family households. There were, however, more people living alone than previously, possibly a reflection of the increased death rates in the 1720s. The adult children (and one nephew) were, in eight out of 10 cases, young men from farming families whose labour was useful there. Additional labour was provided by 16 servants, nine of them men. The numbers of people living alone keep the mean household size below four (3.75 on 44 households). The largest household was that of Benjamin Pountney which consisted of the head, his wife, Luke Bennet a 'manservant', nephew John Pountney, 19 year old son Benjamin, and three younger children aged between five and 14 – a total of eight.

The community, then, was apparently growing in spite of an increase in burials in this decade. With an estimated population of 165, the annual death rate was still below 28 per 1,000.

Listings in the rest of the first Easter Book, which ends in 1756, are less satisfactory. The best is that for 1743, which even so is noticeably less thorough than the seventeenth-century entries, frequently being confined to the head of household and his wife. There are, for instance, only seven servants recorded. Supplementing this list with information from Poor Rate collections and disbursements, we arrive at a figure which can only be taken as a guide to population totals. The compilation produces a total of 160, of whom 37.5 per cent were children.

By the end of the period, the total village population was probably closer to 200. A head-count based on parochial data for 1767, which includes no servants or adult children, totals 171. Certainly the increasing growth rates of 1740–60 could be expected to have resulted in a population increase. In the last decade of the period growth was at its most rapid. A population of 200 would mean that in the 1770s Highley experienced a death rate of 22.5 per 1,000 (i.e. on the low side of the normal range); while birth rate at 42.5 per 1,000 was at the top of the nationally observed range.

This accelerated growth at a period immediately before industrial development is interesting, for although extractive industries such as Highley's are necessarily dependent on geology, Levine has shown how demographic factors were capable of influencing the timing and pattern of industrialization.[11]

Judicious use of the Easter Book in conjunction with other sources can, then, throw at least some light on household size and structure. It suggests a community of small households, with a degree of social differentiation in their formation. The better-off were more likely to keep adult children at home, and to keep resident servants. We may be seeing here a shift in the practice of service: resident 'service in husbandry' continued, but the evidence – too slight to do more than raise a possibility – suggests that its social base may have been changing and that by the eighteenth century the children of the landholding class were less likely than they had been to leave home for a period of service on other local farms.

[11] D. Levine, *Family Formation in an Age of Nascent Capitalism* (New York and London, 1977).

Table 5.3   Bridal pregnancy and illegitimacy 1620–1779

	bridal pregnancy*	illegitimacy ratio
1620–59	22.2%	4.1%
1660–99	27.3%	5.4%
1700–39	23.8%	3.4%
1740–79	17.9%	8.1%

* defined as an interval of 8.5 months or less between marriage and first baptism.

We have seen that baptisms of illegitimate children in the sixteenth and early seventeenth centuries were very few. Table 5.3 shows illegitimacy rates for this period to be considerably higher. Just as in the earlier period Highley's illegitimacy rates were at odds with nationally observed trends, so in this period – or at least in its first half – the figures are at variance with those found elsewhere.[12] Just as in Highley there was no peak in bastardy at the turn of the seventeenth century, neither was there a trough in mid century. Only in its marked rise in the second half of the eighteenth century does Highley fit the national bastardy curve. Illegitimacy ratios are consistently high, and represent a minimum figure when we consider that they represent only those cases recorded in the parish register.

In fact registration of bastardy seems to have been reliable throughout the period. Where other documentation survives relating to bastardy cases, the relevant baptisms are without exception found in the register, with an indication of illegitimacy. In the period 1620–59, the illegitimacy ratio was 4.1 per cent. There is no sign of a falling-off of illegitimacy in this period which elsewhere marked its nadir. However, it has been suggested that falling rates during the Interregnum might have had more to do with changing registration practices than with Puritan controls on sexual behaviour.[13] If this is the case, then the ratio in Highley, where registration of baptisms was at least as good in this period as before 1640 and if anything rather better than after 1660, may not actually have been so unusual.

[12] P. Laslett, K. Oosterveen and R. Smith, *Bastardy and its Comparative History* (London, 1980), p. 14.
[13] K. Wrightson, 'The nadir of English illegitimacy in the seventeenth century' in Laslett, Oosterveen and Smith, *Bastardy*, pp. 176–91.

The low-point in illegitimacy in the period was in fact in the first 40 years of the eighteenth century (though Highley's 'low' could have been a 'high' in other, less bastard-prone areas). At this time, Highley's rate approached most nearly, though still exceeded, the national rate. Between 1740 and 1780, the ratio climbed to 8.1 per cent, a figure only reached nationally in the second half of the twentieth century.[14] It was in this period that age at first marriage for women fell from a consistent mean of 27 years to only a little over 23. This inverse ratio between age at marriage and illegitimacy rates indicates that we cannot look to late marriage as a possible explanation of rising bastardy ratios. Neither does the evidence support the view that illegitimate fertility merely followed the trend of legitimate – certainly not if the latter is measured by mean completed family size.

Table 5.3 also includes rates of prenuptial pregnancy. These are lower than in the pre-enclosure period and are, interestingly, lowest of all in the period of highest illegitimacy. Illegitimacy, then, had become more frequent but bridal pregnancy less so. This lends support to the hypothesis that what we see here is a change in moral regulation in the community. In the pre-enclosure period, sexual activity before marriage was commonplace at all levels of village society: Pountney, Palmer and other Group I brides were pregnant as well as those from cottager families. In the later seventeenth and eighteenth centuries, pregnant brides were not only less usual, but were also exclusively from poorer families. This argues a change in mores among the village elite of tenant farmers, and an increase in their ability to enforce this morality on the rest of village society. At the same time, illegitimacy became increasingly confined to women who had more than one bastard, or who came from 'bastardy-prone' families: in other words, those who were not 'respectable'. Thus what had been a village-wide morality became, like much else in the community, increasingly dichotomized.

So far, then, we have arrived at more conclusions about what were not the causes of illegitimacy than what were. The high and rising bastardy rates were not linked to late first marriage – rather the reverse. They cannot be explained in terms of generally rising fertility. To gain any further insight it is necessary to supplement aggregative analysis by reference to the individuals involved.

[14] Laslett, *Family Life and Illicit Love*, p. 113.

The mothers of illegitimate children in Highley may be divided into three categories. The first are those who have come to be known as 'sparrows'; those women who, apart from the baptism of their child, are not mentioned elsewhere. Secondly there is a group of singletons – women born or resident in the parish whose families had no close links with other illegitimacy, and who bore a single bastard. Finally, there is a group comprising repeaters; those who were themselves illegitimate; and those whose close relatives had also produced bastards.

'Sparrows' form 27.5 per cent of all single mothers throughout the period. Although the surnames of these women are not found in Highley, they are met in other surrounding parishes. Sometimes we can even specify their home parish. An agreement between the parish officers of Highley and Stottesdon records that the latter will provide for the child of Sarah Goodman, which was baptised at Highley in 1779.[15] Many of these women were probably servants, temporarily employed and resident in Highley.

The singleton mothers form another 27.5 per cent of the total. They were either baptised at Highley, or known to be resident there with their families. In this group, the social position of the woman's family is generally known, and we see the increasing concentration of bastard-bearing in landless and artisan classes.

The largest group is of the 'bastard-prone'. Firstly, there are the repeaters: 38.5 per cent of all illegitimate children were born to mothers who had more than one bastard. Their contribution to the increasing illegitimacy ratios, especially in the later eighteenth century, is crucial. Exactly half of all illegitimate children in the period 1740–79 were born to repeating mothers, and no less than 70.8 per cent to mothers in this group as a whole. Besides repeaters, this group includes women who were themselves illegitimate. Ann Bennet, baptised in 1730, was the daughter of Mary Bennet alias Jones, whose name suggests that she may herself have been illegitimate. Ann in turn baptised a bastard in 1751. Only close relationship between mothers has been used as a criterion for inclusion in this group, for at least in the seventeenth century kinship networks were still sufficiently dense for links of some kind to be demonstrable between the majority of the population. Even so, some families can be shown to have had more than their share of bastard-bearers. Sisters Anne and Alice

---

[15] S.R.O. 4123/P/53–61: Bastardy bonds.

Charnock produced three illegitimates at the beginning of the period; then their first cousin Mary Charnock in 1653, and niece Margery Charnock in 1679. The Wilcox family display a similar tendency to produce (and marry) bastards, as figure 5.3 demonstrates.

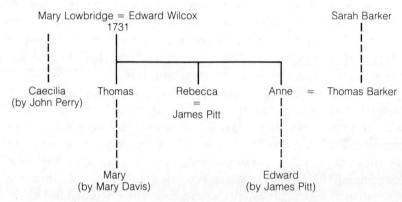

Figure 5.3 Wilcox family, with illegitimate offspring indicated by broken lines

Mary Lowbridge was from a relatively prosperous farming family, one of the very few eighteenth-century single mothers from this class. She had an illegitimate daughter when clearly not much more than 20. Two years later she married Edward Wilcox, who was not the father of the first child. Her youngest, legitimate daughter Ann also had an illegitimate child by her brother-in-law, a relationship which besides being adulterous was also incestuous (brothers- and sisters-in-law being at the time within the proscribed relationships for marriage). Ann was already pregnant when in 1777 she married Thomas Barker, who was himself illegitimate and who had as a child been a parish apprentice in the Wilcox household.[16]

The Wilcoxes were relatively well-to-do bargeowners. Although these families exhibiting a succession of bastardy links were often poor, it was clearly not only poverty which placed families at risk. The Wilcoxes were, however, not really part of the village elite: they were not extensively involved in farming, but made a good living from barge trade and the inn which they kept beside the river.

Where poverty does seem to have been universal was among the

[16] S.R.O. 4123/P/1: Highley Overseers' accounts, 1724–61.

repeaters. All those whose children were born after the commencement of the earliest Overseers' accounts in 1724–25 appear as receiving parish relief. In the seventeenth century Mary Moore, who had baptised four illegitimates at Highley and was almost certainly the mother of a fifth, was buried in 1670. It was recorded that she was 'a poor wandering woman who died in the parish.' This was clearly not true, in the sense that 'wandering' was usually used in the register: her first child was baptised in the parish 11 years earlier. Perhaps the parish authorities wished to disclaim responsibility for a woman who was notorious.

The subsequent careers of mothers of all groups are hard to follow. Axiomatically, we know nothing more about the 'sparrows'. We cannot say whether those women who had borne a bastard were less likely than average to marry, because migration rates are too high for the statistical likelihood of any woman marrying to be determined. Only one of the repeating mothers subsequently married at Highley, although in most cases these women did die in the parish – more frequently in fact than other mothers of bastards. Having had more than one illegitimate child does seem to have been something of a barrier to eventual marriage, even if having made one 'mistake' was not.

No Overseers' accounts survive for the seventeenth century to trace the careers of women who had children during the first half of the period. The Charnock sisters were still in the village, and apparently living together in 1632, when they received a charitable bequest from the will of Richard Palmer. If any degree of opprobrium attended bearing illegitimate children, it did not extend to withdrawing charity. Nor did it routinely result in appearance at church courts, for only a minority of bastardy cases of the period appear in the Bishop's Act Books.

After 1725 we know that single mothers, particularly repeaters, were supported by the parish, often for much of their lives. Mary Bennet alias Jones, who had children in 1730 and 1733, received poor relief from at least 1755 until her pauper burial in 1784. There is evidence that these women lodged in the homes of local farmers (presumably acting as servants), and their parish relief payments went straight to the head of the household, depriving the women of autonomy over even this meagre income.

The potential claim on parish funds made overseers keen to establish the mother's parish of settlement. When Ann Walford, who had accompanied her parents on their move to Abberley in Worcestershire, returned to Highley and became (or already was) pregnant in 1759, letters were exchanged establishing that Abberley would pay the ensuing expenses.[17] Similar arrangements were made in other cases, and it appears to contradict the view that single pregnant women were always removed to their place of settlement. Provided suitable financial agreements were reached, this was not invariably the case.

Singletons were more frequently supported by their families, and apparently more likely to marry, and therefore less the concern of Overseers. Unlike the church courts, the parish officers' interest was purely financial, and their chief concern to establish paternity and hence responsibility for maintenance.

The parish register records the identity of fathers of illegitimates in less than a third of all cases, and no Highley bastardy cases have survived in the depleted Quarter Sessions records. Even when the name of the father is known, it does not always help to establish the kind of relationship within which conception occurred. Often the men came from other parishes and nothing else is known about them. Other cases are more enlightening. Some do appear to be instances of 'marriage frustrated', the phrase used by Levine who sees most illegitimacy as a result of courtship dislocated by adverse economic circumstances.[18] In these cases the parties were generally young, and were free at least to contemplate marriage. William Goodyear, for instance, was 22 and single when he fathered a child in 1745. He eventually married a different woman nine years later, when his circumstances had presumably improved. But youth was not always the reason for failure to marry: William Foxall was a widower of 63 in 1653 when Mary Charnock, aged 41, had his child; and he was able to marry someone else the following year.

In fact there is no case of a couple subsequently marrying after producing an illegitimate child, although one would expect some instances of this if indeed most bastards were conceived between couples intent on marriage but prevented by outside agencies. Another problem with the 'marriage frustrated' explanation is that sometimes parish pressure on the father, in the form of a maintenance order, produced a marriage. There are two cases in the early eighteenth century where evidence of this survives. In

[17] S.R.O. 4123/P/53–61: Bastardy bonds.
[18] Levine, *Family Formation*, chapter 9.

both cases, marriage finally took place a couple of months before the baptism of the child. It looks as if personal disinclination rather than circumstances had prevented marriage in the first place.

Furthermore, not all couples were free to marry or enter a courtship. Thomas Wilkes, who fathered a child in 1733, was a 35 year old married man with five legitimate children; and there were other instances of adulterous relationships. There are no indications of long-term extra-marital relationships in this period: the repeaters for which fathers are named had children by different men.

In several cases it may well be that the loss of a job, lack of available housing, parental disapproval and so on prevented an anticipated marriage. There is slight support for this view in the average age of women having a first illegitimate child. Although the number of cases, particularly in the seventeenth century, is quite small, this mean age does seem to have fallen from nearly 27 years before 1740 to 22 in the years 1740–79. In other words, women were bearing illegitimate children at, or slightly below, the age at which they would have been seeking marriage partners. But in some cases couples clearly entered sexual relationships with no prospect of marriage. And if pregnancy could be the result of normal courtship disrupted, one would expect to find prenuptial pregnancy rates higher than those prevailing during the period when, it seems, sexual activity was not a recognized part of courtship for the majority.

The children themselves frequently vanish, with their mothers, from parish records. Numbers were buried as infants, but a mortality rate for bastards alone is impossible to compute, given the very high mobility of their mothers. Those who remained were often made parish apprentices at an early age. Thomas Barker's mother married and left Highley when he was just six years old. The child remained in the village as a parish apprentice in the Wilcox household. Some apprentices could be sent a considerable distance, like John Moore who went in 1671 to Pitchford, about 25 miles away. Only a tiny minority of the illegitimate children baptised at Highley actually remained there all their lives.

Bastardy ratios, then, were high throughout the period, even by the standards of Shropshire, a known area of high illegitimacy. It is tempting to view the post-enclosure increase in bastardy as at least in part a reflection of increasingly unsettled economic conditions for the poorer inhabitants: numbers of landless labourers grew;

mobility was high; and the likelihood of marriage being prevented by economic factors increased. But not all illegitimacy can be explained in terms of the pauperization of the labouring poor. Some poor families were never involved in illegitimacy while others of a similar, or somewhat higher, financial status were particularly bastard-prone. There does, therefore, seem to be some factor other than the purely economic which made them particularly at risk.

Church courts, secular courts and parish officers continued to be involved in the attempt to regulate morality and provide for the child – and in view of the claims made even so on rate-payers they were likely to have encouraged marriage, to say the least. In the later eighteenth century fewer brides were pregnant but more illegitimate children were born, which may indicate a growing resistance to these pressures, as well as a continuation of what appears to be a seventeenth-century shift in attitudes towards the acceptability of pre-marital sex.

Whatever its causes, the consequences of illegitimacy for the community as a whole were considerable, for payments to single mothers and expenses of maintaining and apprenticing bastard children formed a major part of all parish expenditure on poor relief in the eighteenth century.

6

A Local Oligarchy

In this post-enclosure period, status within the community was closely associated with wealth; and wealth was in turn dependent upon the possession of land. The amount of land held was much more important than whether it was owned or rented. In fact the elite group which had emerged by 1700 were almost all tenant farmers. The increased importance of the parish as an administrative unit meant that this group, which provided the parish officers, had considerable influence within the community. In addition, they were direct employers of labourers who were increasingly dependent on wages alone.

For most of this period, the landlord/tenant relationship was the basis of many social relationships in Highley. Principal tenant farmers sub-let individual fields, and sometimes whole farms. In addition, most labourers and cottagers now rented their houses from local landlords; and in the case of the former, accommodation began to be 'tied' to the job, adding a new dimension to the relationship. However, the same chief farmers and local landlords were themselves the tenants of absentee landlords, with whom they had to negotiate terms for the renewal of leases, and who controlled to some extent the uses to which they could put their land.

Certain important parish offices like the churchwarden and overseer of the poor were increasingly restricted to the most prosperous section of the community. Churchwardens provide the best example of this. In the early part of this period, the churchwardens could be yeomen, husbandmen, artisans or cottagers, as they had been in the pre-enclosure period. In the 1620s and 1630s, a rota system appears to have operated which depended on houses, not individuals: William Perks served in 1634 'for the house he lives in', together with Richard Harris 'for the Wood End'. Thus women, if heads of household, were included, but appear not to have served – in 1628 the warden was 'Francis Dovey for Elizabeth Low, widow'. Elderly men, too, nominated younger relatives in their place. Brian Penn was warden in 1632 for his father-in-law. Interestingly, the wealthiest villagers appear also to have preferred to nominate someone else to serve their year in office, as did Thomas Lowe of Borle Mill and Thomas Pountney of the Rea. The office seems to have been regarded as much as an imposition as a privilege at this date.

Unfortunately, churchwardens are not recorded between 1637 and 1679. By the last two decades of the seventeenth century, the office had become almost exclusively the preserve of the principal farmers of the village – only one man of the 15 who served during this time, on a rota which resulted in a year in office every nine years, was not a farmer. By the end of our period, the size of the group eligible for this office was even more curtailed: only 10 men were called upon to provide the 20 churchwardens needed between 1763 and 1772 (the last complete decade of the period for which wardens are recorded). The same men head the list of tithe payments and Poor Rate contributions during the same period. The same shrinking of the group drawn on for the office of churchwarden is apparent in other offices, notably overseer of the poor: churchwarden is merely the most consistently documented.

This elite group was virtually self-electing, for in the eighteenth century the parish vestry, which consisted of about a dozen chief landholders, appointed wardens and overseers from their own ranks. At the meeting held on 9th April 1765, the vestry described itself as comprising 'the major part of the inhabitants of the said parish' – which numerically it certainly did not.[1] The same attitude is displayed in the memorandum in the parish register of 1678. Giles Rawlins, the vicar, had left money 'to be set forth yearlie by the Churchwardens' for 'the best use of the poor of the Parish at the discretion . . . of the best sort of the said parish.'

The 'best sort' in their role as churchwardens had more influence in village affairs than might at first sight appear. One of their duties was to present cases to the church courts, and there are signs that if the wardens were unwilling to proceed, offences went unpunished. In 1771 the case against Thomas Wilcox was dismissed, in spite of his having admitted fathering an illegitimate child, because the

[1] S.R.O. 4123/P/2: Overseers' accounts and vestry minutes, 1762–1801.

Cross and Church at Ripley South East View 1794.

Jn⁰ Fleming D.D
Patron 1777.

Sam⁰ Borrowes M.A.
Patron & Incumbent 1793.

Tho⁵ Jordan Propr⁵
and Impropriator 1793.

The Beancrofts formerly
Proprietors here.

Plate 5 The parish church in 1794. From Add. MS. 21018, folio 251. Reproduced
with permission of The British Library.

churchwardens did not appear.[2] In 1748 Thomas Brewer and Thomas Dorsett were cited by the vicar for refusing to present John Hill to the court for offences which were part of a disagreement between Hill and the unpopular vicar.[3]

Although Quarter Sessions records for this period are incomplete, they do indicate that only men from this same group were elected jurors. The few surviving mentions of parish constables date from the early nineteenth century but show that this office too was organized on the basis of a rota of principal farms in respect of which their occupiers served for one year.

However, it was in their role as overseers of the poor that 'the best sort' exercised most influence. They collected the parish poor rate, and of course decided the destination and amount of parish relief paid to individuals. In addition they were responsible for applying the conditions of the Act of Settlement, and could (and did) examine paupers and order their return to another parish. They questioned unmarried mothers and imposed maintenance payments on the fathers of their children; they were responsible for arranging the apprenticeships of pauper children; in short, there were for the poor few areas of life which the overseers could not regulate.

Thus a wide range of powers and responsibilities became concentrated into the hands of a group of men which for most of this period comprised only 20 per cent or so of all heads of household in the community.

The hierarchical structure of village society, and the way in which it was largely determined by the occupation of land, is illustrated even in the lay-out of the parish church. A plan survives (undated but c.1775) showing how by the end of our period large pews at the front were reserved for particular farms (not individuals), with a careful gradation to smaller pews for lesser properties, and finally 'cottage seats' at the very back. Various faculties were granted by the Bishop's court to allow prominent parishioners to re-arrange pews in order to enlarge their own even when, as in 1757, this meant moving the pulpit and the font.[4]

Throughout the period, these chief farmers continued to employ live-in servants, with whom their relationship was often quasi-

[2] H.R.O. Acts of Office, Box 41, vol. 160.
[3] H.R.O. Acts of Office, Box 41, vol. 159.
[4] H.R.O. Register of Bishop Beauclerk, 1755–74.

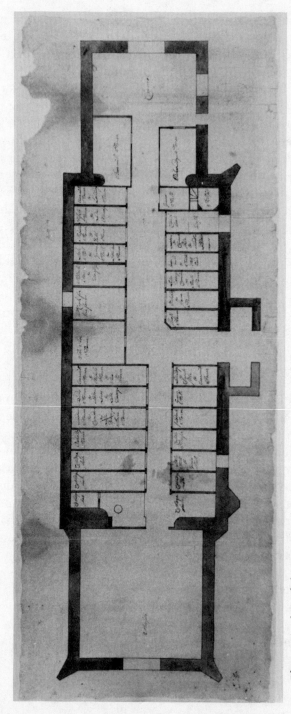

Plate 6 A plan of the pews in the parish church, undated but c.1775. Note the gradation from large farms at the front to cottage seats at the back.

(Photograph: Shropshire Record Office, Shrewsbury)

paternal. In reply to the bishop's Articles of Inquiry in 1716, the churchwardens stated that 'the Parishioners duly send their children and servants to be instructed by the Minister'.[5] We still find instances well into the seventeenth century of servants' Christian names only being used; for example one servant was described as 'Margaret the servant of Thomas Harris' in the same way that his daughter would be designated 'Margaret the daughter of Thomas Harris'.

Servants worked, ate and slept in close proximity to the family, at least during the first half of our period. The witnesses' depositions recalling the 1620s and 1630s show how servants worked alongside their master, asking him questions: Christopher Rowley was hay-making with Thomas son of Richard Palmer his master, and asked him 'what there was to be set out' (in tithe). They were privy to their masters' conversations: James Powis heard the vicar 'demand tithe pay of George Peirson, who said he had but little hay and could not well spare it'.[6] All servants quoted, even the women who might be expected to be more narrowly concerned with domestic matters, knew exactly how much their masters paid for different types of tithe, and several had been sent to take tithe payments in cash to the vicar. Although it is only details concerning tithes which have come down to us, they do illustrate something of the relationship between masters and their resident servants in the seventeenth century.

Private charity, which had been a feature of pre-enclosure society, appears to have declined during the first 50 years of this period. Giles Rawlins' bequest to the poor of the parish in 1678 mentioned above was the last of this type of charitable bequest. Similarly no bequests to individual poor recipients were made after 1651, when Richard Rowley left corn to eight poor villagers. Since such bequests had previously been quite common, this cessation would appear to mark a change in the attitude of the more prosperous towards the poor of the community. The cohesive social structure of the pre-enclosure period had been undermined by the increased stratification of village society and, above all, by the high levels of geographical mobility among tenant farmers. Similarly, no bequests to individual servants are found after the 1670s. It may be no coincidence that the same period saw a

[5] H.R.O. Articles of Inquiry, 1716: printed schedule and MS replies.
[6] P.R.O. E 134 21 & 22 Chas II Hil. 29.

hardening of official attitudes, with the 1662 Act of Settlement designed to regulate the movement of the poor from parish to parish. By the late seventeenth century in Highley, the emphasis in poor relief was firmly on institutionalized provision rather than private charity.

Although some parish-organized system of poor relief must have been in operation during the seventeenth century, records of it do not survive. The first detailed accounts begin in 1724, by which time poverty was perceived as a problem in the community.[7] Highley parish officers used the Act of Settlement from the beginning to rid themselves if possible of those likely to be a charge on the parish: indeed even before the Act, in 1657, a dispute between Highley and neighbouring Alveley over which parish was responsible for Ann Jenkins, a poor widow, had reached the court of Quarter Session at Shrewsbury.[8]

We have seen how numbers of poor had risen until, in the 1720s, a considerable proportion of all adults buried were recorded as paupers. These were not all in regular receipt of parish relief, however: in 1725, for instance, only two individuals claimed payments (of 10d a week) throughout the year. The majority of payments made by the overseers until about 1760 were 'casual' – occasional amounts for coal or house rent, or small allowances not in cash at all but in goods like a peck of malt or clothes or shoes. The parish also lent goods: 'Lent widow Crowther a pair of sheets three weeks' (in 1741). Sometimes occasional payments were made to men who were too ill to work – 'when he was sick'. Paupers were buried and parish apprentices clothed out of the poor rate: in 1744 Margery Malpas was buried at parish expense and her illegitimate son John provided with 'shurts, a pair of clogs, pair of shuse, stockens, pair of briches', presumably prior to being apprenticed. Most payments were made to the elderly and infirm, widows and single mothers. There are a few signs, though, that younger men were beginning to be in a position to claim parish relief. In 1752 the overseers 'paid Barker over his pay 1s 1d'.

Nevertheless, total payments hardly ever exceeded £20 per annum until the 1760s, when a steady rise began. In the last year of the period, 1779–80, total payments in poor relief were £34 14s 3d.

[7] S.R.O. 4123/P/1: Overseers' accounts, 1724–61.
[8] R. L. Kenyon (ed), *Shropshire County Records: Orders of the Shropshire Quarter Sessions* (Shrewsbury, 1908).

The rise was largely due to an increase in the number of 'pensioners', those in receipt of regular cash payments, usually of a shilling a week. In accordance with the 1697 Settlement Act, these paupers wore a distinguishing badge on their clothing. 'Badging the poor' cost two shillings in Highley in 1761. In addition to cash payments, however, paupers had still to appeal to overseers for fuel and clothing and for ex gratia payments when they were particularly 'in want'. They were not allowed a fixed 'pension' over which they had complete control, but were obliged to make several representations a year to the parish officers and to receive some relief in goods rather than in cash.

To supplement the money available, and to use the capital of sixteenth- and seventeenth-century bequests to the poor, it was decided in 1744 to purchase two acres of land where Robert Evans, a local brickmaker and builder, built 'a substantial dwelling house', very soon divided into two.[9] Rents arising from these cottages were used to buy bread which was distributed to the poor on Sundays (provided that the recipients attended the service and took the Sacrament, when available). Although these houses were known as The Poors Houses, they seem at no time during this period to have been used to accommodate poor people, but merely to provide a regular return – a rent of two guineas a year – on the accumulated capital.

Every attempt was made by the 'best sort' running parish affairs to minimize the burden of poor relief on those paying the poor rate. Single mothers were questioned to discover the identity of the child's father, who was then obliged to pay maintenance; families and individuals likely to become chargeable to the parish were 'examined' to ascertain their place of settlement, and could be deported like the Deuxhill family who were returned to Stottesdon in 1682. Appeals were made by the parish against relief orders imposed on them: in 1764, for example, the vestry meeting of eight farmers decided to send the overseer to Shrewsbury 'to appeal against an order granted for the relief of Margaret Shinton to pay her ten shillings a week'. This must be the order for 'the payment of 10s weekly to . . . an impotent poor woman afflicted with foul disease' which was quashed in 1764 as a result of the appeal.[10] In

[9] S.R.O. 4123/Cy/1–5: Highley charity deeds, 1744–1820.
[10] L. J. Lee, *A Full List and Partial Abstract of the Contents of the Quarter Sessions Rolls 1691–1800* (Shrewsbury, ND).

fact no-one received anywhere near as much as 10 shillings a week: two shillings seems to have been the absolute cash maximum during this period.

Ironically, letters and journeys involved in removing paupers, appealing against relief orders and disagreeing with other parishes' overseers about responsibility are expenses which feature prominently in each set of accounts. Provision for the poor was seen as a burden by those householders who contributed to the poor rate, and by the overseers for whom the job meant considerable time and trouble. For the poor it meant frequent appeal to the authorities and little opportunity to exercise personal control over budgeting. It provided a lever for social control: those who did not attend church, for example, did not receive bread.

It must also be remembered that those in regular receipt of parish relief were only the very poorest: there could also be hardship amongst those who did not qualify. A change of circumstances, old age or bereavement, could very easily bring destitution. Thomasin Childs was the daughter of a man who rented the lord of the manor's chief farm: she never married, and after the death of her parents received parish relief for at least 30 years until her death (and pauper burial) in 1752. Richard Esps had rented the same farm, yet came 'on the parish' in old age. The new seven-or nine-year leases did not provide the same security for old age or for widows as the old three-life tenures had done.

Landless families had always been the more vulnerable to poverty in old age, and during this period the number of landless, whether artisans or labourers, grew. Increased illegitimacy in the eighteenth century meant that a significant number of paupers were single mothers and their children. Men temporarily unemployed or unfit added to the numbers of occasional claimants. Although amounts were never large (other Shropshire parishes often spent much more[11]), the period 1725–80 saw a fourfold increase in expenditure on poor relief in Highley. In this whole period between enclosure and industrialization there appears to have been a change in attitude away from individual philanthropy towards communal responsibility. The attitudes of the poor themselves, with their 'P' for pauper badges, public doles of bread and so on, can only be conjectured.

[11] J. Hill, *A Study of Poverty and Poor Relief in Shropshire 1550–1685* (unpublished thesis, Liverpool University, 1973).

Thus one aspect of 'good neighbourliness' – private charity – appears to have declined in importance during this period. Another feature of the pre-enclosure community had been the system of small informal loans of a few shillings or even pence in which most villagers took part. After 1620, these small loans either ceased, or were no longer regarded as worth recording in wills. Such loans as are recorded are both larger and more formal, being invariably secured by bond. They were rarely between neighbours, as the casual small debts had been. Other large loans were those raised by mortgages from the mid-seventeenth century.

In fact the formality of 'business' contacts increased considerably during this period: besides bonds and mortgages, the more prosperous villagers were involved in carefully drawn-up marriage settlements, leases and sub-leases to farms and fields, deeds of sale of property, and so on. This increase in formal contracts was necessarily paralleled by a rise in literacy levels. In the sixteenth century, even the wealthiest tenants of the manor were often illiterate. Throughout this period, we see an increasing class-bias in literacy: although there were exceptions, by the eighteenth century most farmers could at least sign their names, while as far as it is possible to tell, poorer men remained largely illiterate. The only socially unbiased set of signatories is in the marriage register from 1756. Between that date and 1779, just over half of all bridegrooms (and a quarter of brides) signed their names. Literacy was directly related to socioeconomic position, with signatories almost exclusively farmers and tradesmen.

Some Highley men had business interests outside the village. Richard Palmer at the time of his death in 1633 owned a house and tannery in Bewdley. In 1764 Edward Wilcox, a bargeowner, was building a house at Abberley in Worcestershire, and also owned property across the Severn at Alveley. He would also, of course, have had dealings with those whose goods he transported on the river.

We must not forget the importance of the Severn to communications in this period. River traffic was considerable: in 1756 there were 75 barges operating out of Bridgnorth, and a further 10 based in the villages between that town and Bewdley.[12] In the 1770s alone, four bargemen drowned in separate incidents at Highley.

[12] W. Watkins-Pitchford, *The Port of Bridgnorth* (Reprinted from *The Shrewsbury Chronicle*, 1974).

Some villagers may have worked as bargemen, if only temporarily: certainly several had small boats which they used on the river. George Steward and his brother went out late one night in 1771 in their boat to search for coal, presumably dropped from laden barges coming down from the mid-Shropshire coalfield. George was drowned when the boat capsized.[13] During this period the Ship Inn, also owned by the Wilcox family, was established to take advantage of trade from the river. Highley was in fact situated beside the main artery for trade and communication in Shropshire.

Although business contacts between Highley inhabitants and elsewhere were both more frequent and more formal than they had been in the pre-enclosure period, the geographical areas encompassed remained on the whole similar. Mortgagors, landlords and creditors were mainly residents of the local market towns and surrounding villages. Men travelled to, or had links with, towns and villages up and down the Severn. Attendance at Archdeaconry headquarters at Ludlow or the Bishop's court at Hereford, and at Shrewsbury Quarter Sessions, sometimes necessitated longer journeys, particularly for parish officers. Otherwise long journeys seem only to have been undertaken in exceptional circumstances, like the 'four years or so' that William Jefferys had spent 'in the late King's army' during the civil wars.[14] This absence of any mention of long journeys is surprising in the light of the frequency with which the people of even more remote Myddle at the same period seem to have travelled to London, for example.[15]

Some contacts with people living elsewhere were not to do with business: they were simple friendships. 'Friend', as a description of, for instance, a beneficiary in a will, was a term not found in the pre-enclosure period. Friends first appear around 1630 in wills. In fact the first to be thus described is the 'well-beloved friend Mr Francis Dovey' in the will of Alice Harris, 1628. For the will-making class, friends to some extent replaced the more distant kin and close neighbours when it came to choosing overseers and executors. They appear to have been quite unrelated to testators, and usually lived in other nearby villages rather than in Highley itself. It is tempting to see in this phenomenon an increase in

[13] S.R.O. QR 79/10: Inquest on George Steward, 1771.
[14] P.R.O. E 134 21 & 22 Chas II Hil. 29.
[15] R. Gough, *The History of Myddle* (London, 1981) and D. Hey, *An English Rural Community: Myddle under the Tudors and Stuarts* (Leicester, 1974).

importance to the individual of selected relationships rather than those pre-determined by kinship or even by geographical proximity. Towards the end of this period, in 1771, two friends of Joseph Cook were appointed as his executors and in fact were given virtually complete authority over his estate and its disposal: clearly for Cook friendships were important relationships.

Perhaps as a result of increasingly marked social stratification within the village, Highley yeomen turned increasingly towards 'horizontal' social contact with other yeomen in the surrounding area rather than 'vertical' friendships within their own parish. These friends attended social events together, and visited each others' houses. In 1723 the vicar, John Higgs, went to the horse races at Tettenhall with a group of friends.[16] In 1669 Richard Weaver, a 71-year old yeoman from Kinlet went to visit William Rowley, whom he had known for many years, when Rowley was on his deathbed. They talked of local news, including the current dispute between vicar and parishioners.[17]

The records of this dispute offer further evidence of social contacts during the mid-seventeenth century. Witnesses from several neighbouring parishes testified to their knowledge of Highley, its farms, customs and inhabitants. Men who had once lived in Highley but had moved away were recalled to testify, often from quite considerable distances, like Leominster in Herefordshire and Churchill in Worcestershire. Contact between these men and people in Highley seems to have been maintained in the meantime, at least to the extent that their current whereabouts were known.

Of course, not all relations within the community or with the neighbourhood were friendly: disputes and quarrels, even fights, continued. In the absence of court rolls after 1618, our knowledge of disputes between neighbours is less than in the pre-enclosure period. The end of strip-farming removed one frequent source of discord: we have seen how frequently quarrels arose over land boundaries. However, the church courts of the seventeenth century still detail feuds and fights between villagers. In 1682, John Matthews was presented for 'striking wounding and hurting with a bill one John Lyde, servant of Rev. Mr John Burton' in the churchyard. We are not told the cause of the fight, but like those

[16] Bodleian Library MS. ENG.MISC.e.344: Diary of John Higgs, 1723.
[17] P.R.O.E. 134 21 & 22 Chas II Hil. 29.

noted earlier it apears to have been spontaneous, and occurred virtually on Matthews' doorstep.[18]

In the early part of this period, one source of discontent was the rhymes and jokes which some villagers told against others: in 1622, for example, Thomas Charnock had 'raised a foolishe scandalous rime to the offence of divers of the parishioners.'[19] Some members of the community were regarded, at least by the 'better sort', as disreputable; and gossip about and condemnation of them, reached the courts. Catherine Lawrence was presented for being 'a very idle and lewde person' who drank (presumably in the ale house) during the time of church services.[20] In 1615 there was 'a common fame' that Alice Charnock had been delivered of an illegitimate child which had then been secretly buried in a garden.[21] Lying 'under a common fame', without there being necessarily any supporting evidence, was regularly the justification for presentment at court.

Quarrels between vicars and parishioners, severally or collectively, were a common occurrence. We have already mentioned the dispute between all the principal landholders and Giles Rawlins, which dragged on from about 1667 to Rawlins' death in 1678. The parishioners insisted that tithe hay had customarily been paid not in kind but as a cash 'composition': the vicar wanted to collect in kind. All sorts of extraneous charges were subsequently brought in, but this remained the kernel of the disagreement. One of the parishioners described Rawlins as 'a contentious man' who 'quarrell'd with divers poore men and undertennants about theire custom and constrain'd them for feare of suits to alter the same'.[22] Certainly the surviving evidence suggests that Rawlins had behaved unreasonably. In any event, the quarrel was long, bitter and divisive.

There was also discord between Richard Higgs and his parishioners in the mid-eighteenth century. He was accused in the diocesan court of fathering a bastard child on Elizabeth Pountney, widow, and retaliated by accusing her of not having paid her Easter dues for the previous six years. This seems to have marked the

[18] H.R.O. Acts of Office, Box 43, vol. 171.
[19] H.R.O. Acts of Office, Box 36, vol. 138.
[20] H.R.O. Acts of Office, Box 36, vol. 136.
[21] H.R.O. Acts of Office, Box 36, vol. 133.
[22] H.R.O. Depositions, Box 2, vol. 4.

beginning of a series of disagreements between Higgs and the rest of the parish: he presented John Hill to the courts, and the churchwardens for not having done so themselves. Higgs in turn was reported for having failed to hold services at the appointed times; for 'vain Cursing and Swearing', and finally for 'going down on his knees in his own house on the Sabbath day calling upon God that a Curse should fall on some of his Neighbours and afterwards praying that a curse might fall upon the whole Parish in General'.[23]

In 1762 Elizabeth Coomby, widow, was found guilty at Quarter Session of attempting to defame another vicar, Dr Fleming, by alleging that he had sexually assaulted her.[24] Whether this was part of a similar feud, an attempt at blackmail, or even a genuine grievance, it is impossible to guess, as no evidence survives.

The frequently stormy relationships between vicar and parishioners seem to have owed more to secular causes than religious differences. In fact parishioners seem to have taken changing shades of religious opinion in their stride. When Giles Rawlins was ejected at the end of the Civil War, his replacement was Robert Durant, one of the signatories to Richard Baxter's Worcestershire Association of the 1650s, many of whom were, like Durant, removed at the Restoration, and who later chose official nonconformity.[25] Parishioners testified during the court cases of the 1660s that Durant was 'godly', 'honest' and 'of good reputation', and it seems that no repercussions followed this change of direction of religious leadership in the parish. Villagers seem to have been largely indifferent to the doctrinal position of their vicar.

In fact there is no sign of religious fervour in the parish during this period. The returns of the Compton religious census of 1676 state that there were 'no Papists, no Nonconformists' in the parish. The answers to the Bishop's Articles of Inquiry of 1716 similarly report 'We have no Dissenter of what Persuasion soever in our Parish, or any Meating of Dissenters that we know off.'[26] The occasional presentments at church courts for non-attendance at

[23] H.R.O. Archdeacons' Visitations, Box 44, vol. 158.
[24] S.R.O. QR 44/6: Judgement against Elizabeth Coomby, 1762.
[25] G. F. Nuttall, 'The Worcestershire Association: its membership', Journal of Ecclesiastical History, I, 2 (1950), pp. 197–206.
[26] H.R.O. Articles of Inquiry, 1716.

church seem to indicate a lack of enthusiasm for services, rather than religious dissent.

The vicars Rawlins, Durant and Burton between them spanned the period from 1635 to 1720. In some ways they retained something of the involvement in village life of their pre-enclosure predecessors. They lived in the parish, and farmed their glebe lands. Rawlins made a list of his farm implements in 1675 which runs to 53 items and shows minute concern with day-to-day farming. Burton's probate inventory lists considerable crops and stock on the vicarage premises. But all were university-educated men, and not locally born as Thomas Oseland had been. This increasing social isolation was accompanied in the eighteenth century by absenteeism. The churchwardens of 1716 could report that 'our Minister resides personally upon his cure', but after the death of John Burton in 1720, this ceased to be the case.

Subsequent vicars rented out most of the vicarage house and lands and visited Highley only for church services. John Higgs records in his diary travelling to Highley from his home at Quatt to preach, and for burial and baptism services. He was succeeded by his son Richard, who also held more than one living and was not resident. Dr Fleming, the final vicar of our period, was another pluralist, and active in county administration. The social (and literal) distance between priest and people in the eighteenth century was immeasurably greater than it had been in the sixteenth century.

Thus quarrels between neighbours were by no means infrequent, and were if anything even more likely between villagers and someone like the vicar in a position of authority. It is possible that less violence arose from these disputes than had been the case in the sixteenth century: but the changing nature of the evidence in the post-enclosure period prevents any firm conclusions. Fights may well have continued unreported in the absence of manor courts.

The nominal ownership of the manor of Highley changed hands frequently during this period, always to absentees after Thomas Lowe sold it in the 1650s. No records of manor courts have survived: probably none were held, for they are not referred to elsewhere in any way. In any case, they had primarily been concerned with regulating communal agriculture. Ecclesiastical and county courts continued to exercise social control. So, more arbitrarily perhaps, did the local oligarchy which we have seen in charge of administration at parish level, as well as reporting (or deciding not to report) misdemeanours to the courts.

The church courts were primarily concerned with church attendance, sobriety and propriety. They continued to order public penance for the mothers – and occasionally the fathers – of illegitimate children, or for those 'living incontinently'. Pre-marital sexual relations were sometimes punished even after marriage had taken place. Those who worked, or set their servants to work, on a Sunday even at haymaking or harvest, were liable to be punished. Similarly drinking, shooting or playing football or 'chuck' on Sundays were punishable offences.

At least in the first half of the period excommunication, the most severe of the penalties imposed by the court, had considerable effects. It cut the offender off from all social or familial contact. Several villagers were accused in the 1620s of eating and drinking with Walter Holloway; they answered that they had immediately ceased to do so upon learning that he was excommunicate. By the eighteenth century it had become the practice for those who could afford to do so to commute their penance by a cash payment: the ignominy of doing penance in local churches was reserved for the poor. But although their sanctions may by this time have lost some of their force, the church courts continued to operate and to impose these sanctions throughout this period.

In addition, sanctions at village level were imposed. Many individuals depended upon discretionary payments by overseers of the poor, a potential lever for the control of their conduct. The parish stocks were in use until at least the 1750s. National legislation implemented at local level also gave parish officers a degree of control over one very important aspect of behaviour – the freedom to move at will from place to place.

There is almost too much evidence of geographical mobility in the seventeenth and eighteenth centuries. Parish registers, fiscal listings and parish administrative records present a mass of changing names as individuals and families arrived, left and died out. Any attempt to quantify and illustrate the degree of mobility must be partial. Some sections of the community may have been more mobile than others, and certainly some are less historically visible. It is easier to trace the careers of men than of women (who changed their name at marriage and rarely feature in lists of heads of household). Yet men, who were less likely to move as a result of marriage, were probably less highly mobile. In 1672 only 41 per cent of heads of household in Highley had been born in the parish: only 45 per cent were natives in 1779. Furthermore, the great majority of these individuals were men, and the percentage was almost certainly less for women.

Some of even the 'static' two fifths would move later in life, leaving little more than a quarter of the inhabitants who lived out their lives in the village. We lack a complete listing of inhabitants before the nineteenth century to enable an exact figure for those who moved at some time to be established: but all the indications are that mobility rates in Highley accorded well with findings elsewhere. Clark found that, in the period 1660–1730, 70 per cent of men in rural areas had moved at some time in their life, and 75 per cent of women.[27]

Table 6.1 shows the number of children baptised at Highley and surviving childhood, by birth cohort. The most noticeable feature of the table is the consistently high 'disappearance rate', of those who are never recorded again in Highley after their baptism. The

Table 6.1   Emigration 1620–1779

Decade	Number in cohort	Last rec. at baptism	Last rec. as adult	Buried Highley	Buried Highley (%)
1620–29	27	16	1	10	37
1630–39	43	33	3	7	16
1640–49	48	38	4	6	12.5
1650–59	47	30	6	11	23
1660–69	35	24	3	8	23
1670–79	34	22	5	7	20.5
1680–89	37	28	6	3	8
1690–99	33	26	3	4	12
1700–09	29	23	1	5	17
1710–19	44	28	9	7	16
1720–29	51	35	5	11	21.5
1730–39	51	36	6	9	18
1740–49	60	37	16	7	12
1750–59	58	40	11	7	12
1760–69	54	40	10	4	7
1770–79	66	43	17	6	9

[27] P. Clark, 'Migration in England during the late seventeenth and early eighteenth centuries', Past and Present, 83 (1979), p. 66.

cohort of 1620–29 had the lowest percentage of emigrants in this category at 59 per cent. Thereafter the figure was never below 60 per cent, and the cohorts of the period 1690–1710 reached a peak of 79 per cent emigration. Thus a large proportion of those born in Highley continued to leave early in life – they did not marry, bear children or die in their native parish, nor remain long enough to be mentioned in any other documentation there. This continues the pattern of early emigration noted in the pre-enclosure period, when the mean of decadal percentages for those not recorded after baptism was 63.4 per cent.

In the pre-enclosure period, however, most of these young emigrants left in adolescence while their parents remained behind in the village. In this period, and particularly in the eighteenth century, increasing numbers left in childhood when the whole family migrated. For most of the period the percentage of those born in the parish who stayed into adulthood – to marriage or child-rearing ages – remained small, even though this figure includes women marrying at Highley and then leaving. In fact most female children baptised at Highley did not marry there. Interestingly, however, the numbers of those last recorded as adults rose after 1740: this may reflect an improvement in the registration of marriages after 1754, or an increased willingness to move even after marrying and having children.

This increased mobility of whole families is reflected both in the numbers of those leaving in adulthood, and in the very reduced proportion of those who were both baptised and buried at Highley. With the exception of the 1620–29 cohort, which again appears as the most stable, those born and buried in the parish were never more than a quarter of the total, and usually considerably less. Thus we can gain some idea of the extent of migration among those born in Highley: two thirds regularly left in childhood or adolescence; others went as adults, leaving only some 10–20 per cent to be buried in their birthplace.

Of course, not all emigration involved those who had themselves been born in Highley. Some people moved more than once in their lives, and for them Highley was a more or less temporary place of residence. Table 6.2 illustrates another aspect of migration. It lists numbers of 'new fathers' by decade. Consistently less than one third of those men had themselves been born in the parish: the means of means for the cohorts of the seventeenth century is 31.8

Table 6.2   Mobility of fathers of children baptised 1620–1779

Decade	Number of 'new' fathers	Number baptised at Highley	Number buried at Highley
1620–29	14	7	7
1630–39	19	6	6
1640–49	21	8	11
1650–59	14	5	8
1660–69	8	2	3
1670–79	12	4	9
1680–69	14	3	6
1690–99	11	3	2
1700–09	10	5	4
1710–19	17	1	4
1720–29	21	6	14
1730–39	20	5	12
1740–49	16	5	7
1750–59	26	3	8
1760–69	17	8	10
1770–79	20	3	8

per cent, for the eighteenth century only 26.7 per cent. Further-more, less than half of these men, on average, remained in Highley until their deaths. This represents one significant difference from the picture in the sixteenth century, when over half of the 'new fathers' remained until their deaths, while an even clearer majority had been themselves born in the parish.

Throughout the period, the baptism register includes those we have called 'transients', who baptised one or at most two children in the parish and then disappear from the record. Figure 6.1 shows that there were some transients in every decade, with a clear peak in the 1630s. Between 1630 and 1639, nearly 40 per cent of all couples baptising a child were transients. They were most probably labouring families, employed on short-term contracts.

Although we cannot place too much reliance on flutuations from decade to decade because of the small size of overall numbers, nevertheless some periods – notably the 1620s and 1630s – do seem to exhibit certain characteristics on all of our tables. It is therefore worth looking at these decades in more detail. The 1620s seem to continue the pre-enclosure pattern, where migration rates were high among adolescents, but where those who settled in Highley

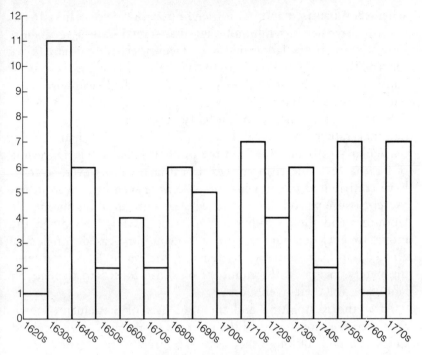

Figure 6.1   Number of transient parents, 1620–1779

showed a marked tendency to stay there for life. There were also very few transients during this decade. Enclosure, however, was well advanced by mid-decade, and one might expect increased mobility as a result. In fact the real increase in migration came during the 1630s. Numbers of transients increased dramatically: 76 per cent of children baptised left in childhood or adolescence, and only 31 per cent of the 'new fathers' recorded remained in Highley until their deaths.

Some of the transients were described as 'wanderers' or 'travellers' – part of what Clark calls 'the multitude of poor migrants on the tramp' in the decades before the Civil War.[28] Some may have been undertaking long-distance migration, like the parents of Richard Woodefinde, an infant buried in 1637/8, 'whose father and mother were wanderers' and who would seem to have abandoned the child. Others travelled around the area for years: Thomas Evans and his wife were described as 'wandering people' when they baptised a child at Highley in 1634, and again

[28] *Ibid.*, p. 57.

when they baptised another in neighbouring Chelmarsh in 1642.

Other transients, while not vagrants, stayed only a very short time, apparently in labouring jobs. Twenty-eight new fathers are recorded between 1630 and 1639; of these, only eight were both baptised and buried at Highley – altogether 11 had been born there and 10 would be buried.

Some of this increased mobility was undoubtedly due to national rather than local causes. The late 1620s had been a particularly difficult time, and the poor were suffering the results of bad harvests and rising prices. Local factors, however, seem to have contributed to the situation. We have seen how even in the pre-enclosure period there were signs of a group of highly mobile labourers and their families in the area. As Highley joined the move to enclose, numbers in this group increased. Enclosure created, at least initially, a demand for more labour: it also ultimately increased the numbers of those forced to depend on labouring for their livelihoods.

After the Restoration and the 1662 Act of Settlement, which restricted the movements of the poor, vagrants more or less ceased to be recorded, although short-stay labourers were a feature of the rest of the period. Mobility also began to increase higher up the social scale. In the pre-enclosure period, when farms had been held for terms of three lives, an heir remained to inherit the property. As more farms fell into the ownership of absentee landlords who let them on much shorter leases, we begin to see the movement on a much larger scale of families of yeoman and husbandman class. The depositions of witnesses in the tithe disputes of the years around 1670 include brief biographies. Nineteen of these witnesses gave evidence of having lived for some time in Highley although they had subsequently moved elsewhere. Of the 15 Highley residents called, only four had been born in the parish and had lived there 'for the most part' ever since. Although some witnesses had spent time in the village as servants, the majority had been in some landholding capacity.

The Easter Book lists of householders exclude the poorest families in village society, and do not name servants – the most mobile of all groups. The lists include all the principal farmers of the parish who would in the earlier period have represented the most stable element of the community. Easter Book entries demonstrate that in the eighteenth century there was considerable movement even among farmers. Only half of the families in Easter Book lists of 1696–98 were still represented (either by the same individual, a widow or a son) 10 years later. Thirty years later, in 1726, only 12 of the original 35 families were still represented, a figure which by 1743–44 had fallen to six. In less than 50 years, 83 per cent of the families of the late seventeenth-century listings had completely disappeared.

Those families who left (or occasionally died out) were replaced by immigrants. Twenty new families appeared between 1706–08 and 1726. This was a period of considerable movement, as also indicated by the drastically reduced percentage of 'new fathers' born at Highley for the decade 1710–19 in Table 6.2 Fifteen years later, only half of these new families remained, but they had been joined by 13 more arrivals. The turnover of whole families, even among the more prosperous sections of the community, had clearly become rapid. At least 12 of the new arrivals between 1706–08 and 1726 rented substantial properties, and belonged to a group which before 1620 would have been very unlikely to move as a family from a parish in which they had settled.

The Settlement laws rarely presented a problem for this group. They were unlikely to become a charge on the parish, at least until old age, and in any case usually rented property worth more than £10 per annum. Occasionally the movements of tenant farmers can be traced around the district. Robert Adams, baptised at Chelmarsh in 1719, lived in Billingsley from 1742 to the end of 1751. He may well have rented a farm there on a nine-year lease. Early in 1752, he took up another nine-year lease on Churchyard House in Highley.[29] Five children had been born to Adams and his wife at Billingsley, and a further one at Highley. He did not live to renew his lease or move on, for he died at Highley in 1757.

Occasionally even men who had occupied considerable premises could fall into difficulties when they moved. Thomas Beetley was in Highley for 'almost two years' around 1726, renting Borle Mill for £20 a year. He, his wife and three children then went to Kidderminster, where by 1729 they were likely to become chargeable to the parish and were removed to Highley as their last place of settlement.[30]

Labourers and servants continued to make frequent moves, in

[29] G.R.O. G/6 D2153/649: Lease to R. Adams, 1752.
[30] S.R.O. 4123/P/11: Removal order, 1726.

spite of the settlement laws. The young single farm worker, whether live-in servant or farm labourer, had few problems in moving. Witnesses' depositions show how servants came from the immediate neighbourhood to work in Highley in the seventeenth century. The same pattern continued to the end of this period: the examination of John Venables in 1773, for instance, states that he had previously lived at Kinlet, but that his last place of settlement was at Sottesdon where he had worked for two consecutive years. As 'an unmarried man not having children', he clearly worked his way around the district wherever work became available.[31]

Married men with children were theoretically in a more difficult position: parishes would be less willing to have them gain a settlement. The steady numbers of transients, however, suggest that labouring families were able to move from parish to parish, although they ran the risk of removal in the case of illness or unemployment. As wives automatically gained a settlement via their husbands, the practice of a couple setting up home in the husband's parish was reinforced. Although no longer the prime cause of adult mobility, marriage was still a major reason for moving, especially for women.

Nevertheless, Table 6.3 shows a considerable increase during the period in endogamous marriage. No figures are presented for the period 1690–1720, for during that time the vicar seems to have been operating a 'marriage shop'. Numbers of marriages rose dramatically, especially after 1700 when 15 or 20 couples married each year rather than the usual one or two. In the first decade, 1690–99, home parishes are usually stated, especially for bridegrooms: after 1700 this is rarely the case. Most of these marriages took place by licence, and couples came from all over the Shropshire part of the diocese of Hereford. The vicar, John Burton, may well have been a surrogate, able to grant licences,

Table 6.3   Number of marriages with partners resident at Highley, 1620–1779

	Both	Bride only	Groom only	Neither	Total marriages
1620–89	7	19	6	6	38
1720–55	17	17	3	11	48
1756–79	30	11	2	0	43

[31] S.R.O. 4123/P/8: Settlement examination, 1773.

which would have initially have drawn couples to Highley. He also seems to have been less than scrupulous about marrying couples within the prohibited seasons like Lent.[32] Between 1700 and 1720, when Burton died, it is practically impossible to distinguish between 'normal' marriages and these extra ones, and to include all marriages performed during this period in our table would be very misleading.

In the seventeenth century, only 18.4 per cent of all marriages were between partners both of whom were living in Highley at the time of marriage. In the final years of our period, after the new format for registration introduced by Lord Hardwicke's Marriage Act of 1753, practically 70 per cent of all marriages were endogamous. We must make some allowances for possible over-estimation as a result of the new format: a space for place of residence was left on the printed page, and occasionally it seems that 'this parish' was entered with more regard for convenience than for accuracy. Even so, considerably more Highley residents chose partners from their home village than was previously the case. There are several possible reasons for this. The village population had increased, thus providing a greater choice of marriage partner within the community. Furthermore, kinship networks had become much less dense, which meant that choice of partner was less restricted by degrees of prohibited relationships. Flandrin found that in rural France the proportion of endogamous marriages rose significantly in larger villages.[33]

In marriages where only one of the partners came from Highley, it was usually the bride who was the local inhabitant. It was unusual for a man to bring his bride to his own village for the wedding itself, although the couple frequently set up home there. Some of these marriages of Highley men to women from elsewhere can be traced in the registers of surrounding parishes. Figure 6.2 indicates in diagrammatic form the geographical area drawn upon for marriage partners, showing the parishes where these marriages have been traced. While naturally not exhaustive, this does indicate something of the area of the marriage market. The sketch map (see p. 152) also shows the home parishes of those marrying a Highley partner at Highley itself.

The map shows an inner ring of parishes within a 10-mile radius.

[32] H.R.O. Acts of Office, Box 41, vol. 153.
[33] J.-L. Flandrin, *Families in Former Times* (Cambridge, 1979), chapter 1.

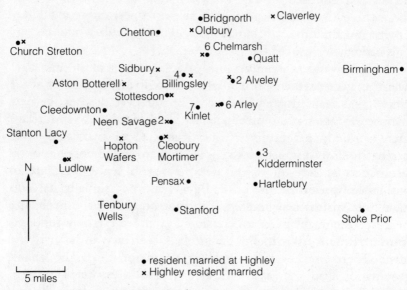

Figure 6.2   Homes of marriage partners, 1620–1779

The nearest of these, those bordering on Highley, supplied several marriage partners each. Others towards the fringes of the inner ring, like Tasley, Claverley and Cleedownton, provided only one each. The parishes outside the 10-mile ring should also include three others at even greater distances: Rewl in Gwynedd; Newport in north Shropshire; and Kingscliff, Northants.

Those who married partners from within the inner ring might be of any social position: all these parishes were within walking distance and within the area drawn upon for servants, for instance. In fact the same area comprises the usual extent of business and social contacts, and the movement of farmers and labourers alike. Those who took partners from a greater distance, however, were almost exclusively prosperous yeomen. The bride from Rewl married Robert Lowe of Borle Mill in 1620; Martha Peirson of the demesne farms married a grazier of Kingscliff; John Pountney of the Rea married Elizabeth Fownes of Stoke Prior in Worcestershire and eventually settled there himself. Curiously, the geographical area drawn upon appears to shrink in the later part of the period:

not only were there more endogamous marriages, but the area of the marriage market itself was more confined to immediately neighbouring parishes. This may have been largely due to the decrease in numbers in the yeoman bracket – the tenant farmers of the eighteenth century did not aspire to the gentry as did the Lowes and Pountneys of the seventeenth century.

Whether they moved before or after marriage, most people born in the parish did as we have seen leave long before their deaths. There is little evidence of the ultimate destination of those last recorded as infants. Wills of their parents sometimes indicate that they were living in other nearby parishes, but more frequently there is no indication of their whereabouts. Occasionally even the parents themselves seem unsure. In 1723 John Ellis left a small bequest to his son Thomas 'if he come again into this countrey within the space of three years'. In this case, no contact seems to have been maintained between Thomas and his family, probably because of the distance over which he had moved: those who moved within 'this country', which we may take to be roughly equivalent to our 10-mile ring, usually did maintain some contact if they left family in their native place. John Roberts in his will of 1627 left money to the poor of Chelmarsh, his birthplace, and bequests to his brother and other relatives still living there. Bequests to the poor of a native parish, rather than to specific relatives there, seem to indicate a sense of identity with the place in spite of years of absence. John Pountney, who had lived at Stoke Prior for many years before his death in 1655, still left money to the poor of Highley in his will.

A few local boys, like John Pountney himself, and James Longford who has been traced as a pupil at Old Swinford Hospital School in Stourbridge in the early eighteenth century,[34] went away to school; far more went into service away from home. Most villagers had family members living at some distance, for after the changes brought about by enclosure and in prevalent types of land-tenure, mobility among all classes was greatly increased. With the end of the three-life tenure, fewer holdings passed from father to son; and shorter leases meant that farmers and their families were much more likely to move in middle life than previously. Those who owned their farms could, like the Pountneys of Green Hall, sell up and move elsewhere. This was also the case with some

[34] Supplied from the school register by the Headmaster Mr C. F. R. Potter.

artisans and cottagers who were forced to join the more mobile group of wage labourers. The demand for labourers increased after enclosure, and attracted some families to the village. There were seasonal variations in this demand, as well as longer-term fluctuations caused by economic conditions and changing agricultural methods. There seems to have been a pool of labouring families who moved regularly round 'the country' as work became available, as well as numbers of servants, drawn from the same area, who spent some time working in Highley.

As a result of these levels of migration among all sections of village society, probably only a quarter of residents would have been born in Highley. Emigration by juveniles remained high – sons had even less incentive to stay on with fewer prospects of inheriting a tenancy – but increasingly through this period we find whole families arriving, staying a few years, and moving on. By the mid-eighteenth century only four of the families resident in 1620 were still represented in the village: Lowes, Pountneys, Fenns and Rowleys. All occupied a lowlier position in the socioeconomic scale than their forebears had done.

Mobility among farming families also resulted in a decline in the importance of settled residence in the community as a status criterion. Wealth was increasingly the determinant of influence. Highley's relatively 'open' nature, the tradition of mobility, and the existence in the area of a pool of labour ready to move in search of work, are factors which may have contributed to its suitability for industrial development.

Such high mobility levels naturally weakened kinship networks within the community, which were not nearly as extensive by the late seventeenth century as they had been in the sixteenth. Since so much migration was over a relatively short distance, however, it did mean that a more extensive network of relationships linked Highley with other parishes in the district. John Matthews, for example, who died in 1716, mentioned in his will a brother living in Arley and a kinsman of Enville, Staffs. He also had a married daughter who had moved away from Highley, and a daughter-in-law whose own family lived in Billingsley.

Kinship networks had already become less dense by the time of the 1672 Hearth Tax returns: the 35 named individuals had 29 different surnames. In fact, even including relationships by marriage, 19 of the heads of household were not related to any other on the list. Fourteen were related to one other, and only three – Stephen Edmunds, his son and son-in-law – to two or more.

It appears that a greater number of second marriages and the increase in endogamous marriage had increased kinship links within the community somewhat by the end of our period. We can arrive at a compiled list of 44 heads of household (which very probably omits one or two short-term residents) in 1779. The list contains 33 different surnames, and although 21 of the individuals were apparently unrelated to any other, 12 were related to one other and 11 to more than one. Many of these relationships, especially in the 'two or more' group, were of affinity: there are never more than two instances of the same surname, but brothers- and sons-in-law make up a considerable number of those related. There still remained, however, about half of the population who were not related to anyone else in the community outside their own nuclear family.

When we turn to the recognition of kin, we find that this nuclear family was still the basic unit in the community. We have seen that by far the most common household structure was that of parents and children only. This predominance of the nuclear family is reflected in the range of kin recognized in wills, which was even narrower than that of the pre-enclosure period.

A total of 36 wills has been traced for the period 1620–1779. Of these, 25 mention sons and 24 daughters. Spouses are mentioned in 22 wills, and grandchildren in 15. For most testators, provision for the immediate family was the over-riding concern. Testators were predominantly male, so the spouse is usually a wife. References to 'my well-beloved wife', 'my loving wife' and so on may have been recognized formulae, but there are other signs of care for and confidence in one's wife. Humphrey Harris, speaking on his deathbed in 1632, said to his wife Elinor 'I do leave unto thee all that I have.' Wives were frequently made executrix, and given considerable control over the future disposition of the estate, although this was more common in the first half of the period than the second. Elizabeth Pountney in 1692 was to receive all her husband's property for her lifetime, and to dispose of it to their children 'as to her shall seem meet and convenient'. Husbands were careful to provide accommodation for their widows: in 1727 Thomas Lowe left to his wife 'the upper part of my dwelling house' with half the garden and half of a small beanfield adjoining it. He, like some other testators, was also concerned to return to his wife 'the goods which I had with her and which she brought to my house when we were married'. In this case, Elizabeth Lowe had worked with her tailor husband, and part of the business was regarded as her own affair: she was to receive 'all her shop goods' and to pay all her own debts.

Widows of freeholders continued to take over the family farm, at least nominally, as they had done in the pre-enclosure period. Joan Palmer appears as head of household on all parish and fiscal listings until her death in 1706 at the age of 85 or more, although her middle-aged sons had in fact been running the farm for most of her 40-year widowhood. It was more difficult for the widows of leaseholders to continue on a farm, however, and in the eighteenth century the widows of relatively prosperous men were sometimes reduced to dependency on parish relief, like the Widow Brooks whose husband was at one time tenant of Borle Mill. Increased numbers of leasehold tenant farmers during this period meant that there were more widows in this position, and in fact after the middle of the seventeenth century there is a marked decrease in wills made by women, which reflects their weakening position in this respect.

Having provided as well as possible for their spouse, most testators concentrated on bequests to their children. Some children had already received their share before the will came to be written. Joseph Cook in 1771, for instance, makes this clear: he gave one shilling to his eldest son 'as he was provided for before'. Unmarried daughters, too, usually received more money than married ones, suggesting that the latter had already received a marriage portion. In one case, a son does appear to have been cut off with the proverbial shilling. John Matthews in 1716 included a terse bequest 'to my son one shilling', without naming the young man or adding any other details. His executors, for 'good reasons' of their own which they did not state but which were almost certainly connected with this disinheritance, refused to act.

Sons-in-law were mentioned in nine of the wills. Sometimes this was in the absence of a son, although daughters too could be given this responsibility. Judith, the youngest daughter of Alice Harris, was made residuary legatee and executrix of her mother's will of 1628, although her older brothers were still living in Highley.

Thurstan Dale in 1632 left most of his possessions to his grandchildren, and chose a granddaughter as executrix.

Particularly careful provision was made for unmarried daughters. They were expected to exercise some personal choice in the selection of a husband, provided that this choice met with the 'consent and good liking' of the executors. This presumably reflects the normal degree of parental influence in the matter. Marriage portions were regarded by testators as vital, and equity between daughters as desirable. John James in 1741 left £30 each to his two single daughters, and in a clause addressed to his son-in-law tells him to 'take to yourself . . . four pounds a year . . . till it come to the value of thirty pounds'.

Younger children were a special anxiety. Humphrey Harris's final spoken instruction was to 'desire his wife to be good unto his two daughters'. George Harris, who died in 1654, left one third of his estate to his wife for her maintenance, and the remainder to bring up his young children until they reached 21. Grandchildren, too, if they had lost one or both parents, received special provision. Richard Palmer in 1632 made extremely detailed arrangements for the apprenticeship of his grandson, the child of his widowed daughter.

Relationships within the family seem, on the evidence of wills, to have been generally warm. Sons-in-law were usually regarded as part of the family, and the step-daughter of Thomas Strefford in 1633 received his whole estate. There is one instance of disharmony within the family in these wills, however, besides the disinherited son of John Matthews; and one with no possible ambiguity. Joseph Cook, who died in 1771, had clearly quarrelled with his son-in-law Samuel Wilcox. Possibly he had never approved of the marriage, for neither he nor his wife witnessed it, and their daughter was living away from home when it took place. In any case, Cook placed £100 with his overseers and instructed them to pay the interest to his daughter and not to Wilcox so that it should not be 'subject to the debts control or management' of Wilcox.

Wills are, of course, an incomplete guide to degrees of affect within the family. In the absence of letters and journals, however, they are the most personal documents we have, and point in the main to caring relationships between spouses, and between parents and children.

Mentions of kin outside the nuclear family are comparatively rare. Nephews, cousins and brothers are mentioned in two wills, and a sister, niece, uncle, brother-in-law and sister-in-law in one each. In six wills we find unspecified 'kinsmen' – the exact relationship being unknown or regarded as unimportant. The range of kin recognized had shrunk, even from the sixteenth century, and the more distant kin were being increasingly replaced by friends. In the main the testator of the seventeenth and eighteenth centuries neither expected his distant kin to administer his affairs or assist his widow and children, nor felt himself obliged to leave some of his possessions to them at his death.

Yet in spite of the high geographical mobility, the increasing stratification of village society, and a decline in some aspects of the neighbourliness which characterized the pre-enclosure community, some ideals of social relations remained. The concentration on the nuclear family and the increased importance of self-selected relationships – both of which may be seen as evidence of increased individualism – are reflected in the memorial inscription of Elizabeth Cook, who died at the very end of our period. Her admirable qualities were listed in order of importance: 'She was a loving wife, a tender mother, a sincere friend, and a good neighbour.'

PART III

The Village
1780–1880

7

Masters and Men

During this period, the development of extractive industries brought considerable changes to the economic, social and demographic structures of Highley. It is, however, difficult to pinpoint the exact beginning of this development, for the earliest surviving evidence, from the 1790s, describes industrial activity already in progress.

Other parishes in the surrounding area experienced some degree of industrialization from about 1780. Quarries and a coal pit were being worked at Kinlet and Stottesdon at this date.[1] Coal miners are mentioned in the parish registers of Chelmarsh from 1774. At Billingsley, the vicar recorded in March 1796 the baptism of a child of John Brown 'at this time resident in the parish . . . with many others who came from the north of England to attempt Opening a Colliery'. A furnace for smelting iron ore was also opened here, on the other side of the Borle Brook from Highley, in 1796 or shortly after.[2]

Two other forges were built in the area, and both had connections with mining developments at Highley. That at Eardington, five miles away, was built in 1778.[3] A later owner also held the lease of one of the most important industrial sites in Highley. The forge at Hampton Loade, a mile up-river, was built in 1796 by John Thompson, who in the early years of the nineteenth century was co-proprietor of Stanley Colliery in Highley.[4] Coal from Highley was certainly used at Hampton Loade.[5]

[1] L. J. Lee, *A Full List and Partial Abstract of the Contents of the Quarter Sessions Rolls 1696–1800* (Shrewsbury, ND).

[2] *Parish Registers of Chelmarsh. Neenton and Billingsley*, Shropshire Parish Register Society: Hereford Diocese, Vol. III, Part 2 (1903), third pagination, p. 36.

[3] W. Page (ed), *The Victoria County History of Shropshire* (London, 1908).

[4] N. Mutton, 'The forges at Eardington and Hampton Loade', *T.S.A.S.*, LVIII (1965–68).

[5] *Ibid.*, p. 241.

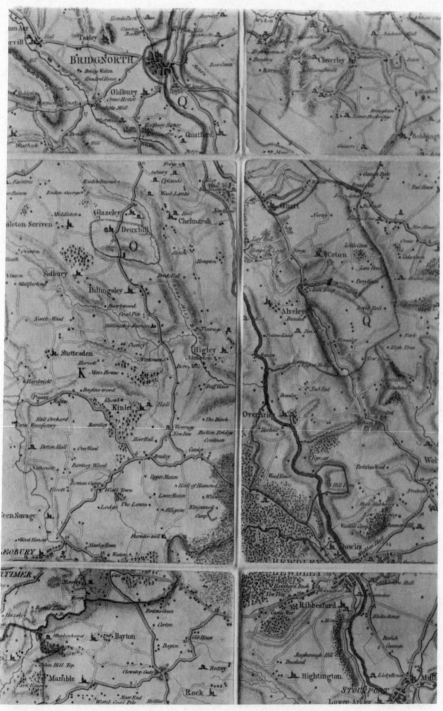

Plate 7 A map of the district in 1808, showing coal pits at Billingsley and similar symbols at Stanley in Highley parish. (Photograph: Local Studies Library, Shrewsbury)

Thus in the last two decades of the eighteenth century Highley was surrounded by new industrial enterprises. A vital stimulus to this development was the opening in 1772 of the Staffordshire and Worcestershire canal, which linked the Severn at Stourport with the industrial Midlands – a link which was extended in 1779 with the construction of the Dudley and Stourbridge canals. This south-east corner of Shropshire now lay on the main route between the industrial centres of Coalbrookdale and the Black Country.

The coal, and most of the stone, mined at Highley lay in deposits close to the river, where two wharves were constructed for the transfer of minerals to lighters. A railway led from one of these to the ironworks and colliery at Billingsley, and was in use by January 1797.[6]

Much of our information about quarrying and coal mining in and around Highley before 1800 comes from the estate papers of Christ Church, Oxford, which owned 20 acres of land at the confluence of the Severn and the Borle Brook.[7] There is a series of surveys of and correspondence about the estate beginning in January 1797, when Dr Henry Macnab and his brother-in-law George Johnson were already operating a quarry and a coal mine. Reference is also made to two other well-esablished quarries in the parish in January 1798.[8]

Macnab had built himself a house near the Severn and the terminus of the railway, and by 1797 wished to extend this and to build cottages nearby for miners.[9] The mine, he said, was currently producing 50 tons of coal a day; although it is not clear whether this was actually on the college estate or is in fact a reference to the mine at Billingsley in which Macnab and Johnson also had an interest. At any rate, the cottages were not built on the estate, although a terrace of stone dwellings for industrial workers was built at New England further up the Borle Brook.

In 1803 the wharf and railway were not working and Macnab and Johnson were in financial trouble, their bankers having foreclosed on the mortgage.[10] Some time after this date, the

[6] Ch. Ch. MS Estates 84/143: Memorandum of survey, 1797.
[7] Ch. Ch. MS Estates 84: Leases, correspondence and surveys relating to Woolstans Wood, Highley.
[8] Ch. Ch. MS Estates 84/163: Surveyor's report, 1798.
[9] Ch. Ch. MS Estates 84/143.
[10] Ch. Ch. MS Estates 84/170: Letter from C. Pocock to J. Bennett, 1803.

'beneficial interest in the lease' was made over to George Stokes, who since 1789 had been co-owner of Eardington Forge.[11] By 1812, Stokes, Macnab and Johnson were all bankrupt. When the stock of the Billingsley operations was advertised in 1814 it included sleepers and rails of the railway which had carried iron and coal to the Severn.[12]

Meanwhile, however, another mine had been opened at Stanley, the area of the parish on the banks of the river. This pit too appears to have been begun at least partly to fuel a local forge. It was owned by John and Benjamin Thompson, who had built Hampton Loade forge in the 1790s.[13] On January 1st 1804, the Thompsons advertised the sale in Worcester of coals 'from their colliery at Stanley' which had proved popular 'last season'; so the mine was in operation at least by 1803.[14] Benjamin Thompson baptised children at Highley in 1808, 1809 and 1811, so it would seem that he lived in the parish and supervized the colliery.

Little can be discovered about the early years of Stanley Colliery: it may have begun some years before 1803. By 1807 a steam engine was used to lower colliers (two boys and a man were killed during this operation) and to wind up coal, and the workings appear to have been quite extensive.[15] There may have been other short-lived mining ventures in the parish in the early years of the century. A piece of land called 'Coalpit Leasow', for instance, seems to be that belonging to Johnson and Macnab by 1802, and purchased by George Stokes by 1810.[16]

After 1812, however, Stanley Colliery appears as the sole survivor, with its scale of operations continuing to increase. In 1813 William Hughes and Joseph Gritton were joint owners, and even issued their own banknotes.[17] Cottages were built to house the miners at Stanley, and the pit continued to flourish well into the 1820s. The stock of the mine was sold in 1824, although it is not certain that it ceased to operate at that date.[18] The census

[11] Mutton, 'Forges at Eardington and Hampton Loade'.
[12] The Salopian Journal, 5 Jan 1814.
[13] S.R.O. QR 236/125: Inquest on Richard Steward, 1807.
[14] Berrows Worcester Journal, 1 January, 1804.
[15] S.R.O. QR 231/78 and/85: Inquests on Samuel Bright and Francis Humphreys, 1808. S.R.O. QR 236/125: Inquest on Richard Steward, 1807.
[16] S.R.O. 1671/: Conveyance from C. Morris to F. Pitt, 1846.
[17] L. Pressnell, Country Banking in the Industrial Revolution (Oxford, 1959), p. 29.
[18] Berrows Worcester Journal, 11 Dec 1823: advance notice of sale.

enumerator of 1831 offered the recent closure of a coal mine as the reason for decline in population.

The register of baptisms begins to record fathers' occupations only in 1813, well after the establishment of mining in the parish, and provides at best a partial indication of its decline. Figure 7.1 shows the number of 'collier' fathers annually recorded, and though of course there were an unknown number of miners who were not the fathers of young families, it does seem to indicate a decline in coalmining after 1825. Some miners who worked outside the parish continued to live in Highley, but in the village itself coalmining on a commercial scale ceased until the sinking of Highley pit in 1878.

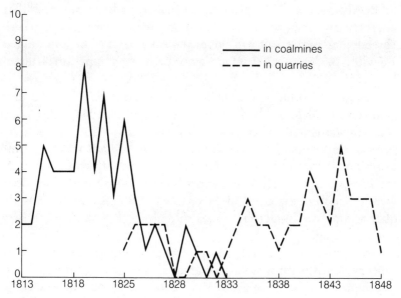

Figure 7.1 Crude annual totals of fathers employed in coalmines and quarries

Quarrying, however, was a longer-lived activity. It had been carried out on a small scale probably for centuries, but the increase in river traffic and the new potential markets opened up by the canal links in the late eighteenth century led to the development of the industry at Stanley. This area of the parish, about a mile from the village centre, was on the west bank of the Severn, and had been mainly used as meadowland until the last quarter of the century. About 1775 the Ship Inn, owned by one of the sons of the bargeowner Edward Wilcox, received its licence here to cater for the river trade. Another son, Samuel Wilcox, began quarrying on his nearby land shortly afterwards.

The earliest record of his activities is in 1797, by which time the quarries were well established. They are probably those noted by Plymley as operating in the parish in 1793.[19] There were at least two: one of grey building stone, and one of red sandstone which was sent to Birmingham for grinding gun barrels and making cider presses. Demand and prices were high, and the works quite extensive.

Another quarry, which belonged to the Reverend Samuel Burrows, supplied a hearthstone to the Silverdale Iron Company in 1797. It was shipped to the Potteries via Stourport, where the Staffordshire and Worcestershire canal joined the Severn.[20] The absentee owner of the Heath Farm, in the same area of the parish, agreed that his tenant would provide stone for the building of Bewdley bridge in 1797 which would also be shipped in Wilcox's barges.[21]

The quarry about which we know most is that on Christ Church land run by Dr Macnab. This was in operation by May 1797 when Macnab was called to account by his landlords, who had not given permission for its opening. Macnab's house had already been built using this stone, and 1500 cu.ft. had also been sent to Bewdley for the construction of Thomas Telford's new bridge there. Forty men were currently employed in Macnab's quarry alone. By 1804 the quarry was no longer in use, although it may well have been opened up again later.[22]

Other quarries, though, continued throughout the nineteenth century. Census returns show a gradual decline of quarrying from a high point probably in the 1830s and 1840s. In 1851 there were 14 quarry labourers in Highley; in 1861 only seven; and by 1881 there were just five.

Highley stone was used extensively to build local houses, as well as Bewdley bridge. In 1839 it was even suggested that the new Houses of Parliament might use stone from Highley.[23] The

[19] B. L. Add. MSS. 21018: undated copy of notes by J. Plymley, 1793.
[20] Keele University Library S.V.141: Minute book of Silverdale Iron Company.
[21] W.R.O. BA 4600/765.
[22] Ch. Ch. MS Estates 84/174: Survey, 1804.
[23] Page (ed), *Victoria County History of Shropshire I*

Coalbrookdale Company purchased sandstone for furnace hearths from Highley[24], and the 'good building stone' of the parish was stressed in a trade directory of 1851.

By 1800, then, a busy industrial centre had grown up in Highley. This was largely based at Stanley on the Severn, where the quarries and coal mine provided employment. Cottages were built for the workers; the public house served locals and bargees passing through the parish. River traffic increased still further with the opening of a tow-path in 1800, and some local men earned their living as bargemen. The Wilcox family continued to run barges out of Stanley, and the colliery had its own boats too: in 1824 there were two barges of 60 tons burden among the stock. By 1820, Stanley had its own blacksmith, carpenter, cordwainer and butcher.

The Census Reports of 1801–31 illustrated this growing involvement in industry. In 1801, only 19 of the 61 families were engaged in 'manufacture and trade': the majority still earned their living from agriculture. By 1811 the position had changed: there were now 49 'industrial' families and only 30 'agricultural' ones. A similar situation was reported in 1821. By 1831, the use of categories appears to have changed, with a large number of families categorized under 'other': in fact, because of the closure of Stanley Colliery there was probably a rough equivalence between those families in agriculture and those in trade and industry.

Figures 7.2 to 7.4 clearly show the decline in importance to the village economy of coal mining, even though, based as they are on occupations in parish registers, they are not a perfect measure. In the years between 1815 and 1824, mining was the single greatest employer: 'labourer' at this date was not used exclusively for agricultural workers. Subsequently, numbers employed in coal mining dwindled steadily. The charts also illustrate the continuing importance of quarrying, and the relatively small but stable proportion of those earning their living from river traffic. Finally, we are reminded of the continual agricultural underpinning of the economy, with the two occupations of farmer and agricultural labourer providing a major source of employment throughout.

From 1841 it is possible to be more precise about the nature of employment. Table 7.1 shows numbers in the main categories of

[24] Dr B. Trinder in a letter, 8 Nov 1983.

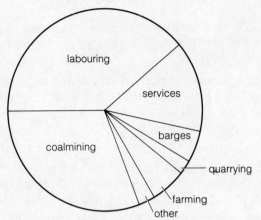

Figure 7.2 Male employment, 1815–24

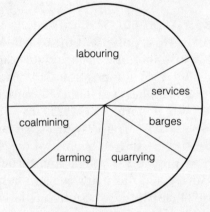

Figure 7.3 Male employment, 1825–34

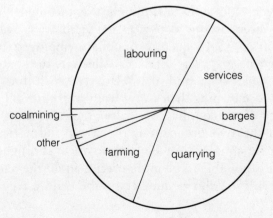

Figure 7.4 Male employment, 1835–44

Table 7.1   Male occupations 1841–81

	agriculture	quarry & coal	services	railway	servants	ret. & prof.
1841	67	9	23	–	23	3
1851	59	20	26	–	11	2
1861	68	9	23	59	1	4
1871	58	12	20	3	3	6
1881	42	63	17	3	5	3

Note: in 1841 distinction between quarrymen and agricultural labourers was not always made in census.

male occupation from census returns of 1841 to 1881.[25] Numbers involved in agriculture remained high, falling off only towards the end of our period. 'Male servants' too were generally live-in farm hands, and some occupations listed under services, like miller and tree-feller, were also quasi-agricultural. The large number of railway workers in 1861 were engaged on the construction of the Severn Valley Railway which opened in 1862. For most of the period, the only resident coal miners lived on the fringes of the parish, and probably worked outside it. However, by 1881 the second phase of coal mining had begun, and this is reflected in the increase in numbers of colliers.

The village economy supported a range of trades. One result of the considerable increase in population in the early years of the century was a demand for new housing. In 1801 there were 48 houses in Highley: 10 years later there were 85. Most of the new additions were short terraces of cottages. Their construction must have provided work for several, and the increased housing stock enabled the village to support its own glazier, plumber, joiner and bricklayers. The increased population provided work for a growing number of shoemakers and blacksmiths, for a tailor and a weaver, and several female dressmakers. There was, however, very little retail trade until the very end of our period. After 1815 a butcher and a chandler are mentioned, and in the census period a small grocer. Three public houses were opened in the 1840s, presumably as a result of relaxed licensing laws introduced in the 1830s.[26] For the most part, goods that could not be produced in the home had to be brought in from outside the village.

[25] P.R.O. HO/107/923; HO/107/1985; RG/9/1847; RG/10/2739; RG/11/2627: Highley census returns, 1841–81.
[26] J. Richardson, *The Local Historian's Encyclopedia* (New Barnet, 1977), p. 270.

In describing the extent of Highley's industrialization in the early nineteenth century, we must not overlook the continued importance of agriculture to the village economy. Even at the height of industrial activity, between 1811 and 1831, between a third and a half of all families were employed directly in agriculture. Pits and quarries, with their associated new housing, were largely confined to one area of the parish, and did not occupy large tracts of productive farm land. Between the 1830s and 1879, agriculture was again the main source of employment. Bagshaw's directory for 1851 called Highley 'a pleasant rural village . . . noted for its extensive orchards and the excellency of its cider', as well as noting the presence of the quarries.

Only on the census returns of 1851 and 1871 is size of farm consistently stated. At the former date, one large farm of 480 acres occupied a third of the farmed land in the parish. There were a further five farms of more than 100 acres. The remainder were either of the smallest viable size, around 25 to 40 acres, or smallholdings of about 10 acres which were supplementary to some other occupation. This represents some degree of engross-ment since the beginning of the century, when most of even the larger farms seem to have fitted what Plymley in 1803 described as the norm for the county of 50 to 100 acres.[27]

Plymley regarded the small farmers of Shropshire, those with 20 or 30 acres, as 'the most wretched and poorest in the community'. Certainly they were in a less favourable position than larger farmers to profit from the vastly increased grain prices during the Napoleonic Wars. Prices in local markets soared during the 1790s: the vicar of Chelmarsh recorded that wheat was sold at 9s 6d a bushel in 1783, and at £1 1s a bushel in 1795.[28] Disastrous though these price rises were for the poor, their effect on local agriculture was stimulating. In 1801 the vicar of Ditton Priors, a few miles to the north-west of Highley, reported that in spite of high prices and apparent grain shortages 'our opulent farmers have stacks of old wheat by them now . . . they care not how high the price of corn is, the higher it is the more their gain.'[29]

Sir William Childe at Kinlet Hall was an innovative and 'improving' farmer at the beginning of the century, and some of his

[27] J. Plymley, *A General View of the Agriculture of Shropshire* (1803).

[28] *Parish Registers of Chelmarsh, Neenton and Billingsley*, first pagination, p. 119, p. 128.

[29] J. P. Dodd, 'The state of agriculture in Shropshire 1775–1825', *T.S.A.S.*, LV (1) (1954).

methods percolated into the surrounding parishes.[30] At least one threshing machine, drawn by three horses, was in use in Highley by 1816.[31] It was probably at this time that some conversion to arable was undertaken: the proportion of arable to pastureland in 1851 was certainly greater than it had previously been. Plymley does not record the acreage of arable in his observations of 1793, but it was clearly important to village agriculture for he notes in detail the prevailing rotation of crops. This was either wheat, barley, clover, wheat; or wheat, turnips, barley, peas, wheat: that is, a 3- or 4-course rotation depending on whether or not clover was grown.

The post-war depression was also felt in Highley. In 1817 the Dean and Chapter of Christ Church were told that the coal mine and quarry on their estate were not working, although operations might resume 'when there is more money in the country'.[32] It was probably during this period that the engrossing of farms took place, as smaller farmers found increasing difficulty. The amalgamation of holdings in the hands of a few prosperous families is also shown by the Tithe Award of 1842.[33]

By 1871, two large farms of over 400 acres each dominated village agriculture. Interestingly, too, six farmhouses were uninhabited – three of which fell into disrepair and were later demolished, while a fourth became two labourers' cottages. This suggests a decline in agricultural fortunes by 1871, which is a little early to be attributable to the 'great depression' of the 1870s, which in any case was much less severely felt in Shropshire than in many other counties.[34] Saul points out that corn producers were much more badly affected than dairy and livestock farmers.[35] In fact, wheat prices had begun to fall in the 1860s, and it is probable that we see in Highley's case an adverse outcome of conversion to arable.[36]

Because of the census returns, we are able during the latter part

---

[30] Plymley, *General View*.

[31] S.R.O. QR 266/74: Inquest on Henry Burrows, 1816.

[32] Ch. Ch. MS Estates 84/190: Letter from J. Bury to R. Morell, 1817.

[33] H.R.O. Highley Tithe Award, 1842.

[34] G. E. Fussell, 'Four centuries of farming systems in Shropshire', *T.S.A.S.*, LIV (1) (1951–52).

[35] S. B. Saul, *The Myth of the Great Depression* (London, 1969).

[36] E. L. Jones, 'The changing basis of English agricultural prosperity, 1853–73', in *Essays in Agrarian History II*, ed W. E. Minchinton (Newton Abbot, 1968).

of this period to make some estimation of the contribution of women and children to the village economy. Figure 7.5 gives numbers of women in employment as stated in census returns, and indicates the proportion who were domestic servants. Women with a job became more frequent during the second half of the nineteenth century, but were still a minority. Those in domestic service were usually young and single, in the 16–30 age group. Most other work open to women was also based on domestic crafts; nurse, housekeeper, charwoman, and so on. Sewing provided other occupations: there were several dressmakers, a mantua maker, shirtmaker and lacemaker. Virtually the only other female occupations were teaching or shop- and inn-keeping. Women agricultural workers are rarely mentioned, although some women probably worked on the land occasionally, for instance at fruit and potato picking. Other women probably also did part-time work, like laundry, not recorded as a full-time occupation.

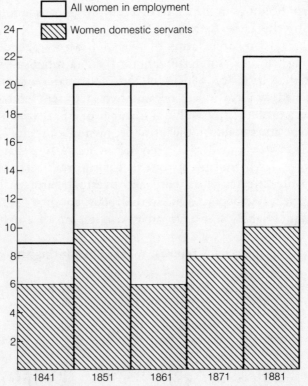

Figure 7.5 Employment of women (over 15 years old), 1841–81

Census returns also show a decline in the numbers of children under 16 in full-time employment. All employed girls were in fact domestic servants, and their numbers dropped from eight in 1841 to zero in 1881. The youngest recorded girl 'in service' was nine, although the majority were 14 or 15 years old. Numbers of boys in work similarly decreased, from 13 in 1841 to five in 1881. In 1841 and 1851 boys of 9 and 10 are recorded as farm servants. Later, most working boys were at least 12, and several were in occupations which acknowledged their youth – apprentice shoe-maker, postboy, ploughboy, etc. In 1881, when there was renewed coal mining activity in the village, three boys were employed as miners, but all were 15 years old. Younger boys had been used in the earlier mines. Samuel Bright, who was killed by falling when descending the pit shaft in 1807, was only 11 years old.[37] William Garbett, killed at Stanley Colliery in 1820, was only 10.[38] There is no record of women miners at Highley, although women worked underground in the mid-Shropshire coalfield until the Mines Act of 1842.[39]

Clearly the agricultural and industrial elements of the village economy cannot be completely separated. The evidence suggests that coal miners in Highley formed a separate, usually immigrant, group who did not, as did the miners of rural north Worcestershire, combine mining with seasonal agricultural work.[40] Nevertheless, their presence provided increased scope for local tradesmen and probably, as in the mid-Shropshire coalfield, the higher wages paid to miners had some effect on the wages of agricultural workers. Plymley noted in 1803 that the best agriculture in the county was practised in industrializing areas, where the price of land and crops was pushed up by the presence of a ready market. However, partly because of the sporadic nature of industrial activity during the period, agriculture in Highley was never swamped – geographically or economically – by industry. The Tithe Award map and apportionment show a basically farming community, with some of the signs of the first phase of mining development already fading from the landscape.

In the pre-enclosure period, when a rough equivalence between

---

[37] S.R.O. QR 231/78: Inquest on Samuel Bright, 1807.
[38] S.R.O. QR 282/189: Inquest on William Garbett, 1820.
[39] B. Trinder, *The Industrial Revolution in Shropshire* (Chichester, 1973).
[40] R. E. Evans, 'The Wyre Forest Coalfield' (Bewdley Museum information sheet, ND).

the amount of land held and degree of wealth enjoyed could be assumed, it was relatively easy to discern the financial hierarchy of the rural community. This became more problematic after enclosure, when the rise of the absentee landlord in particular presented a complication. This was compounded during the industrial period by the emergence of a whole new group of industrial workers and tradesmen.

A small group of substantial farmers, usually tenants, remained the village elite. Fifteen men between them contributed virtually all of the poor rate for 1799.[41] Those who are shown in the Easter Book (to 1830) as having resident servants comprise a similar-sized group, varying between 11 and 13.[42] Here the chief farmers were joined by the coalmasters: Dr Macnab in the 1790s, Benjamin Thompson after 1805, William Hughes around 1815. Industrialization, however, swelled the group by only one or at most two at any time. The great majority of incomers were manual workers. Thus the size of the elite group relative to the population as a whole shrank, from about 21 per cent at the turn of the century to 13 per cent in 1811 and 1821, and to less than 12 per cent in 1831. In the 'census period' from 1841 to 1881, after a brief rise in mid century which owed more to the decline in numbers of industrial workers than to any increase in absolute numbers, the percentage of men in this prosperous group continued steadily to fall. (See Figure 7.6)

There were also more internal variations of prosperity within this group than had been the case in the earlier periods. Although some farms continued to be owned by absentee landlords, one of the most significant developments in the pattern of landholding in Highley throughout the whole period of this study was the reversal of the trend towards absentee ownership brought about by the rise in fortunes of the Jordin family.

William Jordin was born at Neen Savage in 1715: he came to Highley shortly before 1752, and married there two years later. In 1754 he was already one of the largest contributors to the Poor Rate. He rented Cresswell's New House at Netherton and Borle Mill Farm, and by 1767 also owned a smaller property. In 1779 he was renting some lands belonging to Bridgnorth Corporation and a portion of the great tithes of the parish, as well as the other

[41] S.R.O. 4123/P/2: Highley overseers' accounts, 1762–1801.
[42] S.R.O. 4123/Ti/2: Highley Easter Book, 1756–1834.

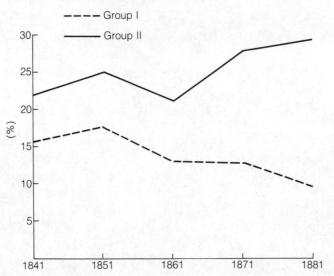

Figure 7.6   Group I and group II households as a percentage of all households, 1841–81

properties.[43] Then in the same year Jordin bought the New House estate. Thus at the beginning of this period his family was possibly the wealthiest in the community, although the difference between them and other well-off farmers was not great – Joseph Cook, for instance, paid more in tithe in 1779 in respect of the old demesne estate.

William Jordin continued to add to his property. He bought two cottages and land near the Borle Mill, and apparently other land too. By the time of his death in 1796 there was a considerable estate to be handed over to his sons William and Thomas. (see Figure 7.7) In the favourable economic circumstances of the war years, both sons prospered. As was the case during the inflation of the late sixteenth century, Highley's chief farmers were able to profit from high prices. However, in most cases they were now tenant farmers, whose landlords were able to raise rents in a way that had not been open to the Littletons in the earlier period. Nationally, in fact, most tenants' rents doubled during the Napoleonic Wars.[44] The Jordins were already owner-occupiers of at least a substantial part of their holdings, and could afford to buy more as they became available. William, the elder son, bought cottages and land in 1803,

[43] S.R.O. 4123/P/2.
[44] P. Horn, *The Rural World 1780–1850* (London, 1980), p. 56 and pp. 73–4.

Plate 8 Netherton House, built for Richard Cresswell shortly before 1678, and the home of the Jordin family from the mid eighteenth century. (Photograph: Local Studies Library, Shrewsbury)

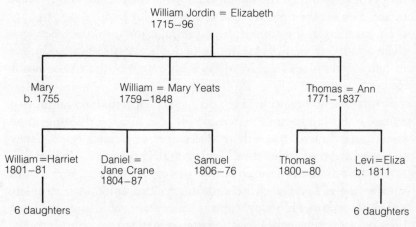

Figure 7.7   The Jordin family

1808 and 1821.[45] Thomas built a new house at Netherton in 1799, the year of his marriage, and bought more land in 1808. Other purchases almost certainly took place of which record no longer survives.

Thus in the 1820s and 1830s when the economic climate was less

[45] S.R.O. 1671/: Deeds of sale between W. Jordin and T. Gitton, 1803; W. Jordin and J. Williams, 1808; W. Jordin and Messrs. Dyer, Pitt and Craig, 1821.

favourable for farmers, the Jordins were better able than their neighbours to withstand any slump, and were able to proceed with enlarging their estates at the expense of the smaller tenant and owner-occupier. By 1834, William had bought Highley Farm, the ex-demesne: he now paid tithe on four large farms, and was lord of the manor. Thomas paid tithe on two farms and two large parcels of land. The New House estate was mortgaged for £5,000 in 1833, possibly to fund this expansion, for there is no other evidence of possible financial difficulties.[46]

By this time the brothers had two adult sons each. Thomas died in 1837, and William made over the New House estate to his elder son, another William. Thus by 1842, it was the four Jordin men of the third generation who occupied among them almost half the farmed land of the parish. This kind of elevation in the status and wealth of one family at the expense of their neighbours, brought about by a combination of acumen and circumstance, was a feature of the period in many regions.[47] Elsewhere in Shropshire, new rising gentry like the Jordins profited from the depression by buying out landlords who could no longer find tenants for their farms.[48] For the community as a whole, the most important feature of the Jordins' rise was that they remained resident in the village.

The 1841 census shows six Jordin households, employing 13 resident servants and a governess. William Jordin the younger (1801–81) was described as lord of the manor and principal landowner in a directory of 1851: in 1856 he was listed under 'gentry'.[49] For almost the first time in its history, Highley had a resident squire. In 1851, William and his brother Samuel, living in the New House at Netherton, farmed 682 acres, nearly half of the parish total. William took an active part in village affairs: he was instrumental in setting up the village school in 1863, for example. In the last years of his life, he helped to determine the future course of village development by agreeing to rent land to the Highley Mining Company. In January 1878 Jordin ceremonially cut the first sod of the new shaft – the working of which was to change the whole structure of the community.[50]

[46] S.R.O. 1671/: Mortgage by W. Jordin of an estate at Highley, 1833.
[47] G. E. Mingay, 'The agricultural revolution in English history: a reconsideration', in *Agrarian History II* ed Minchinton.
[48] Dodd, 'The state of agriculture'.
[49] Bagshaw, *Directory of Shropshire* (1851): *Kelly's Directory of Shropshire* (1856).
[50] *The Bridgnorth Journal*, January 1878.

William's heir, in the absence of a male descendant, was John Beddard, who had originally been his farm manager. When the estate, which represented only the property of the older branch of the Jordin family, was finally broken up and sold in 1945 it consisted of 572 acres of land and 28 houses.

The Jordins' position of pre-eminence in the community coincided almost exactly with our present period. They were never more than minor gentry, and were never able to exert the kind of influence exercized by their titled neighbours in other parishes of the county. Nevertheless, their rise represented a significant change in the distribution of wealth and influence in Highley. Their position in village society was never challenged. By 1836, only 10 men living in Highley qualified to vote, including the vicar and three members of the Jordin family. There were also three members of the Wilcox family who, although never reaching the status of the Jordins, established themselves in this leading group throughout the period.

The Wilcoxes, too, owed the beginnings of prosperity to one man, the bargeowner Edward Wilcox who died in 1764: but unlike the Jordins they did not rely solely on agriculture for their advancement. One branch of the family (all of whom lived at Stanley, the new centre of industry and commerce in the parish) continued to operate barges; another combined farming with quarrying; while a third ran the Ship Inn. Together with the occasional coalmasters, and the vicar, the Wilcoxes were the only members of this prosperous group of a dozen or so families who did not derive all their income from the land.

The next group is less easy to define. In it we must include those smaller farmers whom Plymley regarded as in 'the most wretched' straits, and whose income may indeed have been less than that of the more successful artisans. So in our second group we can include all those, like innkeepers, shoemakers and blacksmiths, who carried on a trade – sometimes in addition to farming a smallholding – as well as those farming less than about 30 acres. Both small farmers and village craftsmen in the late eighteenth century probably had an annual income of between £30 and £50 per annum.[51]

The percentage of men in this group rose during the nineteenth century. Some farms shrank or were broken up, thus leaving more

[51] Horn, *Rural World,* p. 24.

small farmers. In 1851, nine of the nineteen farmers held 30 acres or less, with a mean farm size of 15 acres. The men with five or 6 acres could not support a family by farming alone: in fact two were also agricultural labourers, one a cordwainer and one a maltster. Half the farmers at the 1881 census had a mean farm size of only 13.4 acres. The dichotomy between large landholders and those eking out, or supplementing, a living (which had been exacerbated by the post-war depression) remained marked.

The largest rise in this group, however, was in the number of those providing the increased range of services expected as the century progressed. After mid century these included a sub-postmaster, a station master, a marble mason, and always three or four innkeepers, in addition to the butchers, blacksmiths and shoemakers recorded throughout the period. The small farms and businesses were nearly all family-run. In many cases, sons followed fathers in the family trade. Where this was not possible, there are distinct indications of a desire to avoid 'sinking' into labouring occupations: the son of Thomas Walford, a small farmer in 1861, did not work on the family farm but was a blacksmith. Similarly the sons of William Kirkham, an innkeeper in 1851, were an apprentice blacksmith and a postboy. With this group being apparently self-recruiting, there were correspondingly few opportunities for labourers to join its ranks.

Figure 7.6 shows numbers in both groups as a percentage of all households during the census period. Both percentages dropped in 1861 because of the additional presence in the village of large numbers of railway navvies. Thereafter, however, although the proportion of Group I households steadily fell, that of Group II households rose until in 1881 they comprised nearly 30 per cent of all households. Both groups combined, however, never made up more than 40 per cent of the total during the census period: during the 'industrial' decades earlier in the century it was almost certainly considerably less. The majority of men in Highley remained labourers, working on farms or in the collieries and quarries. The Easter Book for 1818 lists 88 households: in only 10 cases is it not possible to discover occupations (although two were almost certainly colliers and another two farm labourers). Six of the householders were widows. Of the remaining 72, 48 men were miners, agricultural labourers, or 'labourers on barges' – exactly two thirds of the total.

Figure 7.8 shows the proportion of heads of household in the census period who belonged to our third group, the labourers. In fact, it under-represents this group somewhat, as several widows headed households otherwise composed of labourers, and several labourers were lodgers in other households. The percentage of all heads of household who were agricultural labourers is also indicated, as until 1881 this category was by far the largest subdivision of the group.

The most noticeable feature here is the sharp decline in the percentage of agricultural labouring heads of household in 1881, when the opening of the new colliery was already having an effect

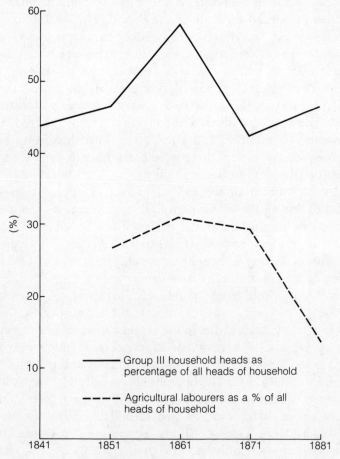

Figure 7.8 Heads of households in socioeconomic group III

on the occupational structure of the community. In fact, 43 per cent of all employed males had been farm labourers in 1871: by 1881 this had fallen to just over 20 per cent.

One reason for this was the persistence of the tradition of the live-in 'servant in husbandry'. Easter Book entries between 1793 and 1830 show a fairly consistent 10 or 12 resident 'men' on village farms, rising in 1807 as high as 18. In 1841, there were 23 male servants living in. After mid century, numbers fell markedly. So although resident servants had begun to be replaced by married labourers as early as the pre-enclosure period, the tradition of service lingered well into the nineteenth century. It was only in the second half of the century that the old order finally gave way.

Most of the resident male servants of the census period were young: the mean age of those recorded in 1841 was 22.5 years. Since ages for adults were given only to the nearest five years, the true figure may have been even lower. All were unmarried. When a live-in worker married, he left to set up a home of his own, becoming an 'agricultural labourer' rather than a 'male servant', and probably also accepting a reduction in his standard of living.[52]

Throughout the period, however, the majority of farm labourers were non-resident. Some distinctions are drawn in census returns between types of farm work, although for the most part those specialists distinguished as such were carters and wagoners. Few farms in Highley were large enough to employ a range of specialist workers, and most agricultural labourers must have performed a range of tasks.

There are indications that not all farm labourers living in Highley actually worked there. By mid century the decline in industry had left vacant housing: four houses stood empty in 1841 and at least 10 in 1871. It is probable that houses existed for more families than the village economy could support. In 1851, when farmers entered on their census returns the number of labourers they employed, there was a total of 28: yet 42 men and boys gave their occupations as agricultural labourer. By 1881, when less labour-intensive farming methods had reduced the number of labourers needed, a maximum of 18 agricultural labourers would seem to have been employed in Highley itself, although 28 lived in the village.

In 1793, farm labourers in Highley were paid 8d a day plus their

[52] A. Kussmaul, *Servants in Husbandry in Early Modern England* (Cambridge, 1981).

keep.[53] In addition, most of them kept a pig, which had replaced the cow as the poor man's only stock. Four shillings a week, with or without meals, was a very poor wage, and inflation forced it up, though probably not in line with rising prices. By 1803, Plymley assessed the average agricultural worker's wage in Shropshire at seven shillings a week rising to nine shillings during harvest.[54] This was below the national average of 10 shillings a week estimated by Burnett.[55] Agricultural wages continued to rise (if less quickly than prices) during the Napoleonic Wars: in Highley there was the added stimulus of alternative industrial employment. In addition, some labourers had large gardens whose produce could supplement the family diet. Their wives and children, too, could add to the family income by part-time work. In September 1827, for example, the wife of Richard Dodd, a labourer, spent the whole day 'leasing' (gleaning) and returned home only at 7 p.m.[56]

Even so, agricultural labourers and their families lived in relative poverty for much of their life-cycle: the young couple had children who could not yet contribute to the family income; the older man could find his wage cut as infirmity, especially the rheumatism which particularly affected farm workers, curtailed his ability to work. Labourers were not able to retire, and had to work as long as their health permitted: in the census returns there are several labourers aged between 70 and 78.

It is difficult to compare the relative financial positions of farm workers and coal miners. Benson points out that variations in wage rates between areas, and between the different types of mining employment, make any estimate of miners' wages difficult.[57] As a guide, he finds that the better-paid miners in small coalfields at the beginning of the nineteenth century were earing 12 to 15 shillings a week. We do not know what Highley miners earned, though it seems probable that they were paid a little more than farmworkers, as they were in the mid-Shropshire coalfield, in order to attract workers in spite of the appalling conditions.[58] Miners, on the other hand, seem to have had fewer opportunities to supplement their

[53] B.L. Add. MSS. 21018: Plymley, 1793.

[54] Plymley, General View.

[55] J. Burnett, A History of the Cost of Living (Harmondsworth, 1967), pp. 164–5.

[56] M. C. Hill (ed), Abstract of the Quarter Sessions Rolls 1820–30 (Shrewsbury, 1974).

[57] J. Benson, British Coalminers in the Nineteenth Century: A Social History (Dublin, 1980).

[58] Trinder, Industrial Revolution.

earnings than had farm labourers. Like labourers, they faced the problem of declining earning potential with age.

Certainly coal mining seems to have been largely a young man's occupation. By the start of the census period there were few colliers left in Highley, but all those remaining were relatively young. In 1881, the 51 coal miners in Highley had a mean age of only 28.1 years. In all probability, the miners of the first industrial phase had been similarly young men. Of those colliers working in Highley between 1813 and 1825, it is possible to discover the ages of less than a dozen: all but one were under 30.

In contrast, the quarrying workforce was not only diminishing, but was also ageing. In 1851, the mean age of quarry labourers was 42; in 1861 and 1871 it was 53.1 and 52.4 respectively. In terms of wages, there was probably little difference between labouring in a quarry or on a farm: certainly by mid century quarrying was no longer attracting young men into the industry.

There was almost no movement between the three chief types of employment in this labouring group. Most of the coal miners moved on when Stanley Colliery closed: few of them had been recruited from the village in the first place. With one exception, those labourers recorded between 1813 and 1820 who remained in Highley until the census period 20 or 30 years later continued to be employed as farm workers. In 1871, there were nine employed sons living with farm labouring heads of household: eight of them were following their fathers' occupation.

If there was little movement within the group, there was virtually no upward mobility from it. Apparently only one man progressed from farm labourer to farmer during the period. In 1819, Thomas Edwards was a labourer living at Netherton. By 1821 he had taken over as tenant at Woodend Farm, now reduced to just over 30 acres. Unfortunately, there is no evidence as to how this came about. Most men who began their working life as labourers ended it in the same way.

At the end of this working life, there was a real possibility of joining our final group, the paupers. Detailed records of individual recipients of parish relief cease in 1800–01. Thus only in the first 20 years of our period can we see just who were the official poor. A majority of claimants at this date were women. Widows, unless their husbands had been among the most prosperous, were particularly vulnerable. Mothers of illegitimate children were also regular claimants. In some cases, spinsters whose parents were dead fell 'on the parish': their ages ranged between 16 year old Elizabeth Charles in 1785 and the sisters Ann and Sarah Wilks, aged 68 and 59 in 1800. Women without a male provider, then, were in a particularly difficult situation.

During this period, several of the male claimants are known to have been elderly, like 76 year old Thomas Detton in 1784, or too ill to work, as in the case of Richard Wall, aged 54, whose illness and subsequent burial are recorded in relief payments in the same year. Those claiming relief also included some young men, either unemployed or with wages in need of augmentation in the crisis years of the 1790s. The official poor were in the main, though, composed of the elderly and the infirm, and those women and children with no male support.

After 1801 there is less indication of the composition of this group, although its size was noted in Parliamentary enquiries of the early nineteenth century. In 1803 it was reported that 17 adults and 14 children received payments on a regular basis, and six adults occasionally.[59] This accords well with the last detailed parish accounts of 1800-01, when a total of 32 individuals received relief. Thus at the beginning of the nineteenth century, one in eight of the village population depended at least in part on parish relief payments. The size of the group does not seem to have increased at the same rate as the overall village population, probably because most incomers were men in employment and their families. Some orders of removal were implemented against miners and their families, and it is likely that the new arrivals were where possible prevented from gaining a settlement in Highley.[60]

Parliamentary returns for the years around 1815 show a decline in numbers of paupers in Highley, although it is not clear whether or not children were included in the figures.[61] The percentage of the total population in the group at this time fell to between 5 and 8 per cent if the returns are accurate, although others may have received casual relief.

In 1834, Highley became part of the Cleobury Mortimer Union as a result of the Poor Law Amendment Act, and most paupers were sent to the workhouse there instead of being supported by

[59] *Abstract of the Answers and Returns Relative to the Poor*, HC XIII (1803-04).
[60] Trinder, *Industrial Revolution*.
[61] *Abridgement of the Abstract of the Returns Relative to the Poor*, HC XIX (1818).

outdoor relief. Thus numbers in this poorest group actually living in the parish declined, although Highley's own Workhouse Cottages were apparently sometimes used to provide rent for charitable purposes, and sometimes as temporary accommodation particularly for single mothers and their children. Those for whom 'workhouse' is recorded as place of residence in the burial register make up 11.2 per cent of all burials during the period 1835–50, though this is likely of course to over-represent the proportion in the population as a whole.

Thus it appears that something under 10 per cent of the village population were officially paupers, with a peak of perhaps one in eight around 1800. Those in receipt of poor relief were not, of course, the only poor in the community. Changing criteria might have affected the size of the group as much as changing circumstances of its members. In fact the majority of the labouring population probably lived in some degree of poverty.

Figures 7.9 and 7.10 can do no more than provide an indication of the overall changes in the distribution of wealth during our period. Firstly, it is not always possible to distinguish between labourers and small craftsmen in the 1799 Easter Book listing which provides the basis for Figure 7.9. In 1881, the census returns upon which Figure 7.10 is based do not give information specifically about paupers: the group designated as Group IV is made up of heads of household who were widows living alone, or with young children or lodgers. Nevertheless, certain broad outlines of the shifting economic balance are illustrated, the chief of which is the rise in numbers of the 'middle class' – small farmers and local tradesmen – at the expense of Group I, whose numbers declined largely on account of the increasing predominance of the Jordin family.

Thus the polarization of wealth in the community which was a feature of the post-enclosure period continued in a modified form. More families fell in the socioeconomic scale than rose: those who did rise did so spectacularly. In terms of land held – and probably wealth – William Jordin replaced half a dozen farmers of the earlier period. No long-term resident of Highley got rich from industrialization, although one of its effects may be seen in the proliferation of crafts and trades in the nineteenth century. During the first 30 years of the century, the influx of colliers broadened yet further the base of the economic pyramid of the community.

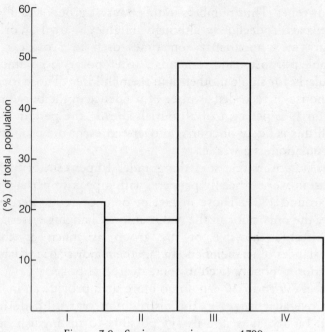

Figure 7.9 Socioeconomic groups 1799

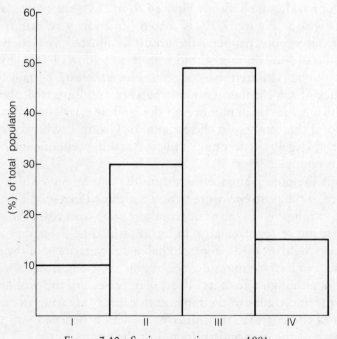

Figure 7.10 Socioeconomic groups 1881

By the mid-point of the period, land ownership in the parish was more or less divided between the Jordin family on one hand, and a few absentee landlords on the other. The last of the small tenements which had remained owner-occupied after enclosure were finally sold – usually to the Jordins.

The classic division of the eighteenth century (in Highley as elsewhere) between farmer and labourer remained: but in the nineteenth century it was complicated by further divisions between Squire and farmer; by the availability of industrial as well as agricultural labouring employment; and by the growth in numbers of small tradesmen in the village.

8

Growth and Decline

As a result of the industrial developments of the first years of the nineteenth century, Highley's population doubled. According to Archdeacon Plymley, there were 215 inhabitants in 1793.[1] This had increased by the turn of the century to 273, and then jumped in the next decade to 484. Subsequently, it fell back to levels not much greater than those of the late eighteenth century. (See Figure 8.1) Such immigration and emigration clearly affected the demographic structures of the community.

Figure 8.2 – which gives simple decadal totals of baptisms and burials – reflects the jump in total population between 1800 and 1819. Even before immigration, the natural trend of the community was towards growth, with baptisms outnumbering burials. In the early years of the nineteenth century, burials increased much less markedly than baptisms, reflecting the change in age-structure brought about by the influx of miners. Indeed burials in the 1850s, when the total population was less than three quarters of its 1811 peak, exceeded those of the decade 1810–19. In the last decades of our period baptisms were decreasing and the two totals again approaching parity: Highley was an ageing community, and deaths might actually have outstripped births for the first time in 300 years had the second wave of miners not arrived from shortly before 1880.

During the years of expansion Highley experienced high fertility rates. Table 8.1 shows annual rates of baptism per 1,000, both in actual census years and estimated on mean population size at consecutive censuses per decade – although it should be stressed that figures for individual years, though precise, represent a short-term situation open to several distorting effects.

As one might expect, the birth rate (for which the baptism rate is

[1] B.L. Add. MSS. 21018: Undated copy of notes by Archdeacon Plymley, 1793.

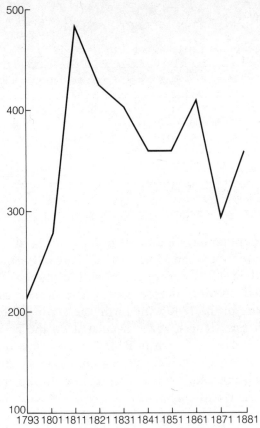

Figure 8.1 Population of Highley, 1793–1881

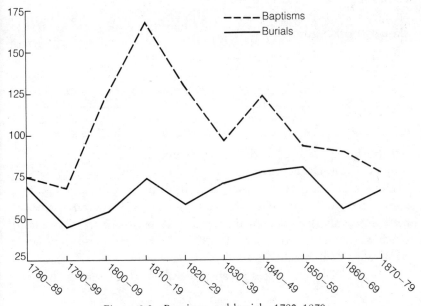

Figure 8.2 Baptisms and burials, 1780–1879

Table 8.1　Baptism rate per 1,000, population 1790–1879

1790–99	1800–09	1810–19	1820–29	1830–39	1840–49	1850–59	1860–69	1870–79
28	35	37	33	27	34	24	26	24

1793	1801	1811	1821	1831	1841	1851	1861	1871
27.9	36.4	55.9	33.0	27.2	27.7	22.2	46.6	27.3

obviously a minimum figure) went up during the decades of immigration to more than 35 per 1,000. Many of the newly-arrived miners and their wives were apparently of fertile age. This rate was not sustained: during the rest of the century, except for a temporary rise in the 1840s, the birth rate gradually fell.

The death rate figures, again calculated on the basis of census population totals and shown in table 8.2, are consistent with this picture of an influx of largely young immigrants. After 1800 the death rate fell markedly and remained low during the period of initial industrialization. The only other period with a comparably low death rate was the 1860s, when the railway navvies had for a time a similar effect on age structure. The 'natural' agricultural community had a lower birth rate and a higher death rate because all ages were represented: immigration by a young working group skewed both figures.

Table 8.2　Burial rate per 1,000, population 1790–1879

1790–99	1800–09	1810–19	1820–29	1830–39	1840–49	1850–59	1860–09	1870–79
18.75	15.1	16.3	14.0	18.6	21.4	21.1	16.0	20.4

It is not possible to determine whether the families of coal miners were larger than those of the agricultural population. Miners were highly mobile, and in only a few cases can a completed family size be discovered. We can, however, compare birth intervals (not related to position in family) for both sets of workers. During the period 1800–30, miners' children were baptised at a mean interval of 28.2 months, and those of agricultural labourers at a mean interval of 31.1 months. Miners' families may therefore have been slightly larger than those of agricultural workers.

Among the population as a whole fertility was rising in the early nineteenth century: birth intervals were somewhat shorter than in the pre-industrial period, and completed family size increased to 4.75, in spite of the frequency with which marriage was broken by death. In the period 1830–79 mean family size increased still further, to 5.3, although mean birth intervals lengthened somewhat and age at first marriage rose. One reason for this was increased duration of marriage. Furthermore, although most women had reached their mid-twenties before they began to bear children, they continued (as table 8.3 shows) to do so into middle age.

Table 8.3   Age of mother at birth of last child, 1830–80

Age	N
39	1
40	4
41	4
42	6
43	3
44	1
45	3
46	0
47	4
48	0
49	2

Mean = 43.2 years

Both age at first marriage and its duration clearly affected marital fertility. In the first half of this period we must rely for age at marriage on those partners identifiable as having been baptised at Highley. This gives a group of 29 men and 32 women, whose mean age at first marriage was 26.7 years and 23.8 years respectively. As this is very similar to marriage age in the period 1740–79, it appears that industrial development in the parish did not have the effect of further lowering marriage age in the settled community from which the group is drawn.

During the second half of the period age at marriage is often recorded, notably from 1838–45 and after 1860. Thus we have a larger group of 38 men and 54 women. Marriage age rose to a mean of 28.4 years for men and 25.2 years for women; this is a significant rise which suggests that the economic stagnation in the community did delay marriage.

In fact, in spite of marrying later, couples in the second half of the period were on average married longer: mean duration of marriage in the first half (to 1829) was 25.4 years, but 28.7 years in the second, despite the exclusion of some lengthy marriages which continued beyond 1880. Some couples were married for a very long time: several marriages of over 50 years are recorded. Edward and Susanna Harris, for example, were married in 1769 and remained married for 56 years until the latter's death in 1825 at the age of 88.

Yet throughout the period 47 marriages are known to have been broken during their fertile period by the death of one of the partners. Sixty per cent of these were in the first half of the period, when they helped to lower completed family size. In 39 of the 47 cases it was the wife who died. In 10 cases, the evidence suggests death in childbirth or its aftermath. Although numbers of women at risk had increased considerably with the growth in population, it does appear that child-bearing had become more rather than less dangerous in Highley.

Several young men were thus left with small children to care for. Thomas Barker's first wife died in June 1790, the month in which the couple's sixth child was baptised. His second wife died in May 1794 at the time of the birth of their second child. Thomas married for a third time in November 1795. Other widowers left with a young family were similarly quick to remarry. This was not always solely to obtain a housekeeper: all three of Thomas Barker's wives were pregnant when he married them.

Some of the 39 young widowers apparently left the village: very occasionally others died themselves within a couple of years. But 29 of them remarried: many, like Thomas Barker, did so as quickly as possible. The interval between bereavement and remarriage is known in 22 cases: eight remarried within one year, nine within two years, and only five after more than two years. Some, indeed, were married again within three or four months. This raises questions about the quality of marital relationships: it also highlights the very real difficulties of a man having to work long hours without a partner to care for his children.

These men were not of course the only widowed in the

community: marriages were frequently broken after their fertile period. Thus second and third marriages were quite common. During the period 1838–79, when marital status of brides and grooms was recorded, 18 per cent of all marriages were registered as second marriages for one or both parties. When we consider not only orphans but also the illegitimate, we see that numbers of children living with only one – or perhaps neither – of their natural parents were considerable.

The declining death rate during the early decades of industrialization has been pointed out. This is not to suggest that Highley became a healthier place because of industrial development. Table 8.4 shows mean age at death for those aged over 15, as well as mean age at death overall. Figures before 1813 are calculated on the basis of family reconstitution; those after 1813 on stated age at burial. Both adult age at death and, most noticeably, overall age at death declined during the industrial period, and rose steadily after 1830. Age at death was at its lowest during the decade 1810–19, when coal mining was at its height: average life-expectancy at birth was less than 25 years; and even those who reached adulthood could barely expect to live to 50.

The figures for overall mortality are of course very much affected by the incidence of juvenile mortality. (See figures 8.3 to

Table 8.4 Mean age at death, 1780–1879

	1780–89	1790–99	1800–09	1810–19	1820–29
Adults	58.8	53.3	51.7	49.75	55.3
N	24	20	24	35	37
All	28.5	31.1	29.4	24.2	36.1
N	51	35	44	75	57

	1830–39	1840–49	1850–59	1860–69	1870–79
Adults	52.6	58.8	60.2	59.4	56.4
N	52	47	57	37	51
All	39.3	36.8	43.2	41.0	43.2
N	71	77	81	55	67

8.5) The decades of industrialization were the first ones in which child death took over from infant death as the major part of juvenile mortality. After a high of 22 per cent in the 1780s, infant mortality was generally around or below 10 per cent – a much more favourable situation than at any time since the mid-seventeenth century. Deaths of children aged one to 15, however, rose, culminating in a peak of 17.7 per cent of all children baptised in the decade 1840–49. The evidence suggests an epidemic, or series of epidemics, in this decade, when burials of children made up 26 per cent of all burials (and infants comprised another 13 per cent). Some years were worse than others: of the 11 burials in 1848, seven were of children.

The population growth of the early nineteenth century did not, then, lead to a rise in infant mortality. Children, though, would seem to have been more at risk at the height of mining. Of course, a

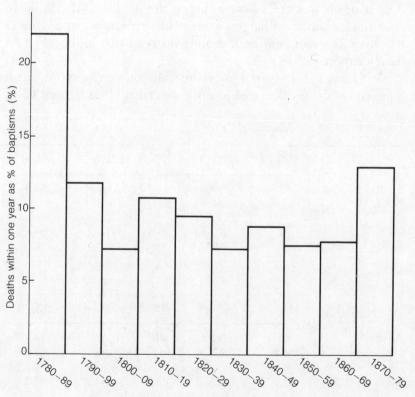

Figure 8.3   Infant mortality, 1780–1879

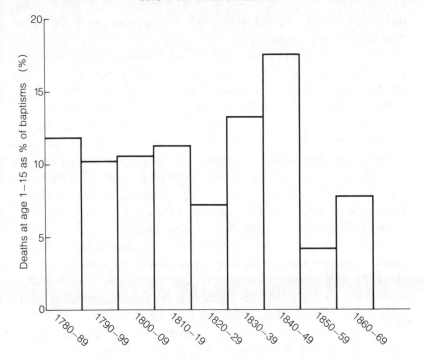

Figure 8.4   Child mortality, 1780–1869

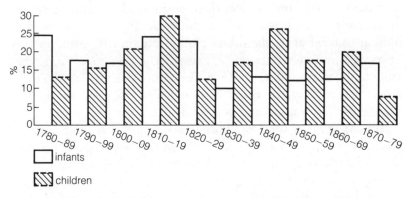

Figure 8.5   Juvenile burials as a percentage of all burials, 1780–1879

'young' population would naturally increase the numbers at risk. The significant change in patterns of juvenile mortality was the way in which deaths of children became more frequent than those of infants. One in every five or six children born continued to die before adulthood: most families could still expect to lose a child and, increasingly, a child of perhaps six or nine years old rather than a new-born infant.

From the beginning of this period, some medical care was available: a midwife and a doctor were called to paupers at parish expense; other poor were paid to 'sit up nights with' the sick. In 1784 the parish paid for the inoculation of Richard Meredith and his family.[2] Yet no practising doctor was resident in the village, and medical care for those not claiming parish relief was prohibitively expensive – the Meredith family's inoculations cost 15 shillings, probably two weeks' wages for most. The ability to pay for medical attention was not always enough: four of the six daughters of Squire William Jordin succumbed in succession to what family tradition insists was tuberculosis.

Coroner's inquests into sudden deaths dealt with a surprising number of cases where people dropped dead in orchards, fields and barns. Not all victims were elderly. Thomas Guest, found dead in an orchard in 1821 was 35 years old; Thomas Lowe died of an 'apoplectic fit' in a barn in 1786 at the age of 44.[3]

There continued to be quite frequent fatal accidents: 16 are recorded in inquests between 1800 and 1830 alone. The Severn continued to be a danger. Men fell from barges and were drowned, or simply slipped and fell in from the bank. Certainly more fatalities occurred on the river than on the roads – but the river was much busier. Children died in domestic situations; scalded by boiling water, burnt when their clothes caught fire, or in one case 'drowned in a stone cistern'.[4] The elderly, like the young, were vulnerable to accident. In 1828 William Cheshire, aged 78, fell down the steps of the Borle Mill and died; 67 year old Thomas Walford fell in a pond and was drowned.[5]

But the greatest increase during this period was in accidents at work. Between 1805 and 1820 nine men and boys died in this kind of accident, seven of them in coal mining. Pit accidents were of two kinds: some died by falling down the shaft while being raised or lowered on a 'trunk'; others when coal or earth crushed them in small roof falls. Mining was a more hazardous occupation than

---

   [2] S.R.O. 4123/P/2: Highley overseers' accounts 1756–1801.
   [3] S.R.O. QR 152/18: Inquest on Thomas Lowe, 1786. M. C. Hill, *Abstract of the Quarter Sessions Rolls 1820–30* (Shrewsbury, 1974).
   [4] Hill, *Quarter Sessions Rolls.*
   [5] *Ibid.*

agriculture (although one boy was killed by a threshing machine in 1816), and must have given rise to several serious injuries as well as to recorded fatalities.

The demographic evidence all points to a change in the age structure of the community after 1800, brought about by wholesale immigration. Unfortunately, we can only assess age structure with accuracy for census years after 1841, as illustrated in figures 8.6 to 8.10.

One feature of all diagrams except that for 1881 is the small percentage of those in 15–19 age group as compared to the other five-year spans of childhood. Adolescents clearly continued to leave the village in search of work, and the net loss of young people was increased by the decline in resident farm service.

The largest group of adults was consistently of those aged 20–29. In many cases married agricultural labourers were replacing younger live-in servants. The greatest fluctuations are seen in the proportions of those aged over 50, which rose to 25 per cent in 1871 at a time of economic decline, and fell to 16.2 per cent in 1881 with the arrival of coal miners and their families.

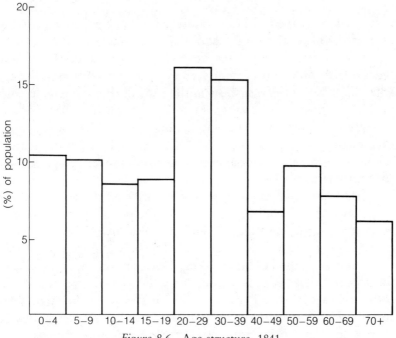

Figure 8.6   Age structure, 1841

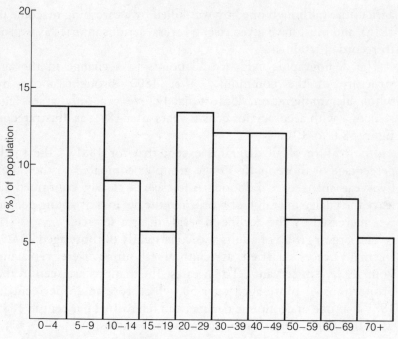

Figure 8.7   Age structure, 1851

In 1841, after the falling birth rates of the 1830s, less than 30 per cent of the population were children – the smallest percentage of any of the census years. The birth rate increased in the 1840s, and one explanation for this can be seen in the large numbers in the 20–40 age bracket. Its effects show in the 1851 diagram where, in spite of higher juvenile mortality rates in the previous decade, an increased proportion of the population were children under nine. Otherwise, the population in 1851 was not such a predominantly young one: there was a smaller percentage in the fertile age groups, and more elderly.

In 1861 the large number of navvies affected the age structure, and contributed to the 46.6 per cent of the population in the main working groups between 20 and 50. But by 1871 we find a community more weighted towards higher age groups. Without the activities of the Highley Mining Company towards the end of the decade, village population was set to decline still further. But in 1881, change had already begun, and Highley was a much younger community. Nearly two thirds of the population were under 30 years old. The proportion of 15–19 year olds increased as

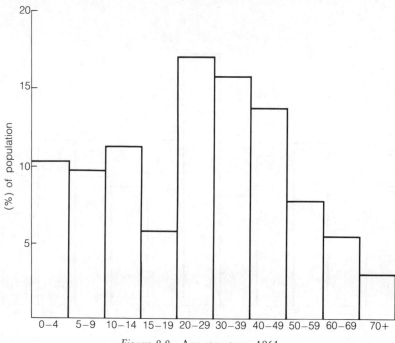

Figure 8.8 Age structure, 1861

employment opportunities improved. Young families arrived, with the result that 35 per cent of the population were children under 15. If it were possible to construct similar diagrams for the years between 1800 and 1830 (and mobility prevents even tentative representations in this form) they would probably show the characteristics of 1881 in an even more marked way.

Demography and immigration affected the size and structure of households. In 1793, according to Plymley, there were 49 houses in Highley for the 215 inhabitants.[6] In 1801 there were 48 houses and a population of 274 – an increase in mean household size from 4.4 to 5.7 in eight years. Pressure on housing was great, as provision of new houses lagged behind the arrival of industrial workers. The first miners must have found lodgings with local families, as many of the railway navvies and later miners did. In fact the 48 houses of 1801 housed 61 families: at 4.5 the mean *family* size remained much as before, and the increase in household size was due almost entirely to the sharing of accommodation.

[6] B.L., Add. MSS. 21018: Plymley, 1793.

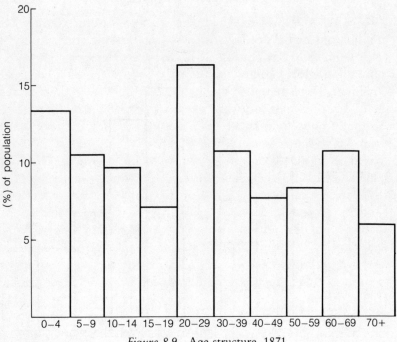

Figure 8.9   Age structure, 1871

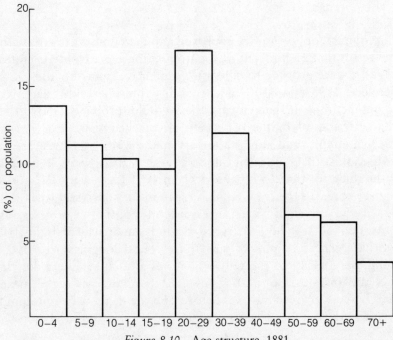

Figure 8.10   Age structure, 1881

By 1811 the pressure had been relieved somewhat by the building of numbers of new houses – the housing stock rose in 10 years from 48 to 85. Thus by 1811, in spite of the great increase in population, most families had their own house: the 85 houses were inhabited by 86 families. Mean household size, as illustrated in table 8.5, conceals one discrepancy between 1801 and 1811. Although household size remained the same, family size jumped from 4.5 to 5.6. The evidence suggests that the first immigrants shared accommodation with local residents to whom they were not related; and that when houses became available they filled them with families larger than those of the agricultural population. In 1881 miners frequently shared their homes with members of their extended families until separate households could be established, and it seems that much the same thing happened in the opening years of the nineteenth century. This is further suggested by the fact that although the total population fell by 60 between 1811 and 1821, the number of separate families increased from 86 to 97.

Mean household size only reached five at times of considerable immigration; the decades of industrialization, the 1860s, and again in 1881. At other 'normal' times it was four and a half or below. This, though, is still higher than mean household size in the late seventeenth century. Industrialization in Highley, far from reducing households from large extended-family groupings to nuclear family units, had at least at some stages of its development an opposite effect. Lodgers and distant kin were far more likely to be present in households at times of industrial expansion.

At such times there was much overcrowding. The new houses built between 1801 and 1811 were small, with at most two bedrooms, and existing housing was in many cases old and dilapidated. The result was living arrangements like those detailed in a Quarter Sessions case of 1827.[7] Sarah Botfield, a widow, slept at the house of her nephew Thomas Botfield. Botfield, his aunt, his

Table 8.5 Mean household size, 1793–1881

1793	1801	1811	1821	1831	1841	1851	1861	1871	1881
4.4	5.7	5.7	5.9	4.8	4.3	4.5	5.0	4.3	5.2

[7] Hill, *Quarter Sessions Rolls.*

wife and children all slept in the same room. Sarah was probably also accompanied by her seven-year old illegitimate daughter. In another house in the same row, the home of Lewis Jones, William Jones and his father John shared a bed which also included on the night in question George Detton of Chelmarsh.

It is only during the census period that we can accurately assess household composition. Even the 1841 census is of little use as relationships to the head of household were not stated. Prior to that, the Easter Book for 1818 suggests that a minimum of 10 per cent of households contained lodgers or adult extended family members (excluding servants), although by this date the Easter Book was less comprehensive than it had been. The list of 1793, which can be checked against Plymley's figures, is better, and shows an overwhelming majority of nuclear family households. Thirty of the 49 households were of this type. A further seven heads of household were widows (with or without children), and six were widowers. Only six households were not of the basic nuclear type. In only one case was an elderly parent specified as resident. Three single women apparently lived alone, two with children. The remaining two households consisted of three elderly sisters living together in one case, and two elderly unmarried brothers together in the other.

The nuclear family household similarly predominated in the census period. From 1851 to 1881 a majority of heads of household were, as one would expect, married men. Their proportion declined from nearly 75 per cent in 1851 to under 65 per cent in 1881. Conversely, the percentage of households headed by widows and widowers rose, from 16.5 per cent in 1851 to 24 per cent in 1881. In each census a handful of single men – between seven and 10 per cent – headed households. Most of these were men well into middle age, who in fact never did marry, and who were more likely to come from the farming class than any other. Single or married women heading households were rare: women were only likely to head households when widowed.

In most cases, identifying the head of the house must have been straightforward: but occasionally such identification is enlightening as to familial authority. Often, a widowed mother was designated head even if her children were middle-aged, as long as they were not married. But sometimes a single son was regarded as head, as with Richard Rowley, aged 23 in 1851, who lived with his 61-year old mother. Presumably the matter was decided by economics. For even a widow with son, daughter-in-law and grandchild in the house could still be classed as its head if, like Elizabeth Lewis aged 69, she was a shopkeeper with an independent income.

Usually, elderly men retained their position whatever their marital status, but occasionally there are signs of a son taking over from his father as the latter aged. In 1871 Henry Barrett, a single man of 22, was head of a household which also contained both his parents. His father was 71, and presumably no longer earning.

In the census period we are able to classify households according to their composition. Table 8.6 shows percentages of households in each of four categories: 'nuclear', containing a single individual or married couple with or without children; 'Three-generation', where either a grandchild or elderly parent is present; 'wider kin', where other relatives such as siblings, nephews and so on are included; and 'non-kin residents' where the household includes unrelated lodgers, 'nurse-children' etc. (servants are excluded).

For most of the period, a majority of people lived in simple nuclear households. However, three-generation and extended family units were by no means unusual. A wide range of relatives was housed – uncles and aunts, nephews and nieces, and most frequently unmarried brothers and sisters.

As in the first half of the period, unmarried siblings quite frequently set up home together: Decimus and Caroline Burrows shared a home all their lives, in spite of several moves of house. In other cases, single individuals lived with married siblings, often on a long-term basis. Samuel Jordin lived all his life with the family of his elder brother William. Throughout the period, several households contained unmarried brothers, brothers-in-law or uncles of

Table 8.6 Household structure, 1851–81

	Nuclear (%)	Three-generation (%)	Wider kin (%)	Non-kin residents (%)
1851	57.3	12.2	18.3	12.2
1861	48.7	4.9	14.6	31.7
1871	61.8	14.7	13.2	10.3
1881	44.3	7.1	18.6	30.0

the head. It seems that single men, with their earning capacity, were more welcome than single women, for whom domestic service remained almost the only alternative.

Because of the high incidence of second marriage and of illegitimacy, a significant proportion of nuclear families contained children who were in fact step-children of one of the couple. Similarly, an orphaned or illegitimate child might well be housed by its grandparents: in other cases a child might live with its grandparents to relieve pressure on accommodation at home and to help the elderly. Letitia Robinson, aged 10, lived with her grandmother in 1861, although her parents and four younger siblings lived elsewhere in the village.

The proportion of households containing lodgers naturally rose at times of increased employment, in 1861 and 1881. The figures for 1881 are particularly interesting as they probably mirror the situation during the early years of the century. Numbers of nuclear families were fewer than at any time, including 1861 when the navvies were present. Not only was the percentage of households with lodgers high, but so too was that of households with a wider range of kin, as extended families lived together until separate accommodation could be found.

Thus the nuclear family household was far from universal, although it predominated. Highley's inhabitants shared their homes with a range of kin, with servants, or with lodgers. Very few lived alone. There were never more than three single-person households in any census. Those who remained unmarried tended to live with other family members. Because women continued to bear children into their forties, most elderly widows (who outnumbered widowers) still had unmarried offspring at home well into their old age. Other old people moved in with married children, or took in lodgers. We must not forget, though, that over this picture of familial care for the elderly falls the shadow of the workhouse, where some of the unsupported elderly must have gone. Nevertheless, as in the first half of the period, overcrowding would seem to have been more of a problem than loneliness.

Overcrowding there undoubtedly was, although pressure on housing had eased after 1830. The largest households tended to be those of the better-off, who kept servants. Their children, too, remained at home longer than those of the poor. The size and formation of labourers' households followed a cyclical pattern. One example will illustrate the extent of these changes over the life-cycle of the family. The abbreviated census details illustrate the evolution of one labouring family. (See table 8.7)

The Burgess household of 10 in 1851 was in fact one of the largest in the village. Few families retained their offspring so long, but the older children here were boys who tended not to leave as early as girls going into service. John and Mary Burgess began their married life with Mary's mother; then for some years the household was nuclear, but shrinking as members left home or died. Finally, John Burgess lived with his son and his son's family in another three-generational household.

Numbers of lodgers rose at times of work-related immigration after 1841. Some households in 1861 has as many as seven navvies and their dependants lodging with them. Immigrants in 1881 were less numerous and less temporary, but even so several households had three or four lodgers. The situation must have been very similar in the 'boom' years at the start of the century.

Thus although the nuclear family unit was the most frequent household type, there is evidence to suggest the existence of a supportive network of kin where the elderly, the illegitimate, orphaned or simply the unmarried could hope to find a home. Lodgers who were not apparently related to the family were taken in to households already too large for the accommodation available. In spite of the new houses built shortly after 1800, households were on the whole larger than they had been in the pre-industrial period.

The influx of miners early in the century clearly affected the demographic structures of the community. It lowered the average age of inhabitants and increased fertility. In the absence of any disastrous rise in infant mortality, Highley was expanding through natural growth as well as through immigration. However, it was not until the second half of the nineteenth century that we find any real improvement in terms of age at death and levels of juvenile mortality over the situation 200 years previously.

After the departure of the miners, the rate of natural increase slowed, and a falling birth rate in an ageing population, together with emigration, brought about a decrease in total population. Demographically, the period between 1850 and the late 1870s may best be compared with the last years of the seventeenth century,

Table 8.7 Burgess household, 1841–81

1841	1851	1861	1871	1881
Sarah Gardiner 60	John Burgess 40	John Burgess 50	John Burgess, widower, 60	John Burgess 69
John Burgess 25	Mary Burgess 30	Mary Burgess 46	Mary Ann Burgess 15	Benjamin Burgess 28
Mary Burgess 25	Thomas Burgess 16	Thomas Burgess 26		Eliza Burgess, daughter-in-law, 36
Thomas Burgess 6	John Burgess 13	John Burgess 23		Bertha Burgess, granddaughter, 10m.
John Burgess 4	Joseph Burgess 11	Joseph Burgess 20		
Joseph Burgess 1	Caroline Burgess 9	George Burgess 12		
	Eliza Burgess 6	Benjamin Burgess 9		
	George Burgess 4	Mary Ann Burgess 5		
	Benjamin Burgess 6m.			

which was also a period of stagnation. In the third quarter of the nineteenth century, Highley and its neighbours in south-east Shropshire all saw a steady decline in population. It needed a further industry-related influx of migrants for Highley to reverse this trend.

9

Squirearchy

We have already seen that Highley's population was by no means a static one, even in the seventeenth and eighteenth centuries when agriculture provided almost the only employment. The coming of industry greatly increased the degree of mobility for it brought large numbers of immigrants who were for the most part short-stayers, without stemming the flow of young single emigrants who continued, as before, to leave the village.

Table 9.1 indicates the numbers of children born at Highley (and apparently surviving childhood) by birth cohort, distinguishing between those who were last recorded at baptism, as adults, or at burial. It is impractical, here and in Table 9.2, to consider decades after 1820 as burial records after the end of our period in 1880 were not used.

Table 9.1   Emigration, 1780–1819

Decade	Number in cohort	Last rec. as infant	Last rec. as adult	Buried at Highley
1780–89	54	35	13	6
1790–99	61	43	12	6
1800–09	107	82	8	17
1810–19	142	110	15	7

In the nineteenth century we are better able to trace those adults who remained in the village. Nevertheless, we still find that over 75 per cent of those children born between 1800 and 1819, when the first phase of industrialization was at its height, were never recorded in Highley again after their baptism. They either left the village in childhood with their parents, or alone as adolescents. In fact of the 110 children of the 1810–19 cohort who were not

Table 9.2 Mobility of fathers of children baptised, 1780–1819

Decade	'new' fathers	baptised at Highley	buried at Highley	Not bapt. or bur. at Highley
1780–89	24	3	6	16
1790–99	19	2	8	10
1800–09	54	7	18	35
1810–19	62	2	8	53

recorded again, only 23 appear to have left alone – that is leaving parents and/or siblings still resident in the village. The remaining 87 apparently left with their parents. Thus although young adults still left to find work or to marry elsewhere, much larger numbers left as children when their families, some of whom spent only a couple of years in Highley, moved on.

This is a fundamental shift in emigration patterns, and one which was identified as beginning in the post-enclosure period, when the loosening of ties with landholding meant that whole families moved more than they had previously done. Industrialization, however, with its demand for a specialized labour force, and with the short-term nature of some of its ventures, made the migration of families vastly more frequent. This is further illustrated in Table 9.2, which shows those new fathers who were neither baptised nor buried in the parish.

Although we know that quarrying and some coal mining were being carried on in the 1790s, the table shows few new couples appearing in the baptism register. This supports the supposition that the quarrying workforce, in particular, was largely recruited from local residents. Yet between 1793 and 1801, total population rose from 215 to 274. Since, as we noted earlier, those born in the period 1750 to 1779 showed a tendency to remain in Highley to adulthood, it may be that the beginnings of industrialization led to an increase in population initially because of a temporary slowing down of emigration rather than massive immigration.

The main period of immigration came with the expansion of coal mining after 1800. Of the 62 new fathers recorded in the decade 1810–19, only two had themselves been born at Highley. Furthermore, few of these men remained in the village for any length of time. Less than 13 per cent of the new fathers of this decade were themselves subsequently buried at Highley – compared with a mean of means of the eighteenth century decades (to 1779) of 45.4 per cent.

This picture is reinforced by Figure 9.1, which shows numbers of transient parents during the first half of the period. Interestingly, this number was lower in the 1790s than it had been in most decades of the previous century, which accords with our suggestion about the nature of the workforce in early industrial developments. After 1800, numbers of transients rose sharply, reaching a peak between 1810 and 1819, when two-thirds of all new fathers were in fact very short-term residents.

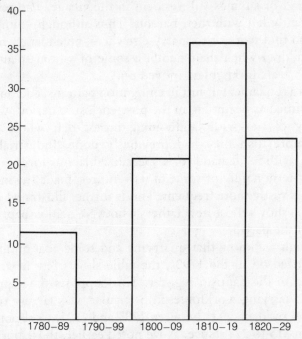

Figure 9.1 Numbers of transient parents, 1780–1829

There must in addition, of course, also have been many other transients who did not baptise a child during their brief stay in the parish. Of the 86 heads of household in the Easter Book for 1818, for example, 16 are not mentioned in parish registers. In addition, those servants and lodgers not recorded by name were probably also for the most part short-term residents.[1]

The Easter Book listings from 1793 to 1830 supply a further indication of the extent of mobility during the period of

[1] S.R.O. 4123/Ti/2: Highley Easter Book, 1756–1834.

industrialization. They too support the view of relative stability between 1780 and 1800. Of the 53 named heads of household in 1793, 40 were still in the village in 1799. Only eight families appear to have left Highley: five heads of household had died but were followed by sons or widows.

By 1807, the total population had leapt to perhaps 400. As before, a nucleus of about 40 families remained. However, since 1799 30 new families had arrived. Several of these new arrivals are known to have been coal miners: probably the great majority were. There is little evidence as to the place of origin of these immigrants. Some had previously worked in mines in Billingsley and Arley parishes, and had apparently been brought in by mine owners from a considerable distance. One of the co-owners, George Johnson, came from Byker in Northumerland, and one of his miners buried at Billingsley in 1800 was also 'of Biker near Newcastle-Upon-Tyne'.[2] Others, according to Billingsley registers, had come 'from the north of England'.

Other miners were more local, coming from the mid-Shropshire coalfield. Luke Hartshorn had come from Broseley, and was sent back there by parish officers in 1817.[3] Sometimes apparently related families arrived together. Four couples surnamed Yeats appear in the baptism registers between 1800 and 1805, none of them natives of Highley. Similarly Edward, John and Thomas Geary all first baptised children in 1809 or 1810 – none had been born in the parish, and none appears to have remained there more than two years.

There was considerable turnover of industrial personnel. Because several small mines and forges were working in this corner of Shropshire, men could move from place to place as economic or geological factors made one mine less attractive, or the prospect of better housing or conditions appeared elsewhere. The miners of the large coalfields are known to have been constantly on the move between pits.[4]

By 1818 mining in Highley was at its peak. Of the 86 heads of household listed in the Easter Book of that year, 40 had arrived

[2] *Parish Registers of Chelmarsh, Neenton and Billingsley*, Shropshire Parish Register Society: Hereford Diocese, Vol. III, Part 2 (1903), third pagination, p. 36.
[3] S.R.O. 4123/P/11–26: Highley removal orders.
[4] M. Pollard, *The Hardest Work Under Heaven: the life and death of the British coal miner* (London, 1984).

since 1807, while 22 of the 71 heads of household of 1807 had left (only three had died in the interim). As figure 9.1 shows, transience remained high during the 1820s. As coal mining folded, emigration began to outstrip immigration. Less than 40 per cent of the families listed in 1818 were still represented in 1830.

Table 9.3 Birthplaces of adults recorded at censuses 1851–81

	In Highley (%)	Less than 10 miles away (%)	More than 10 miles away (%)	Unknown (%)	Total (%)	[N]
1851	33.2	36.8	29.9	0	99.9	217
1861	21.6	28.8	45.3	4.3	100	278
1871	31.9	32.5	33.5	2.1	100	191
1881	25.7	26.0	45.9	3.4	100	231

Throughout this period, a shrinking nucleus of 'original' families remained. Twenty-two of the 53 families of 1793 were still represented 25 years later, and only 11 by 1830. There was, however, a turnover of about half the village population every 10 years or so, with even more short-term immigration not revealed by the Easter Book sampling. Coal mining families were less likely to remain for any length of time than other groups, although there continued to be some transient agricultural labourers, and short leases still meant a high turnover of tenant farmers.

Except perhaps in the very earliest stages of its development, it seems that very few locals were recruited into coal mining. In his history of the industry in the eighteenth and early nineteenth centuries, Flinn quotes a contemporary opinion that colliers must be recruited as boys of less than 13 or 14, otherwise they 'never will become colliers'.[5] This certainly seems to have been practised in Highley: local boys were sometimes taken on, but hardly any Highley-born adult miners can be traced. Mining had its own specialized work force who were brought in when the industry developed, and which left no room for the entry of local adults.

Quarry men were often recruited locally. Unfortunately, they are indistinguishable from agricultural labourers in the parish register until the mid 1820s. From then until the beginning of the census period 18 quarrymen were recorded, most of whom were

[5] M. W. Flinn, The History of the British Coal Industry Vol 2 (Oxford, 1984), p. 339.

born in the immediate neighbourhood – four in Highley itself, five in Chelmarsh, two in Alveley, and so on. Half the group remained in Highley for more than 20 years, and none was a particularly short-term resident. In several cases sons followed fathers as quarrymen. They were in general a much more stable group than miners, and quarrying provided more employment for local men than did the much more extensive coal mining industry.

The advent of mining brought dramatic increases in levels of mobility in Highley: but the extent of migration among the purely rural community became no less after the onset of industrialization. Highley-born young people continued to leave to work elsewhere: their employment opportunities were less enhanced than might be supposed from the scale of industrial development.

During the census period it is easier to assess mobility of all inhabitants, not just heads of household or those featuring in parish registers, and to add for the first time an actual geographical dimension since we have relatively reliable information about the place of birth of immigrants. Table 9.3 deals with place of birth of those inhabitants over 15 years of age in census years from 1851, when exact parish of origin was first recorded.

Regularly less than a third of all adults living in Highley had actually been born there. There was still considerable movement within the 10-mile radius which had long been a significant area. There was also increasing migration from a wider area, especially after the coming of the railway in 1862. The presence of the navvies in 1861 and miners in 1881 accounts for much of the rise in the percentage of longer-distance migrants in those years.

The railway navvies were drawn from all over England and Wales. Although temporary, their presence must have had a profound effect on village society as their numbers were large. Navvies and their families accounted for 106 of the village population of 407 in 1861. The navvies themselves were born in 23 different counties of England and Wales, and one in Ireland (in addition to some unidentifiable place names, and nine men who did not know, or choose to divulge, their birthplace). These counties ranged from Yorkshire in the north to Somerset and Surrey in the south; from Wales in the west to Suffolk and Norfolk in the east. Only three were relatively local men from south Shropshire.

Birthplaces of wives and children of navvies show that the men had travelled widely before arriving in Highley. From the birthplaces of his children, for instance, it seems that George Walter, aged 33 and born in Buckinghamshire, had previously worked in Doncaster, Caerphilly and Worcestershire. John Thompson, born in Norfolk, had lived at Wednesbury in Staffordshire, Breconshire and Cardiff, all within the previous eight years. Seven of the children of the navvies had been born in France. Gangs of British navvies first went to France to build the Paris and Rouen railway in 1841, and many stayed on until the 1850s constructing other railways in Normandy and Brittany.[6]

Children's birthplaces also suggest that some members of the Severn Valley Railway construction gang had worked and travelled together. The majority, however, had been gathered together from all over the country for this job. They clearly lived an itinerant life, and many were either unmarried or unaccompanied by their families.

The impact on the community of such a group of immigrants must have been great. Navvies' drunkenness and rowdyism were legendary, although we have no evidence of disturbances they might have created in Highley.[7] Some managed to get vacant cottages: others lived in a specially-built barrack house at Stanley. But many more lodged with local families. These were men who had travelled all over the country, and sometimes overseas, and their impact on a local population who had in the main been born less than 10 miles away cannot have been negligible.

Some navvies were in Highley by 1859: the Severn Valley Railway was opened in 1862. Perhaps the 106 navvies of 1861 represented a short-lived peak in their numbers. Nevertheless, for something like four years, a quarter of Highley's population was made up of 'strangers'.

The coal miners of 1879 onwards represent a different kind of immigration. Coal mining in this second phase continued until 1969, and the families of some of the immigrants of 1881 are still represented in Highley. In all, in 1881, 126 of the total population of 363 were miners and their families. Not all miners were immigrants: six of them, mostly young men, had been born in Highley itself. The majority of the 58 miners, however, had come from elsewhere. A handful was drawn from the surrounding rural parishes like Glazeley and Billingsley. Another small group came

[6] T. Coleman, *The Railway Navvies* (London, 1976), pp. 203–4.
[7] *Ibid.*, pp. 28–9.

Plate 9 Station-master and staff on the platform at Highley Station. The arrival of the railway in 1862 widened social and commercial horizons.

from places where there was already a mining industry established, within about 20 miles of Highley, like Dudley, Madeley and Lindridge. The majority, though, came from further afield, some from Flint and Cheshire and the largest group from the area of the Potteries in Staffordshire.

In addition, the birthplaces of these men's families show that many of them had previously worked in the Potteries. Eighteen miners' dependents were born at Silverdale near Stoke-on-Trent, and a further 12 within a mile or two. Matthew Viggars, who was a director of the Highley Mining Company, was also the owner of Knutton Manor Colliery in Silverdale,[8] and in fact the first housing built in Highley for this generation of miners was called Silverdale Terrace. Once again, the mine owners were bringing in men from their other areas of operations.

In fact the 1881 census shows many of the characteristics which, earlier evidence suggests, applied to the first phase of coal mining in Highley. Some related family groups arrived together. Frederick Evans was born in Flint, although he had subsequently worked at Silverdale. His younger brother Norman and sister Alice lived with his family in Highley, and next door was Richard Evans, also born in Flint and who had also been living at Silverdale. Elsewhere

[8] *Kelly's Directory of Staffordshire* (1870).

Plate 10 Highley Colliery photographed in its early days. Note the piles of pit props waiting to be taken underground, and the rural surroundings of the mine.

in the village was the family of Joseph Evans (born Flint) whose children were all born at Silverdale. Thus almost certainly four brothers, with the families of three of them, had been previously in the Potteries together before coming to Highley. Similarly it is difficult to believe that Isaac, Noah and Jabez Lawton, all born at Wolstanton, were unrelated.

Another similarity was that although some local men were recruited into mining, they were all young. Typical were the two sons of Benjamin Lucas, who was not himself a miner, aged 15 and 19. Significantly, the young locals were described as 'colliery labourer' not as 'collier' as were the immigrants, and it is probable that they were not employed underground but on surface work and construction. The skilled miners were all brought into the village from outside.

In the 'normal' years of 1851 and 1871, a third or less of the adult population had come to Highley from a distance of more than 10 miles – and many of these were born less than 15 miles away. Table 9.4 shows these longer-distance migrants by socio-economic group. Group I has a disproportionate share of these migrants. Professionals like the vicar were likely to travel greater distances, and farmers too were prepared to travel to take up a farm. Both agricultural labourers and small tradesmen and craftsmen moved

Table 9.4   Longer-distance migrants by socioeconomic groups

	I	II	III	IV	Total
1851	20	13	32	1	66
1861	15	21	26	2	64
1871	20	16	30	3	69
1881	8	18	24	2	52

frequently within the 10-mile radius, but less frequently from further afield. Group III also includes servants, however, who were quite regularly brought from considerable distances.

In some cases this can be explained by a knowledge of family circumstances. In 1851, for example, Elizabeth Burrows, widow of the vicar, employed a servant born at Ombersley in Worcestershire. Her son was at the time vicar of Ombersley. Similarly in 1871 William Jordin employed a farm bailiff born at Hartlebury in Worcestershire, which was also the birthplace of his wife Harriet Jordin.

Some servants were joined by younger relatives, a prudent measure to ease the start of a girl's life 'in service'. In 1871 Emma George aged 22, born at Stottesdon, lived in at the Jordins', as did 12-year-old Mary George, born at the same place. Most female servants had been born in the rural parishes around Highley, although by the last decade of the period there are signs that the populous Black Country to the east was beginning to provide some domestic servants. Male servants were more likely than female to originate outside the 10-mile area, like Austin Waldron, a single man of 50 in 1851, who was born in Ireland.

The surrounding area of south Shropshire still provided a significant proportion of Highley's adult population. Agricultural labourers in particular were likely to travel within this radius, particularly before the coming of the railway in 1862. Table 9.5 shows the birthplaces of agricultural labourers, and comparison with Table 9.3 underlines how consistently more were born in Highley than was the case with the adult population as a whole. In the later years of the census period, we find somewhat more labourers from outside the immediate area. As with servants, there are indications that farm workers were brought in by an employer who had connections with a particular area. Jesse Lane, a principal farmer, came from Kineton in Gloucestershire. A group of farm employees also came from that area: there was a shepherd from

Ford, a couple of miles from Kineton; two single labourers from 'Gloucestershire'; and a waggoner with two small children born at Willersey in the same small area. Since immigrants from Gloucestershire were otherwise rare, it looks as if Lane had brought his own work force with him.

Table 9.5   Birthplaces of agricultural labourers

	In Highley	Less than 10 miles away	More than 10 miles away	Total	[N]
	(%)	(%)	(%)	(%)	
1851	35.0	42.5	22.5	100	40
1861	45.7	42.8	11.4	99.9	35
1871	40.6	29.7	29.7	100	37
1881	44.4	26.0	29.6	100	27

In the main, however, agricultural labourers were, even as late as 1871, the least likely group in the community to travel (or to have to travel) long distances to find work.

So far we have examined only the birthplaces of Highley's adults, since they are easier to relate to occupations and give a better idea of voluntary migration. It is worth, however, briefly considering the proportion of all inhabitants born locally, as this enables a comparison between Highley and other mid-nineteen-century communities. In the two censuses unaffected by large-scale immigration, the percentage of the total population born in Highley was 48.7 per cent and 42.7 per cent. In the large industrial town of Preston in 1851, Anderson found 48 per cent of the population were native to the town.[9] In Horsham, Sussex, on a 10 per cent sample, 45.6 per cent were natives in 1851: there, as in Highley, this percentage had fallen somewhat by 1871.[10] Thus Highley was by no means unusual in its high degree of mobility: what is surprising, perhaps, is that a small, relatively remote rural community exhibited immigration rates comparable with those of expanding urban areas.

This immigration was counterbalanced by considerable emigration. Although 75 per cent of the survivors of the birth cohort of 1830–39 were still in Highley in 1841, for example, only just

[9] M. Anderson, *Family Structure in Nineteenth Century Lancashire* (Cambridge, 1971), p. 37.
[10] D. Constable, *Household Structure in Three English Market Towns* (Reading, 1977).

over 30 per cent were still resident by 1851. Adolescents continued
to leave in numbers: only 10 per cent of those born 1830–34 (and
therefore past adolescence) remained to 1851. Although the
unprecedented levels of migration of the first half of the period
were not sustained, the largely agricultural community of the
second half was still highly mobile. If we work from the 1831
population figure of 404 and assume no migration, growth in the
community as shown in baptisms and burials should have meant a
population by 1841 of 428 – in fact it was 360. With only minimal
industry, Highley was, like so many agricultural communities in
the mid nineteenth century, a village in decline in terms of size.
This is made even clearer if we consider census totals with navvies
and coal miners omitted (in 1861 and 1881).

1831	1841	1851	1861	1871	1881
404	360	359	*301	293	*237

Table 9.6 details migration between successive censuses. It
shows that after a (relatively) stable decade between 1841 and 1851,
it was usual for two-thirds of the inhabitants to have vanished from
the listing on the next census. Using parish registers in conjunction
with census returns, it is possible to distinguish between those who
had died in the intervening decade – a remarkably consistent
percentage – and those who had merely left. Regularly over half
the village's inhabitants could be expected to move every 10 years.

Much of this emigration was by young people aged between 12
and 20, who had always been likely to move. Whole families of all
classes, though, were also highly mobile. Fewer Highley residents
actually owned land in the parish that at any time since enclosure:
farming families, with the exception of the landowning Jordins,
moved at least as often as any other.

Table 9.6 Mobility between censuses

	1841–51	1851–61	1861–71*	1871–81
Died (%)	12.1	11.8	11.6	11.6
Stayed (%)	41.3	29.4	35.9	31.4
Left (%)	46.6	58.8	52.4	57.0
Total (%)	100	100	99.9	100
[N]	356	357	292	293

* Omitting railway navvies

For some families, Highley was one stop on a circuit of villages in the area. Judging by the birthplaces of their children, George Bill and his wife had been in Bridgnorth in 1862, Worfield in 1864 and 1866, and Shifnal in 1868, before moving to Highley by 1870. Craftsmen as well as labourers could be mobile: William Walford, a shoemaker born at Highley and living there in 1871 had nevertheless had children born at Eardington, Glazeley and Billingsley before returning to his birthplace. Tenanted farms changed hands frequently: Hazelwells had a different family in residence in each census year except 1871, when it was empty (although a further, fifth, resident was there in 1870).[11]

A final indication of the levels of migration throughout the period is the very small number of families who continued to be represented in Highley from 1780 to 1880. In fact of those families listed in all sources 1779–80, only two could still be traced in the village 100 years later. One of these, the influential Jordins, died out in that year. Highley had experienced a virtually complete turnover of population in the century.

The most spectacular migration was of the large numbers of coal miners drawn into the village. But individuals born in Highley, and families never involved in inudstry, also continued to move. The new developments employed few local men, and throughout the period young men left to find work more often than they stayed. Young women, too, went into service in other villages and towns: some worked in Highley itself, but in fact the majority of servants employed in the village were born outside it. Tenant farmers moved often, and over considerable distances. Their labourers were more likely to come from the immediate neighbourhood, but were no less mobile.

A nucleus of families remained for more than one generation, but hardly any for more than three. Those who owned land, like the Jordins and Wilcoxes, were more static than tenants. Some labourers and craftsmen lived all their lives in Highley, and were succeeded by their sons and even grandsons. These, however, were the exceptions, for the trend towards whole-family migration which had been increasing in the eighteenth century accelerated in the nineteenth. Very few families indeed were tied to Highley by ownership or long-term tenancy of land. Some men probably left agriculture to work in towns now more accessible than ever

[11] *Kelly's Directory of Shropshire* (1870).

before: after 1862 Birmingham was only an hour or so away by train.

On the whole, between about 1830 and the late 1870s, more people left Highley than arrived. Without the opening of the new coal mine in 1879, Highley would have continued to decline in size into the twentieth century, as did neighbouring Billingsley and Kinlet. As it was, there was a new influx of miners which showed many of the characteristics of the earlier immigration. This time, though, mining activity was to be sustained, and the population would double before the end of the century, and increase more than five-fold in the 20 years after that.

Parish registers suggest an extremely high level of endogamous marriage during this period. Before 1830, no less than 82.6 per cent of all marriages were between partners supposedly both 'of Highley'. Between 1830 and 1880 this fell somewhat to 72.4 per cent. Undoubtedly endogamous marriage was more frequent than in earlier centuries: the village population was greater than at any time in its past, and this, together with weaker kinship networks within the community, considerably increased the choice of partner available.

However, we should be suspicious of some of these apparently endogamous marriages, particularly during the first half of the period. Between 1780 and 1829 90 marriages were between partners both supposedly living in Highley. Yet 37 of these marriages produced no children baptised at Highley. Some of them may of course have been childless, or between Nonconformist couples: but in the great majority of cases the couples are never again recorded as resident in Highley in Easter Book or census listings, or at burial. In two-thirds of these marriages neither party had been baptised in the parish, and their surnames are not otherwise encountered there. In the remaining third, a Highley-born partner married an apparent stranger. Thus although these marriage partners might have fulfilled the three-week residence rule before their wedding, they do not seem to have been genuine inhabitants.

Even in the remaining 53 cases, where at least short-term residence followed the marriage, it is doubtful if both partners had been living in Highley for long prior to it. In 29 of these marriages, neither partner had been born in the village. However, if we assume that these marriages were truly endogamous, and that those not followed by further mentions in Highley were not, we find that less than half of all marriages were endogamous between 1780 and 1829. Later in the century, particularly after 1860, the marriage register appears to be more reliable with regard to place of residence.

Nevertheless, even if only 50 per cent or a little less of all marriages were actually endogamous, this represents a considerable increase over earlier periods. Where places of origin are mentioned, they indicate a wider area drawn upon for marriage partners. Increasingly, industrial towns to the east of Highley are mentioned, like Penn in Wolverhampton (twice), Sedgely, Hockley, Birmingham and Walsall. Distances involved could be greater: one groom came from Dublin, for instance. Towns in north Shropshire and in Staffordshire which had not figured prominently in the seventeenth and eighteenth centuries now did so – places such as Eccleshall, Shifnal, Stoke and so on. Possibly because of industrialization and better communications, more marriage partners came from towns rather than villages: even local towns (Bridgnorth with six, Bewdley three and Kidderminster two) provided more partners than before. The neighbouring villages which had previously been drawn upon continued to be so, but to a lesser extent.

The most noticeable feature of the sketch map (Figure 9.2) which plots these places of origin and shows their direction from Highley as well as a diagrammatic indication of their distance, is how many partners now came from the industrialized east rather than the rural west. This may have been simply because the east was more heavily populated; but it does indicate a shift away from market towns like Ludlow and Shrewsbury, and greater links with the growing Black Country.

There seems to have been little intermarriage between the colliers of the early nineteenth century and local women. Most miners seem to have arrived in Highley with wives and children. Only seven known colliers married in the parish. None of their brides was born in Highley itself, although two came from Billingsley and one from Arley. The two from Billingsley were in fact sisters, born in 1796 and 1799, and at the time of their marriage were living in Highley with their father who was himself a miner. In the main, however, miners' wives were not born locally, either in Highley or its immediate neighbourhood. They were either brought from the immigrants' home area, or themselves the

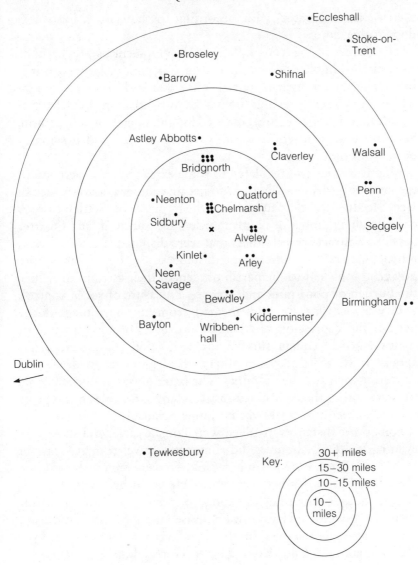

Figure 9.2 Homes of marriage partners, 1780–1879

daughters of temporary (and probably therefore mining) residents.

In spite of the short duration of their stay, some railway navvies and their families did marry locals. In 1861 Ann Page of Highley married William Smith, a 'navigator' from Norfolk who was lodging in her family's house. In the same year Mary Munro married an 'excavator' who, according to the census, lived next door to her family.

The miners of the second phase of development barely had time to settle in Highley before the end of our period. However, it is interesting in the light of our surmise that early miners brought wives from their previous homes to note that in 1879 Samuel Rhodes, a miner of Highley, married Susanna Leigh of Wolstanton, Staffs – an area in which we know many miners had previously been working.

Migration was still regulated to some extent by the operation of the laws of settlement. Those who became chargeable to the parish were frequently despatched to their place of settlement. A considerable number of removal orders has survived, and Quarter Sessions abstracts reveal others that were disputed.[12] The ability to move paupers over often long distances was one of the more powerful tools left to the parish officers in their attempt to reduce the burden of poor rates and exercise a measure of social control.

It was occasionally implemented from the beginning of the period: the depression of 1816–17, however, brought a spate of removals. Five orders survive for 1817 alone. Two categories appear most at risk; the mothers of illegitimate children, and labouring men and their families. The latter must have been unable to work either through illness or, as seems probable in the post-war years, because work was no longer available.

Sometimes distances involved were considerable, and show that even agricultural labourers did sometimes travel relatively far. In 1812, John Price, his wife and six children were removed to Abbey Dore on the border between south Herefordshire and Wales.[13] They had not been in Highley long, for none of the children – not even the 11-week-old baby – was baptised in the parish. Curiously, Elizabeth Ashwood was in the same year removed to Ewyas Harold, about a mile from Abbey Dore, although apparently unrelated to the Prices. Jane Baynham was sent back to Church Eaton, near Stafford; and John Hughes and his family removed to Peopleton, between Worcester and Evesham.

Not all removal orders were immediately carried out. The Prices were allowed to remain until Mrs Price was sufficiently recovered

[12] R. L. Kenyon (ed), *Shropshire County Records: Orders of the Shropshire Quarter Sessions* (Shrewsbury, 1908).
[13] S.R.O. 4123/P/11–26.

from her 'extreme illness' to travel. Elizabeth Ashwood was first ordered to be returned to Morville in Shropshire in December 1811: this order was withdrawn, and in January 1812 that for Ewyas Harold was drawn up. It seems that removal orders were obtained for single women when their pregnancy was known, but that they in fact only left after the birth – a more humane attitude than that shown in parishes where pregnant women were harried over the parish boundary to prevent the child from gaining a settlement.[14] Elizabeth Ashwood was still in Highley in April 1812 when her illegitimate son was baptised. Ann Fenn was ordered on 3rd August 1811 to go to Deuxhill, Salop, although her child was baptised at Highley in September.

Some removals were either never carried out, or were rescinded. The family of William Walford, ordered to Enville, Staffs, in 1784 were still in the village in 1785 and 1789, and apparently stayed until at least 1801.

Implementing orders of removal could be very expensive, since at least one overseer had to accompany the paupers and hand them over at their destination. In 1815, for example, expenses of removals cost the parish £53.

Poor relief was an increasing problem for parish administrators from the beginning of this period. Inhabitants told Plymley in 1793 that poor rates for the parish amounted to about £80 a year, although within memory they had only been £20 to £30 a year.[15] They were quite right. In the year to Easter 1776, £24 19s 6d had been raised: in 1780–1 overseers spent £35 14s 3d. By the mid-1790s, as Plymley was told, the poor rate averaged over £80 a year.

Yet worse was to come, as rising prices brought increased problems for the poor. In 1796–97 the total expended leapt to £159 10s, and in the early years of the nineteenth century over £250 per annum was needed. A peak was reached between 1813 and 1818, when the figure was regularly over £300. Such high poor rates, besides indicating hardship among the poor, helped in some cases to force the small freeholder, already in difficulties, off the land altogether.

In 1790 and 1792 payments to paupers were contracted out: two local men received £48 a year to be responsible for the maintenance

---

[14] G. Taylor, *The Problem of Poverty 1660–1834* (London, 1969), p. 28.
[15] B.L. Add. MSS. 21018: Copy of notes of J. Plymley, 1793.

of the poor.[16] The scheme may not have been successful, as it was soon discontinued. Indeed, it is hard to see how it could have worked, for there was no workhouse and the majority of paupers were not capable of much work. Expenditure was also rising so quickly that agreeing a contract in advance would have been hazardous, and the only way for a contractor to make a profit would seem to be by cutting the amount of relief paid. It was probably fortunate for the village poor that the experiment seems to have been short lived.

The last year for which detailed records of payments survive is 1800–01. These accounts are worth examining for the light they throw on how the poor rate was spent. Weekly 'pensioners', who received poor relief regularly throughout the year, got amounts varying from one to four shillings a week, with a norm of about three shillings – less than half a labourer's wage. In addition, they received small payments for clothing and for coal as the need arose. As well as her weekly payments, Martha Steel was given 'a sheet and cloth to mend her bed-tick' (probably in advance of her lying-in), 'a pair of cards', cloth for a shirt and smockfrock for her son, a shift, two petticoats, shoes and coal. Altogether, including paying for her journey to Bridgnorth and for someone to 'fetch the midwife to' her, Martha Steel cost the parish about £12 9s in the first 39 weeks of the financial year. She was by no means the only recipient – at least another half-dozen women received similar ex-gratia payments throughout the year.

Some claimants were not regular recipients: they were given small sums at odd times when 'in want', or had their rent paid. Other expenses in 1800 included doctors' bills, expenses for overseers' journeys, money for relieving vagrants and wounded sailors, for drawing up indentures, and the county rates.

Altogether, £254 was spent, which represented a *per capita* expenditure of 18/6d from the whole village. Parliamentary reports indicate that expenditure was almost exactly the same in 1802–03.[17] At this time, 13.5 per cent of the total population received relief – considerably more than the national average of 8.6 per cent.[18] Yet few able-bodied men received relief: 38 per cent of all recipients were children: a further 32 per cent were elderly. Of the remaining

[16] S.R.O. 4123/P/2: Overseers' accounts, 1762–1801.

[17] *Abstract of the Answers and Returns Relative to the Poor*, HC XIII (1803–04).

[18] J. D. Marshall, *The Old Poor Law 1795–1834* (London and Basingstoke, 1973), p. 33.

30 per cent, detailed returns indicate a majority as single mothers. Highley's problems were apparently not caused by the necessity of subsidizing unemployed or underpaid agricultural labourers, as they were in 'Speenhamland' parishes. Industry was already present to push up agricultural wages, and those labourers who did not have a legal settlement in Highley were removed at the first sign of problems. Those men who did receive relief were usually occasional claimants, and often elderly. Highley had a higher than usual proportion of elderly paupers – some 32 per cent were over 60, as against 10 to 20 per cent in the 'problem' counties of the rural south.[19] In addition high levels of illegitimacy contributed significantly to expenditure.

Numbers of claimants remained broadly similar in 1813–15, although children were no longer included in figures returned.[20] Because the total population increased, however, *per capita* expenditure fell to around 13/– before rising to its post-war peak of 15/3d in 1818. Nevertheless, because of the nature of immigration, the burden of the poor rate fell on a group whose size had not significantly increased and who, because of falling grain prices after 1815, were less able to carry it.

After 1818 expenditure fell steadily throughout the 1820s, although since we do not know the numbers of claimants it is unclear whether this was because of a fall in their numbers, or whether expenditure was being cut back in the light of falling prices. The decrease was dramatic: only £112 6s was spent in 1832, and only £85 12s in 1834. The community was certainly spending less *per capita* – only 5/7d in 1832, less than at any time since the early 1780s. It is unlikely that numbers of paupers fell so rapidly or so much. We must therefore assume that amounts distributed were severely curtailed.

It is only in the early years of the period that we can see the mechanics of the system of poor relief. Numbers of paupers had increased since the mid eighteenth century: they also received more money per week – two or three shillings instead of 9d or a shilling. There were also far more incidental and administrative expenses: journeys, letters, indentures, court appearances took up far more of the available money than they had done 50 years earlier.

---

[19] *Ibid.*, p. 36.
[20] *Reports of the Select Committee on the Poor Laws*, HC VI (1817); HC V (1818).

If the system had become more cumbersome, it also retained some flexibility. Payments were made as need became apparent. Money was collected in the same way. Plymley reported that 'each farm is called upon to pay a certain sum as often as money is wanted, there being no regular mode of assessment'. In fact the Overseers' Accounts indicate that there was a regular mode of assessment, although collection may well have been irregular as Plymley states. Whether or not this was a more humane system than the more remote bureaucracy that superseded it in 1834 is debateable. Local officers could exercise their discretion and were in a position to detect and relieve distress: they were also given very considerable powers over their neighbours and employees. One of the two overseers in 1800–01 was Dr Macnab, quarry owner and coalmaster. The size of the group which provided the churchwardens and overseers continued to shrink in absolute terms as well as relative to the population as a whole. The demarcations between this group and the rest of the population must have been reinforced by the necessity for the poor of making frequent appeals for poor relief, to argue the need for a new petticoat or mattress cover. The immediacy of the system, one of its potential and quite possibly actual strengths, also gave scope for resentment on both sides of the divide between contributor and claimant.

Whatever the tensions generated in the community by the administration of the old Poor Law (and numbers of removals and apprenticeships, vastly increased poor rates and so on indicate that they grew during the early years of the century), the new Poor Law of 1834 fundamentally changed the situation. The powers of the parish, which had steadily grown and been concentrated in the hands of an ever-smaller oligarchy, were very much curtailed. In one important respect, Highley's autonomy was weakened. It became part of the Cleobury Mortimer Union of parishes; its poor relief was administered from Cleobury; and the workhouse there was to house many of its paupers.

In this respect at least the poor were less fortunate. The old system, for all its potential humiliations, kept them in their own homes, within their own community. Local charities still existed into the 1820s to distribute bread to those in need; and small acts of private charity and mutual aid were still possible.

We do not know what proportion of Highley's paupers entered

the Union workhouse. The old, the sick and the disabled went when they could no longer be looked after or look after themselves. Sometimes this could be long postponed: Nancy Bennet, a 'pauper' (presumably receiving outdoor relief) lived alone in 1851, aged 81. She was buried in 1859, though, from the workhouse. In the case of those with physical or mental handicaps, the workhouse was the only alternative when relatives were unable or unwilling to care for them any longer. Richard Kirkham, an 'imbecile', lived with his widowed stepmother in 1871. In 1877 she remarried and left Highley. Two years later Richard, aged 26, died in Cleobury workhouse.

Until 1865 the cost of maintaining the poor of the parish, whether domiciled in Highley or Cleobury Mortimer, fell to the parish itself. Since Highley was largely a village of labourers and small tradesmen, expenses were probably still high. The decision-making, however, was no longer in the hands of the more prosperous section of the local community. Parish officers lost the powers of administering poor relief, and of moving paupers to another parish or even county. They were no longer responsible for examining paupers, or the mothers of illegitimate children, or for apprenticing the children of the poor.

The best surviving evidence for such apprenticeships is from the first 20 years of the nineteenth century. A total of 22 indentures survives from 1783 to 1818, involving 21 children – 12 girls and nine boys.[21] A third of these children are known to have been illegitimate. Some of the legitimate children were orphans, like Elizabeth Barker, apprenticed at 12 in 1804, both of whose parents were dead. Her half-brother, whose mother remained alive, was apprenticed in the same year, aged eight. Not all apprentices were orphans or fatherless. Two children of George and Eleanor Ashwood were apprenticed in 1790 and 1793: the parents left the village, but one of the children stayed for more than 20 years.

The minimum, and most usual, age for apprenticeship was eight, although some children were not apprenticed until 11 or 12. Most children were apprenticed to local farmers – the same group who provided overseers and other parish officers. Thus the paternal role of the village elite in the affairs of the poor was reinforced. The 'trade' that these children learned can only have been domestic service for girls and farm labour for boys. Plymley was told in 1793

[21] S.R.O. 4123/P/29–42: Indentures 1783–1818.

that the children of the poor were 'occasionally taken upon Honour' but more usually bound apprentice: according to their masters they made 'but . . .indifferent servants'.

Some children were sent out of the parish. John Wall was apprenticed to a carpet weaver in Kidderminster in 1802; Samuel Barker to a moulder in Bridgnorth in 1818; others to farmers in Kinlet and Arley. Those children who remained in Highley, where a parent or other relative might still be living, were probably in a better position than those sent to towns even if they did not actually learn a trade.

The parish apprentices were not the children of miners. In fact the influx of miners in the early years of the century had little effect on the system of poor relief: miners came because there was employment for them, and were rarely destitute. Miners did not contribute to or claim from the poor rates, and thus were not a part of one aspect of the interaction between sections of the agrarian society.

In other respects, too, miners seem to have been set apart from the social framework of the community. Religion did not provide much of a meeting point for the two halves of village society. A Wesleyan Methodist chapel was opened in 1815, at the height of coal mining, and one might expect this to be at the instigation – or at least for the use – of miners and their families. But in fact this seems not to have been the case. The prime movers in building the chapel were a group of local farmers, principally Mr Steward of Borle Mill. Numbers attending the chapel were not large: membership in the 1820s was about 20, and by 1851 the average congregation was reckoned to be 30.[22] In any case, the chapel had been built as far from the mining centre at Stanley as was possible in a small parish, and attendance would have meant a steep uphill walk of two or three miles. The timing of prayer meetings in the early years – 5 a.m. on Sunday mornings – must have been discouraging.

Church attendance continued to be without apparent zeal among miners and labourers alike. In 1793 communion services were held at Easter, Christmas, Whitsun, Michaelmas and before harvest. Numbers attending were usually between three and 10.[23] Similarly, prayers were read on Saints' Days 'when a sufficient congregation assembles, which is not often the case.'

[22] J. F. Wedley, *A History of Methodism in the Stourport Circuit* (Stourport, 1899).
[23] B.L. Add. MSS. 21018.

If the existing poor relief system and organized religion hardly affected the mining community neither, to judge from existing evidence, did other measures of social control. The manor court was briefly revived around 1820, and two court rolls survive.[24] They deal with similar matters to those before their sixteenth-century counterparts – encroachments, soiling the town well, ringing pigs – and read as if the community they regulated was similarly unchanged. There is no mention of any industrial activity.

More surprisingly, there is hardly any evidence in Quarter Sessions records of disputes between, or crimes committed by, miners. Either miners were more law-abiding than their agricultural neighbours or, as seems more likely, control within the mining community was left to its leaders. Certainly the Quarter Sessions do not record any upsurge in crime or disturbance accompanying the onset of industrialization.

One quarrel in 1814 did involve the joint owner of Stanley Colliery, Thomas Gritton, who was allegedly assaulted by Jasper Neth, a labourer. Neth was found guilty, and his counter charge against Gritton was dismissed after the court heard from witnesses who were in fact Gritton's clerk and 'engineer' – that is, the rest of the colliery management.[25] Unfortunately, no other details of the incident survive. But it may be significant that the only case apparently to come to court involved colliery management rather than miners, and was not a matter internal to the mining community.

Most other crime which got to the courts was petty theft. In 1808 Edward Pugh, chimney sweeper (and occasional pauper, born illegitimate in Highley in 1761) served one month in prison in Shrewsbury for stealing 1s 2d worth of hay.[26] John Turner, labourer, was in 1819 sentenced to one year's imprisonment for stealing two £1 notes.

Sentences could be harsh: in January 1828 Thomas Botfield was sentenced to seven years' transportation for poaching.[27] This was the first time that such a sentence had been given in Shropshire for poaching.[28] Harsh game laws, of course, reflect the gulf between

[24] S.R.O. 1671/: Court rolls 1819 and 1822.
[25] S.R.O. QR 259/162; QR 259/158: Case of assault against J. Neth and T. Gritton, 1814.
[26] S.R.O. QR 234/9: Case against E. Pugh, 1808.
[27] S.R.O. QR 313/228: Case against T. Botfield, 1828.
[28] M. C. Hill (ed), *Abstract of the Quarter Sessions Rolls 1820–30* (Shrewsbury, 1974).

landless and landowners, and the determination of the latter to protect their interests. Botfield was unlucky, in as much as eight men were involved in an organized raid, and he was the one who was caught. Apparently he served his sentence and actually returned to his wife and family in Highley, for there is an eight-year gap between births of his children, and the whole family was in Highley by 1841.

In another case a boy of 11 received a sentence of one month, without hard labour, in the House of Correction. This sentence was lighter than usual, presumably in view of the child's age, although in law no distinction was made. This was an opportunist and thoughtless crime, but the case is interesting as it shows 'community policing' in action.[29] The boy, Richard Broom, had broken into a labourer's house by reaching through a broken casement which had been mended with paper. He had thrown a mirror out of the house, dressed himself in the labourer's shirt, hat and corduroy breeches (leaving his own rags behind), and walked off with a silver watch. Several people had stopped the boy; one examined the watch which Broom then threw away; another, seeing and possibly recognizing the clothes, took the boy to the labourer from whom he had stolen them. A third sent a young employee to recover the watch and return it. The case hardly needed to have gone to court. Probably other cases were dealt with by the community in just such a way without going further.

The impression given by Quarter Sessions records is of a community where it was difficult to escape undetected; where petty theft or an occasional fight or poaching expedition were the main extent of crime. Society seems to have been less violent than in the sixteenth century, when manor courts recorded frequent assaults. But since the nature of the legal system and of the surviving evidence had changed considerably, we cannot be sure of this. It may simply be that mechanisms for dealing with this kind of minor disturbance had ceased to be official.

With the decline of the church courts, there was less regulation of morality. Illegitimacy concerned the parish authorities only when they were likely to have to support the child. Efforts were made to make the father contribute to its upbringing, and some maintenance orders survive. Samuel Crane, for example, was ordered in 1818 to pay £1 6s 3d towards the delivery of Martha

[29] S.R.O. QR 312/76–8, 118: Case against R. Broom, 1827.

Clinton's child, and 1/3d a week towards its maintenance thereafter.[30]

Before turning from crime to examine illegitimacy in more detail, it is worth noting two deviant families who feature in court cases for petty crime and in illegitimacy, and who demonstrate the links between poverty and both.

Thomas Botfield, the transported poacher, lived with his wife and children, his aunt and her illegitimate daughter. His own eldest son or stepson was also apparently illegitimate. The Botfields married in 1825, three years before Thomas was convicted. Figure 9.3 shows the recurring links with illegitimacy within the family.

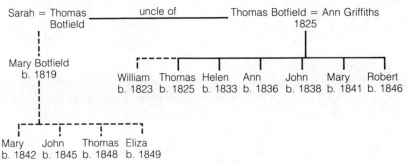

Figure 9.3   Botfield family

Also accused with Botfield but acquitted was John Jones his near neighbour in the terrace of cottages at New England. Jones and his wife were occasional claimants of poor relief from the time of their marriage. In 1801 Jones was paid 'towards the loss of his house'.[31] In 1806 he was in prison in Shrewsbury on 'violent suspicion' of having stolen a quantity of barley, although he was eventually discharged. His wife Elizabeth was imprisoned for one month in 1822 for having assaulted the constable of Kinlet.[32]

The Jones family's links with illegitimacy are many and complex, as Figure 9.4 shows. Two of John Jones's daughters had illegitimate children; a third married a man who had already fathered a child on another woman. A son, George, married two women both of whom had had illegitimate children by other men. Interestingly, the two older Jones sisters were the only locally-born women known to have married coal miners at Highley.

[30] S.R.O. 4123/P/53–61: Bastardy bonds and maintenance orders, 1671–1818.
[31] S.R.O. 4123/P/2.
[32] Hill (ed), *Quarter Sessions Rolls*.

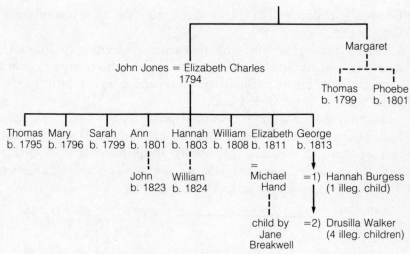

Figure 9.4   Jones family

This is not to imply that poverty, illegitimacy and crime always went together. But in the case of these two neighbouring families, the links are strong. If there was a sub-culture in the community, they were certainly part of it.

During this period illegitimacy levels exceeded even the high rates of the mid-eighteenth century. Between 1780 and 1880, illegitimate baptisms made up more than 10 per cent of the total. Some families were indeed more prone than others to illegitimacy, but it was by no means confined to families like the Joneses and Botfields. In spite of the onset of industrialization, the illegitimacy ratio in the first half of the period, at 9 per cent, was lower than the 12.1 per cent ratio in the second half. Shropshire is recognized as an area of high illegitimacy, but these rates are consistently double the national average.[33]

Figure 9.5 shows decadal illegitimacy ratios throughout the period, and highlights the fluctuations which lie behind the overall figures. In the 1790s, illegitimacy figures soared: nearly one in five of all children baptised was illegitimate. The influx of coal miners cannot be blamed for this 'explosion', as in the main they arrived after 1800. In fact during the decade 1800–09 the ratio fell back to 6.5 per cent. This fall was not due only to the increase in numbers of legitimate births in this decade, for absolute numbers of bastards also decreased.

[33] P. Laslett, *Family Life and Illicit Love in Earlier Generations* (Cambridge, 1977), p. 136.

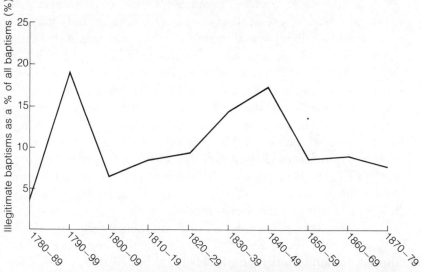

Figure 9.5   Illegitimacy ratios, 1780–1879

After 1830, and the decline of industry, illegitimacy again increased, reaching a high point in the 1840s. Laslett's national sample also reaches a peak in this decade, approaching 7 per cent.[34] Highley in the 1840s experienced an illegitimacy ratio of 17.7 per cent. Thereafter the figure fell to 8 or 9 per cent for the rest of our period.

The first phase of industrialization, then, seems if anything to have decreased the frequency of illegitimacy. It is tempting therefore to relate illegitimacy to economic opportunity in the parish: industrial development provided employment, and fewer couples were perhaps prevented from marrying by adverse economic circumstances. Yet we have noted how few local men were absorbed into mining, and how poor relief records suggest that hardship was as acute after 1800 as before. Food prices remained high, and in addition the pressure on housing became intense as total population grew. The 'frustrated courtship' explanation for illegitimacy and its necessary relation to economic conditions probably played a part in reducing illegitimacy – a 'knock-on' effect from industry may have improved agricultural labourers' opportunities – but it cannot in local circumstances account completely for the abrupt reversal of the trend of the

[34] P. Laslett, K. Oosterveen and R. Smith (eds), *Bastardy and its Comparative History* (London, 1980), p. 17.

1790s. To arrive at a more complete picture, it is necessary to investigate both individual cases of illegitimacy and attitudes towards conventional sexual morality in the community.

A total of 88 women had illegitimate children baptised at Highley between 1780 and 1879. Only 12 (13.6 per cent) were 'repeaters' having more than one child. This was a comparatively low proportion, and did not alone account for the rise in illegitimacy.[35] The problem of studying repeaterdom in any single parish remains, however, for there is evidence that some of Highley's 'singletons' had in fact had children in other parishes. Susanna Rogers, for example, was baptised at Highley in 1769 and had an illegitimate son there in 1797. Five years previously, though, she had had another son at Arley.

Thirty-six (41 per cent) of the mothers were apparently singletons, who had only one child at Highley and who had no other close family links with bastardy, although their families are known to have been resident there. A further 25 (28 per cent) appear in the registers only at the time of their child's baptism. Some were described as 'of Kinlet' or 'of Kidderminster'; others were servants in the parish at the time. The third group, 27 women of the 'bastard-prone', comprised 31 per cent of the total, and included as well as repeaters those women who were themselves illegitimate or whose sisters also bore bastards.

In 28 cases, single mothers subsequently married at Highley, although in only half those cases is it possible to determine if their marriage partner was the father of their child. In fact only five women later married the father, while nine married a different man.

The five cases of marriage between couples who had already produced one or more illegitimate children are interesting. Two of them were between farmers and their servants, where financial considerations do not seem responsible for delaying marriage. In one instance, marriage took place a month after the baptism of the child, and could presumably have occurred before it if both parties so desired. The remaining two couples clearly only regularized a long-term relationship when they married. Mary Botfield had had four children by John Norwood when they married in 1850; Mary Barker and John Stanley married in 1846 when their second child was about to be born.

[35] *Ibid.*, p. 88.

Such non-marital relationships may not have been uncommon. Elizabeth Harris (who had an illegitimate child in 1847) was described in the 1851 census as an 'agricultural labourer's woman'. She lived with Joseph Yeats, a widower. Next door, Drusilla Walker, living with two of her illegitimate children and the daughter of another, was described in the same way, although no adult male was recorded in the household.

Table 9.7 Bridal pregnancy, 1780–1879

	Total Number of brides	Number pregnant	Percentage pregnant (%)	Illegitimacy ratio (%)
1780–1820	56	30	60.7	9.0
1830–79	40	23	57.5	12.1

Pre-marital sexual activity was common. Table 9.7 shows how bridal pregnancy had increased from its low levels of the post-enclosure period to reach those of the sixteenth century. Unlike the earlier period, however, the nineteenth century saw high levels of bridal pregnancy accompanied by high rates of illegitimacy. Of all brides married at Highley who subsequently had children there, between a half and two thirds were pregnant at the time of their marriage. A majority of all young single women in the village became pregnant. In many cases this was followed by marriage: in others, for whatever reason, it was not. Pressure to marry did not always prevail, even in circumstances where there seems to have been little impediment to marriage. In other cases, marriage was never in prospect. George Jarman married in May 1837; in June his wife had a baby; in July another single woman bore Jarman's child. Obviously he cannot have intended to marry both women, and one wonders by what criterion his final choice was made.

Other fathers, too, were themselves repeaters. John Rowley fathered an illegitimate child in 1837 when he was 19-years-old. He did not marry the mother. In 1840 he had another child by Charlotte Broom whom, eventually, he did marry. The brothers Samuel and Edward Wilcox fathered three acknowledged bastards, continuing what amounted to a family tradition of illegitimacy outlined in chapter five.

Table 9.8 Age of women at marriage or at birth of first illegitimate child, 1780–1879

	Mean age at first illegitimate child	[N]	Mean age at first marriage	[N]
1780–1829	23.0 yr.	[26]	23.8 yr.	[32]
1830–79	22.0 yr.	[26]	25.2 yr.	[54]

Table 9.8 shows mean age at first child for single mothers, together with mean age at first marriage. Before 1830, single mothers produced their children at around the same age as others married, lending support to the view that disrupted courtship played an important role in illegitimacy. Yet in the second half of the period, when marriage age rose, age at first illegitimate child fell, leaving a shortfall of over three years between the two figures. In this half of the period we find some single mothers of 14 and 15 years old, whose marriage cannot have been immediately in view. This may reflect the lowering of the age of menarche in the second half of the nineteenth century.[36] It certainly shows sexual activity at an earlier age than is ever recorded in previous centuries.

During the nineteenth century we are better able to trace these illegitimate children and the arrangements made to care for them. Sometimes their mother married and the child was absorbed into the new family – though how completely it is hard to say. In general, when the husband was himself the father of the child born before marriage, it took his surname. But otherwise, the child retained its mother's maiden surname, which of course was different from that of the rest of the family. The relationship of these children to the head of the household was given on census returns as 'step-son' or 'wife's son'.

In some cases, the absorption into the family does seem to have been complete. Thomas Walker became part of the household of George Jones when his mother Drusilla married Jones in 1851. Thirty years later, when his mother had been dead for 10 years and Jones was remarried, Thomas Walker still lived with the new family.

It was quite common for other relatives, usually grandparents, to take care of the child. In 1800 Ann Williams received poor relief

[36] Laslett, *Family Life*, pp. 214–32.

payments for clothing for her grandson – in fact the four-year-old illegitimate son of her daughter.[37] From the census period there are several examples of illegitimate children living with their maternal grandparents but without their mother. In 1841, nine-year-old Thomas Morris and his grandfather of 75 were both lodgers in a local gamekeeper's household. Occasionally the child remained with grandparents although the mother had married and was living in Highley. Other relatives, too, could sometimes be called upon to provide a home for the child. Francis Bentley, baptised in 1843, lived with his maternal uncle's family in 1851.

These relatives who took over responsibility for the child were without exception its mother's family. There is no record of the father of an illegitimate child or his relatives taking care of the child (unless he had subsequently married the mother). Maintenance payments could be exacted, but in the main bastards were the responsibility of the women who bore them, not the men who fathered them.

With illegitimacy so frequent during our period, very many people had 'bastardy links'. Of the 359 inhabitants in 1851, no less than 127 are known either to have been illegitimate, to have had an illegitimate child, or to have been the parent or child of someone who had. When we consider than there must have been others, perhaps not long resident in Highley, whose links cannot be traced, as well as the numbers of couples who married only weeks before the birth of a child, it becomes apparent that a majority of the village population had close personal experience of extra-marital conception and its consequences within their own immediate family.

This raises questions about attitudes towards bastardy. If personal experience of illegitimacy was so widespread, what degree of social stigma can have attached to it? Less, one might suppose, than in a community where pre-marital pregnancy was relatively infrequent, as it had been for instance in early eighteenth-century Highley.

It looks as if attempts to regulate village sexual morality had broken down during this period. Pre-marital sexual activity was now clearly more widely tolerated: one interpretation of the long-term trends in moral regulation in Highley is offered in the next chapter.

[37] S.R.O. 4123/P/2.

For whatever reasons, illegitimacy had begun to increase from about 1740, and once high rates were established they were to a large extent self-perpetuating. Those who were themselves illegitimate were more likely to bear bastards in their turn. Social attitudes towards sexual morality, too, must have been to some extent determined by the kind of widespread links with illegitimacy which have been described. If, as seems likely, the Church had exercized any influence over sexual morality, this influence waned with the secularization of social relations in the nineteenth century.

Church attendance was no longer obligatory, and for the first time there was an alternative place of worship in the parish, although as we have seen neither church nor chapel was particularly crowded. On 30th March 1851 some 22 per cent of the population attended morning service at church or chapel.[38] Church courts had more or less ceased to operate from the beginning of the period, and after 1834 the importance of the parish as an administrative unit drastically declined. The moral authority of the vicar must have dwindled too in such circumstances, although his social authority probably remained. Samuel Burrows was incumbent for over half the period, from 1790 to 1843. Like his predecessors he was university educated and of upper-middle class origins. Unlike them, however he lived in the village and was part of local society: he employed local servants, took parish apprentices, and supervized the farming of his 92 acres of glebe land.

The vicarage and the Jordins' house at Netherton were consistently the two largest households in the village. Burrows and his successor Samuel du Pré, also resident for nearly 40 years, were active in village affairs. With the decline of the village oligarchy and the increased turnover of tenant farmers, the Vicar and the Squire did indeed form the twin pillars of nineteenth-century village society. Kelly's Directory of Shropshire for 1870 reports that the chief landowners are William Jordin Esquire and the Reverend Samuel du Pré. The four 'proprietors' listed are Jordin and his brother Thomas, du Pré, and Decimus Burrows son of the previous vicar. There are just two marble commemorative tablets in the interior of the church; one of Samuel Burrows and his wife, the other of the Jordin family.

The Squire was the landlord of many villagers. Jordins owned the manor house built by Cresswell, the old demesne farm of the

[38] P.R.O. H.O. 129/355: Places of worship census, 1851.

Peirsons, Thomas Lowe's Borle Mill, the Rowley and Palmer farms at Netherton, the blacksmith's shop, and eventually Macnab's house at Woolstan's Wood – as well as at least two substantial houses, an inn and numerous cottages. In 1851, Jordins directly employed at least 17 people. In 1863, William Jordin gave the land for and supervized the establishment of a school for the children of 'the labouring and manufacturing classes'. Its trustees in 1874 were William and Daniel Jordin, Samuel du Pré and Decimus Burrows.[39]

Curiously, we know less about levels of material culture in the nineteenth century than in the sixteenth. Clearly, however, the divergence in type as well as extent of possessions of rich and poor which was identified from the seventeenth century had continued. Differences in life styles are exemplified by a comparison of the Squire's house at Netherton with the cottages built for miners around 1800 at New England. Jordin's house, Netherton House as it had come to be called, had five main rooms on the ground floor and seven bedrooms as well as numerous pantries, sculleries and linen rooms, two staircases and of course the wine cellar. There were extensive gardens, a coach house and stables. The furnishings remained more or less intact until the estate was sold in 1945.[40] There were 22 lots of silver; 20 lots of old cut glass (9 decanters, 11 champagne glasses and so on); and 44 lots of china, including a 70–piece dinner service and 2 early Coalport tea and dessert services. The Jordins had obviously bought locally and well, for most of the porcelain was from Coalport or Worcester and of the late eighteenth and early nineteenth centuries.

The cottages at New England, in the hollow of the Borle valley, were built of local stone in a terrace of 12. They had at most two rooms upstairs and two down, with privies in the garden. The cottages were demolished early in the twentieth century, but photographs show something of their size; upstairs windows seem to be at most 10 feet from the ground. We have seen how overcrowded the houses could be in times of population pressure: but otherwise they were not popular, for in 1851 six of them stood empty. Probably the cottages built for miners at Stanley were similar, and they seem to have fallen into disrepair even more quickly for in 1861, when navvies were crowded into every

[39] P.R.O. ED 7/102: Public elementary schools; preliminary statements, 1874.
[40] Sale catalogue of Netherton Estate, Highley; Nock and Joseland, auctioneers, 28 June, 1945.

Plate 11 A family pose in front of their cottage, one of the terrace built at New England about 1800 to house miners and their families. The cottages were demolished in the 1920s.

available corner of Stanley, at least five houses there and another four elsewhere in the village were empty, and must have been almost ruinous. Sadly, there is no indication of the furnishings of these homes. The cottages were built for industrial workers, but later inhabited by farm labourers, and in size and type were quite typical of the homes of the majority of the village population, for the 'labouring and manufacturing classes' were by far the most numerous throughout the nineteenth century.

The swift and extensive changes in village society brought about by the development of industry are a major feature of this period. Yet Highley was never a mining village in the way that those villages built as virgin settlements around pits in larger coalfields were. It was a rural community half of whose number were, for a time, coal miners. The miners found an existing community, with its own social structure, its church, houses and crafts. Without neglecting to consider the impact of this immigration on Highley, we must nevertheless remember that the existing population in many ways continued to live much as before. Such change and evolution as occurred in the agricultural community owed more to factors like inflation and the decline of the small farmer, the advent of the railway and accessible education, and the reform of the Poor Law than to the activities of coal and quarry owners.

In fact during the period of industrial expansion Highley had two apparently disparate social systems operating in parallel. The points at which they impinged on each other were surprisingly few. The miners lived close to the pit, at a distance from the village centre which was significant if not great. Their community at Stanley had its own public house, its own tradesmen, its own currency – and its own hierarchy of owner, manager, clerk, faceworkers, surface workers and so on. Miners seem to have been remarkably little involved in the machinery of administration and control, at either parochial or county level. There was very little inter-marriage between the two halves of the community, and almost no movement between agricultural and industrial employment.

Social relations within the agricultural sector were dominated by the continued polarization of wealth which had begun in the seventeenth century. Differentiation was sharper than ever between on the one hand a dwindling group of farmers (increasingly freeholders of considerable wealth and status) and on the other a large and growing army of the labouring poor. Ironically, this dichotomy meant that there came to be a greater homogeneity in village society than there had been since the sixteenth century: but it had become a homogeneity of the labouring poor.

10

The Course of Change

We have traced Highley's development over more than three centuries. During that time, there were two major shifts in the village economy, with consequent effects in the dynamics of social relations. The close-knit, stable society of the sixteenth century became the squirearchy of the nineteenth. Some underlying features endured, but principally the story is one of change.

One thing which does emerge very clearly is the extent of this change within the pre-industrial period. Highley in 1700, say, was as different from its sixteenth-century self as it was from the village of the late eighteenth century. Perhaps too much emphasis is laid on industrialization as the great watershed of English social history if as a corollary we are to treat 'pre-industrial England' as one homogeneous and chronologically open-ended whole. This study has shown that, for Highley, enclosure was as powerful an agent for change as was industrialization. Because Highley enclosed its common fields early, we are better able to separate the effects from those of industrial development than is often the case when the two events were chronologically close.

Of course, in some respects Highley may have been unique: the circumstances of the breakdown of the manorial system may well have been more advantageous than usual to tenants because of the financial difficulties of the Littleton family; and certainly the development of mining and quarrying industries followed a different course than would have the advent of factory-based production. In other respects, the course of social and economic change in Highley cannot alone be attributed to purely local factors. Part of the community's experience was undoubtedly common to the country as a whole, and much else probably shared with its more immediate neighbourhood – although conclusions on this part of Shropshire must await more detailed research on the area.

Nevertheless, certain points in the unending process of change and development can be identified as crucial, and it is around these points that the study of Highley has been structured. The most surprising finding is that the end of the manorial system had effects at least as profound as any brought about by industrial development. This emerges if we focus briefly on some of the features of the pre-enclosure community which were lost in the seventeenth century.

Enclosure did not happen in 1620. The breakdown of the manorial system and the enclosure of the open fields was a gradual process which began before 1610: indeed some features of the protracted movement towards enclosure, such as the rise in numbers of peripatetic landless labourers, and the accumulation of considerable amounts of cash by principal tenants which permitted the purchase, improvement and enclosure of holdings, can be traced to the last decades of the sixteenth century. Nevertheless, it is from about 1620 that the effects of the abandoning of communal agriculture are seen.

Prior to that time, Highley's economy can best be described as a semi-peasant one. The family was an important unit of production, but by no means all production was by the family for home consumption. There are indications of wage labour, and of an increasingly cash-based economy with production for sale as well as for subsistence. There was a financial hierarchy, with the inequalities of opportunity inherent in the system.[1]

Yet without wishing to present pre-enclosure Highley as some kind of Utopia, it must be acknowledged that its society was more egalitarian and participatory than it was later to become. Wealth was not the sole criterion of influence: settled residence and perhaps personal reputation appear to have been important determinants too. This was a society in which men known to be needy by their fellows – servants, labourers and cottagers – could be elected to local manor or parish office; and one where such offices carried a good deal of influence, for the community was in considerable measure self-regulatory. There were of course higher authorities both lay and ecclesiastical, but it was local officers who were responsible for reporting offences and, very often, for seeing punishments implemented.

[1] R. H. Hilton, 'Reasons for inequality among medieval peasants', *Journal of Peasant Studies*, 5 (1978).

The open-field system of agriculture imposed a degree of cooperation between neighbours. Its operation, as well as its regulation, required communal activity and collective decisions, and acted to blunt the divisions of the financial hierarchy.

The major theme of the period of enclosed agriculture which prevailed for most of the seventeenth and eighteenth centuries is that of the sharpening of these distinctions. Enclosure did not of itself create a widening gulf between a wealth-based oligarchy on the one hand and a dispossessed peasantry on the other. Bad harvests, demographic stagnation and the creation of a rural proletariat were clearly part of the national experience. But enclosure did speed up and exacerbate the polarization of village society. It provided a catalyst, coming at a time when economic circumstances had encouraged differentiation in village society – when, bluntly, the rich were getting richer and the poor poorer. The consolidating and enclosing of farms, their sale to local men, the division of the common woodland and consequent loss of grazing rights all combined to accelerate the pace of change.

From the period of instability in the land market which followed the sale of the manor emerged the tripartite pattern of absentee landlord, tenant farmer and agricultural labourer. By the end of the seventeenth century the chief farms of Highley were no longer owner-occupied; the smallholding had virtually disappeared and the cottager had become a landless labourer. Tenant farmers enjoyed considerable status and influence. As parish governance became increasingly restricted to a self-electing oligarchy, there was a polarization of power as well as of wealth – and a greater equation between the two. Social distance between most and least affluent, between vicar and parishioners, between employed and employee, grew. At the same time national legislation (and its local implementation) enhanced this division by its increasing use of parish officers as an essential part of the state machinery of regulation.[2]

The effects of changes in the agrarian system were universal, for virtually everyone in Highley was involved in agriculture until the late eighteenth century. Industrialization, however, in spite of the population increase which it brought, was able to be contained both geographically and socially. An industrial community was virtually grafted onto the existing agricultural one, and the points

[2] P. Corrigan and D. Sayer, *The Great Arch* (Oxford, 1985).

at which they impinged on each other were far fewer than might be expected.

The development of coal mining and quarrying did add one new dimension to social differentiation in the village: it greatly increased the numbers of 'men' without much affecting the numbers of 'masters'. There was, too, internal differentiation within the labouring groups. At the same time, Highley's ruling group of tenant farmers was shrinking as its small farms, like others in south Shropshire[3], were amalgamated and as one family, the Jordins, rose to preeminence in village society. Particularly after 1834, the powers of the parish elite, as well as their numbers, were much curtailed. Society was once again as homogeneous as it had been in the sixteenth century, but with crucial differences: the numerically predominant group was now that of the labouring poor; and the autonomy of the pre-enclosure community was greatly eroded.

The overall changes thus broadly outlined were reflected in many areas of social life. They led to shifts in patterns of migration, in kinship networks, in attitudes towards the relief of poverty and even in morality. There is however, one aspect of Highley's sharpening social differentiation which remains to be addressed before any more detailed consideration of these aspects of change.

Throughout the study, the various socioeconomic categories have been called 'groups', rather than classes. This is quite deliberate, if cumbersome, for it is far from clear at what point we can with validity speak of classes in the community.[4] Such a division into 'groups' is a useful analytical tool, but there are drawbacks in its use. Firstly, the consistent use of four such groups should not be taken to imply a similar composition throughout – obviously the yeoman/husbandman/cottager/labourer nexus of the pre-enclosure period is no longer meaningful in the eighteenth and nineteenth century. Most importantly, such a division should not be regarded as indicating a rigid and permanent demarcation between groups. Individuals could and did move between groups during their lifetimes, and some in any case, such as smallholders who also laboured for wages, straddled two categories. Furthermore, some divisions were more marked than others. For much of the period the amount of land held was more important than any

[3] T. Rowley, *The Shropshire Landscape* (Oxford, 1972), p. 146.
[4] R. S. Neale, *Class in English History 1680–1850* (Oxford, 1981).

strict yeoman/husbandman distinction. The division into 'groups', then, is to some extent one retrospectively imposed upon village society in order to achieve a measure of social specificity when discussing individual experience.

As a descriptive term, 'class' does seem applicable to these groups, who shared similar lifestyles, income and life-chances. However, the existence of classes becomes much more problematic if we take a more demanding definition. Did all, or any, of the groups exhibit class-consciousness, the acknowledgement of horizontal ties of class affinity? And were they able to take concerted action in defence of common class interests? Of course, such debates take us far outside the narrow parish limits of Highley, especially if we agree with Laslett that such consciousness and action should be nationwide.[5]

Laslett has persuasively argued that in 'pre-industrial' England only the gentry were free to form a class in this sense, and that therefore we are dealing with a 'one-class' society. Perkin, too, takes this view of the 'old society' pre-dating the late eighteenth century,[6] a social order characterized by vertical ties of patronage and deference (and what Laslett calls the familial base of production where 'every relationship can be seen as a love-relationship'[7]), and where there could be no place for class antagonisms. E. P. Thompson castigates those who hold this 'cosy' view and finds that class-struggle pre-dates, and indeed brings about, the formation of mature class divisions.[8]

So where does this leave Highley? For most of the period, there were no resident gentry and so by Laslett's definition we should have to think of it as an essentially classless society. This rings true for the pre-enclosure period, when a hierarchical structure based on subtle gradations prevailed. Yet it is more problematic in the subsequent period, when the 'best sort' did apparently perceive themselves as in some way differentiated and horizontally bound.

If we accept that only the gentry were capable of forming a true class, we must ignore the power of oligarchies like those in Highley. They could not legislate: but on the one hand they were

[5] P. Laslett, *The World We Have Lost* (London, 1971), chapter 2.

[6] H. Perkin, *The Origins of Modern English Society 1780–1880* (London, 1969), chapter 2.

[7] Laslett, *World We Have Lost*, p. 5.

[8] E. P. Thompson, 'Eighteenth century English society: class struggle without class?', *Socal History* 3 (1978).

those who voted legislators into power, and on the other hand they implemented that legislation, which depended to a large extent on the parish officers who administered it. They were not magistrates: but it was they who reported (or chose not to report) cases to magistrates. The parish vestry saw itself as 'the greater part' of the parish, and acted on occasion in defence of the interests of the rate-paying section of the community. Formal and informal sanctions were largely in their hands, and remained so while the parish was the chief unit of administration and their farms were virtually the only source of employment.

We certainly see the village elite pulling away from the rest of the community in some respects – in their withdrawal from the purely local marriage market, and their increasing tendency in the seventeenth century to form socially horizontal and self-selected friendships with others in similar social positions in the wider neighbourhood; in their aspirations for their sons whom they sent away to school, and in their changing attitudes towards the poor of their parish. Yet these very aspirations, it can be argued, prevented their cohesion into a class distinct from the gentry above and the poor below. It remains a matter of perspectives: viewed nationally, these local elites cannot be seen as constituting a class in anything other than the simplest descriptive sense of the term; but viewed locally, the picture becomes a little different. In Highley, an 'open' village with no resident gentry, this caucus of relatively prosperous farmers – overseers, constables, employers – certainly seem to have displayed (or been perceived to have displayed) a class identity and a measure of class action.

Did the vertical ties of patronage and paternalism in fact prevent the formation of clearly demarcated classes in Highley at this date? We have indeed seen how some of these vertical affinities appear to have weakened after the mid-seventeenth century, when poor neighbours ceased to receive bequests from well-off testators and when the network of small informal loans which had involved most of the community gave way to larger, formally secured business transactions between social equals. In other respects, however, paternalism remained and even, as we shall shortly examine, formed the basis of employment relations during and after industrialization.

But are vertical and horizontal alignments necessarily mutually exclusive? Highley's experience would seem to suggest that they are not. There is of course a limit to what conclusions of such a general nature can be drawn from the study of one small locality: conversely, such studies have been recommended as the way forward towards a more complete understanding of a complex issue.[9]

If, as would hardly be questioned, it is valid to speak of classes in ninetenth-century Highley, then it would appear to be equally valid to do so at any point after about the middle of the seventeenth century. This is not to say that a hierarchical structure was wiped away in 1650 – or indeed in 1750. Wrightson convincingly argues a reassuring premise, and one which has considerable empirical force in Highley's case; that hierarchy and class can exist side by side both as realities of social relations and in individual perceptions.[10]

Paternalism in Highley endured not only through the post-enclosure agrarian period, but into the nineteenth century too. In the seventeenth and eighteenth centuries, the household remained the base of agricultural production, and live-in servants stood in a quasi-filial relationship to the head of the household. Families, of course, can generate envy, competition and bitterness as well as loyalty and deference. Relationships can be seen in terms of familial responsibilities rather better if one is in the position of exacting devotion rather than giving it, especially when, as in the case of post-enclosure Highley, the *pater familias*, changing to his role of parish officer, is responsible for policing and paying or withholding poor relief.

Paternalism extended to the structuring of wage labour relations too. The farm labourer lived in tied cottages; he received part of his wages in the form of food and drink as late as the nineteenth century.[11] Even during the census period, we find agricultural labourers brought into the village by their employers, sometimes following their master over considerable distances. Industrial development did not end the 'old order' in this respect. The way in which extended-family groups followed mine owners from one enterprise to another, as late as 1880, argues a paternalistic aspect

---

[9] K. Wrightson, 'The social order of early modern England', in L. Bonfield, R. M. Smith and K. Wrightson (eds) *The World We Have Gained* (Oxford, 1986), pp. 201–02.

[10] *Ibid.*, pp. 198–9.

[11] B.L. Add. MSS. 21018: copy of notes of J. Plymley, 1793; J. Plymley, *A General View of the Agriculture of Shropshire* (1803).

to the organization of the industry. Coalmasters, too, owned their employees' houses, and seem to have exercized a considerable degree of social control over their workforce. Paternalism in coal mining is not unique to Highley: it was central to the organization of the industry in larger coalfields such as Durham.[12] Charities in the nineteenth century still were organized by employers in their role as local administrators, distributing bread to the deserving poor. The village school was basically the gift of the Squire to the children of the poor. So it was not only the manorial system of the sixteenth century which utilized the 'employer-as-father' concept as a means of social organization: capitalism, whether agrarian or industrial, also structured its labour relations on the same implicit basis.

What we appear to see in Highley with the dichotomizing of society from the seventeenth century is the gradual formation of a class who gathered, or were given, considerable autonomy as a group in running village affairs; who thought of themselves as the 'best sort'; and who looked increasingly to their social peers in a wider area than the village itself. At the same time the old hierarchies, the old vertical ties and responsibilities, lingered on. The effects of this polarization of wealth and influence were felt in many areas of life.

The pre-enclosure community had by no means been an isolated one: servants and some labourers spent short amounts of time in residence; brides had frequently been born elsewhere; and above all there was a high level of emigration by young people. Yet this mobility took place within a stable framework. The settled core remained, and families continued to be represented as sons succeeded fathers on manorial holdings. The end of the three-life tenure changed this. Those who continued to hold land did so increasingly on short leases, which encouraged migration among farmers and their families. The growing numbers of landless were not tied to the community in the way that cottagers had been and they too were more likely to move as a family from place to place in search of work. The height of this mobility came with the development of coal mining, which used an almost entirely immigrant workforce.

The miners had mostly come from a much greater distance than

---

[12] T. Austrin and H. Beynon, 'Masters and servants: paternalism and its legacy in the Durham coalfield' (Durham University working paper, 1980).

that usual for migration, for although mobility had increased, it had largely remained confined to a radius of 10 miles or so around Highley, an area which also encompassed the majority of social and business contacts. The agricultural population of the nineteenth century was also highly mobile, but the frequent moves of farmers, labourers and servants still tended to be within this area until the coming of the railway opened up communications with the industrial west midlands and the agricultural regions to the south. As a result of more frequent migration at all levels of village society, families remaining for more than two generations became rare. Only the landowning Jordins stayed throughout the last 100 years of the period.

As a further result of this increased mobility, kinship networks were never again as dense as they had been on the manor, and settled residence could hardly remain an important criterion for participation in village administration. Most of the tenants of the manor in the sixteenth century were related to several others, and most had been born in Highley. By 1851, hardly any heads of household (except the Jordins) were related to any others, and only 30 per cent claimed to have been born in the village – some of them with apparent inaccuracy.

Kinship links were further eroded by the polarization of wealth which brought economic and social disparity between family branches. We have noted the shrinking range of kinship recognition evidenced in wills, and the associated rise of friendships between unrelated social equals.

The end of the three-life tenure and the thousand-year lease also changed inheritance practices. Sons were even more likely to leave a farm which their father held only on a seven-year lease. Widows and unmarried daughters of these tenant farmers – as well as the tenants themselves – were more likely to fall into poverty in old age. The practice of holding for three lives did much to secure the position of widows, which markedly deteriorated after enclosure. The growing involvement in wage labour did much to devalue the contribution of women to the family economy long before the coming of industry.[13]

The firmer delineation of class boundaries from the seventeenth century onwards meant that social advancement became even more difficult. The acquisition of land became a near-impossibility: even

---

[13] A. Clark, *The Working Life of Women in the Seventeenth Century* (London, 1919).

its retention was beyond most local men. By the census period, the sons of labourers who stayed in Highley were themselves labourers. Others may have left for jobs in the manufacturing centres of Birmingham and the Black Country, but any change of occupation within the village was unlikely. Movement into trade seems to have been barred. Village blacksmiths, shoemakers and so on were as far as can be ascertained the sons of artisans, often in the same trade. They in turn, although possibly managing to rent five or six acres of land to run as a side-line, were not able to break into full-time farming. Indeed most men who combined a smallholding with another occupation were by the eighteenth and nineteenth centuries more likley to be farmers on the way down the social scale than artisans on the way up.

There is evidence to suggest a divergence in demographic experience between socioeconomic groups, although this needs to be tested in larger parishes where socially-specific samples of sufficient sizes can be generated.[14] Demographically, Highley followed pretty closely the patterns of growth and stagnation which have been established as the national experience. Marriage age was relatively high until the second half of the eighteenth century, families averaged perhaps five children born at two-and-a-half-year intervals, infant mortality outstripped that of children until the period of industrialization, and a considerable proportion of individuals were widowed and remarried. There is a danger, though, of averages concealing significant variation both chronological and social.[15] There seems, for instance, to have been a reversal of the sixteenth-century trend of prosperous couples having more children than poorer ones. It also appears that marriages were more likely to be broken early by death in the period after enclosure than they had been before. And the influx of miners from about 1800 had marked effects on the demographic structures of the community, raising levels of fertility and, by their general youth, depressing death rates and changing the age-structure of the community.

It is unfortunate that existing evidence does not allow an examination of household structure before enclosure. However,

[14] This has only occasionally been attempted. See V. H. T. Skipp, *Crisis and Development: an Ecological Case Study of the Forest of Arden 1570–1674* (Cambridge, 1978), chapter 4.

[15] M. Anderson, *Approaches to the History of the Western Family* (London and Basingstoke, 1980), pp. 30–3.

the Easter Book, used in conjunction with other sources, provides
an unusually full picture of households from the last decades of the
seventeenth century. These households were somewhat smaller
than what appears to be the national norm, although the latter
naturally encompasses considerable variation.[16] Here too the
sharpening differentiation of village society can be seen, with more
prosperous households the largest, being more likely to include
servants and grown-up children. Households at all levels, though,
were predominantly nuclear: the presence of other kin was unusual
in this agrarian period. Industrialization appears if anything to
have strengthened links with the extended family group. Mean
household size rose, and both phases of mining development
encouraged immigration by related groups, especially of married
siblings who, at least initially, would appear to have shared a home.
Anderson found that in Preston in the mid-nineteenth century
industrialization had strengthened kinship links and encouraged
the formation of extended-family households.[17] It seems to have
done the same in Highley.

The nineteenth century also saw the final decline of the practice
of resident service in husbandry. Although non-resident farm
labourers had been a feature of the agrarian economy since at least
the last quarter of the sixteenth century, live-in farm servants had
continued to be frequent until the middle of the nineteenth
century. Here, too, there appears to have been a gradual change in
the social composition of the group. In the first century under
consideration, resident service was rather a stage in the individual's
life cycle than an indication of poverty. The children of yeomen
might well spend some time in service. By the eighteenth century
these servants were drawn from a more restricted background;
they were the children of labourers, often parish apprentices, and
expected to continue wage labour after marriage when they ceased
to live in the farmhouse.

Domestic service, however, continued, and by the census period
girls were more likely than boys to leave home for a period of
resident service. Indeed domestic service was virtually the only
occupation open to young single women.

In the pre-industrial period, it was rare for any household to

[16] P. Laslett and R. Wall (eds), *Household and Family in Past Time* (Cambridge, 1972), p. 154.
[17] M. Anderson, *Family Structure in Nineteenth Century Lancashire* (Cambridge, 1971).

include unrelated individuals other than servants. After 1800, lodgers became much more usual. This was naturally the case at times of increased pressure on local housing, such as the years in which large numbers of railway navvies lived in the parish, when some households contained five or six lodgers. But it also seems to have been increasingly common to take lodgers at other times too. There were 14 lodgers in Highley in 1851, and 10 in 1871.

In those periods at which it is possible to explore the formation and structure of families and households, a developmental cycle is clearly discernible. There could be great variations in the size of the residental group at various stages of the cycle: parents of a married couple were likely only to live with them for a few years in old age, at a time when their own children were still at home. Most of their own children (especially among less well-off families) began to leave home from a relatively early age, and the size of the household shrank. However, with fertility continuing into middle age, the elderly quite often had an unmarried child still at home; and in fact few people lived alone.

It is difficult in this kind of study to assess the nature of familial relationships. Such evidence as there is, largely from wills, does not support the view that prior to an eighteenth-century revolution in sentiments we see an essentially 'low-affect' society.[18] Certainly duty was stressed: Margery Holloway's son inherited 'if he deale with me as a son ought to deale with his mother' in 1569. On the other hand, there seems to be an element of mutuality and companionship in marriage, and a large measure of personal choice of marriage partner, at all levels of village society.

The replacement of the relative egalitarianism of the pre-enclosure period by a more clearly defined social and financial hierarchy is also reflected in material standards of living. We see a difference in the type of possessions of the wealthy, rather than merely in their quantity, from the seventeenth century. The more prosperous began to acquire furnishings which were ornamental rather than purely utilitarian. They now owned books, clocks, jewellery, carpets. In many cases their houses were rebuilt or extended in the first half of the seventeenth century. Particular rooms were reserved for particular functions, and we no longer find grain stored in bedrooms and farm equipment with cooking

---

[18] L. Stone, *The Family, Sex and Marriage in England 1500–1800* (Penguin edition, Harmondsworth, 1979), p. 88.

utensils. As far as it is possible to tell, the homes of the poor remained small, often overcrowded (especially during periods of intense industrial activity), and sparsely furnished with functional items.

The divergence culminated in the nineteenth century with a handful of large and luxuriously appointed houses – the vicarage, Netherton House and Hazlewells, rebuilt as a late-Georgian miniature mansion – while the majority of the population lived in small cottages like those hastily built after the turn of the century.

The widening gulf between rich and poor seems to have had its effects on attitudes towards charity and the relief of poverty. The better-off tenants of the manor felt a responsibility towards their poorer neighbours both collectively as 'the poor of the parish' and individually. They left money to servants and ex-servants, and even to individuals who were simply 'poor neighbours'. They lent small sums to the less well-off. Writing of the century after 1580, Wrightson describes the tensions caused by the conflict of these traditional social obligations with the demands of agrarian capitalism.[19] In Highley, these tensions appear to have been resolved in two ways. As we have seen, traditional social obligations were utilized in the regulation of labour by both agrarian and industrial capitalists, via the exercise of paternalism. In other ways, the village elite shifted the focus of their obligations towards the poor firstly away from the individual towards the poor as a class, and ultimately were satisfied to fulfill them through the channels of parish administration. Bequests to the poor disappear from wills, and appeals against the poor rate levy become frequent.[20]

The amount of money needed for poor relief grew rapidly after about 1760. There were more inhabitants without adequate financial support – widows, single mothers and their children and, increasingly, men without employment or with insufficient wages. The poor rate became an increasing burden on a shrinking group of ratepayers, and may well in the early nineteenth century have helped to drive some small farmers off the land altogether. Attempts were constantly made to restrict this burden, by the examination and removal of paupers, by parish apprenticeships, and by frequent disputes with other parishes over responsibility

[19] K. Wrightson, *English Society 1580–1680* (London, 1982), p. 60.
[20] L. J. Lee (ed), *A Full List and Partial Abstract of the Contents of the Quarter Sessions Rolls 1696–1800* (Shrewsbury, ND).

for individual paupers. The potential for the generation of divergence and tension in village social relations is obvious.

Increasing social distance between neighbours is exemplified in the changing relationship between clergy and parishioners. The pre-enclosure vicars were tenants of the manor, and farmed their lands as did the rest of the community. Thomas Oseland had even been born in the parish and had close relatives among his flock. Vicars of the seventeenth century were outsiders, with a much higher level of education than their parishioners. Socially, they were at least on a par with the top stratum of farmers. They did, however, continue to live in the parish and involve themselves in farming activities. Eighteenth-century vicars were absentees who rented out the vicarage house and lands, and who put in only occasional appearances to take services. At least two of the post-enclosure clergy were deeply unpopular, and relations with the others lacked warmth. In the nineteenth century, clergy were again resident and with the squire formed the core of a much-reduced social elite.

With the end of compulsory church attendance and the waning of the powers of the church courts and of the parish as an administrative unit, there was less scope for moral regulation in nineteenth-century Highley. The apparent trends in pre-marital sexual activity throughout the period of this study are interesting, for they too seem to be linked to enhanced social and economic differentiation within the community. In the subtly graduated social structure of the pre-enclosure period, a village-wide morality appears to have held sway. While illegitimacy was not condoned, there was a general toleration of pre-marital sex leading to marriage. Pregnant brides were common, and found at all levels of society. The parish elite which evolved after enclosure apparently made some claim to moral as well as social differentiation, developing its own mores, which precluded pre-marital sex. Thus we find not only a fall in the numbers of pregnant brides, but also that they, and the mothers of illegitimate children, were increasingly confined to the poorer classes. The labouring poor may not have subscribed to this morality, but the parish oligarchy now possessed the means to attempt a more or less successful imposition of it upon them. Those who resisted were increasingly drawn from a group who were not 'respectable'; and it may be significant that this group can also be seen to resist other forms of social control.

By the 'industrial' period, numbers in the ruled and ruling groups had become too disparate, and too many of the mechanisms for moral regulation were being removed from the hands of the rulers for their morality to be able to prevail. Once again, a more homogeneous society produced a more nearly universal morality – one which apparently tolerated pre-marital sex and found illegitimacy an unfortunate but unavoidable corollary of it.

This can be no more than a tentative explanation of the course of change in sexual morality. Nevertheless, it reinforces the suggestion that illegitimacy in particular may profitably be related to a context wider than the narrowly economic.[21] The changes in the incidence of illicit sex in Highley certainly seem to relate more closely to changes in the patterns of social structure and the mechanisms of moral regulation than they do to the more straightforward measure of economic opportunity.

The chief features of the course of social change in Highley, then, stem from the development of much greater economic and social differentials than had characterized the community before enclosure. The relatively stable and egalitarian manorial community, densely interrelated and widely participatory, gave way to a clearly stratified – even dichotomous – social structure from the seventeenth century. For the agrarian community which continued alongside the industrial ventures of the early nineteenth century, the major changes had come much earlier with the formation of a village elite of tenant farmers and the creation of a rural proletariat of landless labourers. Economic circumstances of this later period merely served to accentuate these trends, with the parish elite on the one hand losing authority as other units of administration took over their role, and on the other hand dwindling in size as the Jordin family emerged as major landowners at the expense of smaller farmers.

Industrial developments, in Highley and the surrounding villages, were naturally not without consequences for the population as a whole – Highley more than doubled in size within 10 years, for one thing. Yet in many ways the agrarian community remained surprisingly untouched by these developments. Existing

---

[21] D. Levine and K. Wrightson, 'The social context of illegitimacy in early modern England', in P. Laslett, K. Oosterveen and R. Smith (eds) *Bastardy and its Comparative History* (London, 1980), pp. 158–75. A. Macfarlane, 'Illegitimacy and illegitimates in English history', in *ibid.*, pp. 71–85.

mechanisms for the relief of poverty and for social control were hardly affected. Employment opportunities for local men were not enhanced by the advent of coal mining. In short, industrialization in the area was not for Highley the crucial watershed between a traditional social order and a 'modern' one. In many respects, the old order vanished in the first half of the seventeenth century.

Throughout the long period under consideration, we have been dealing with a dynamic process of change and evolution. It would be a mistake to view the entire period before 1780 (or indeed before 1620) as a single entity, uniform and static. Similarly, development did not stop in 1880 – in fact it speeded up. The second phase of coal mining was longer lasting than the first, and Highley remained a mining village until 1969. Population reached 1,500 before 1914, and thereafter grew more slowly but steadily.

Today Highley is in a 'post-industrial' phase, and is largely a dormitory for those who work in the West Midlands conurbation. Very few of those who live in Highley work in the village. In 1980, only 31 people of a total population of 3,000 were employed full-time in agriculture in the parish. Secondary education has not been available in the village since 1959; the local railway closed in 1963. The loss of autonomy which can be traced through much of the preceding centuries, and which accelerated with the reforms of 1834, is almost complete. Highley has an elected parish council, but in effect most decisions are made and implemented at Rural District Council headquarters at Bridgnorth or County Hall in Shrewsbury. The cohesiveness of the post-1880 mining community has now gone the way of the pre-Victorian autonomy.

There remains much that can never be recovered about life in Highley – or any other community – in the past. Nevertheless, studies of individual parishes like this one can, in several and especially in total, seek to elucidate obscure areas of social experience and to 'give a more human face to the broader processes and interpretative abstractions of historical change'.[22]

---

[22] K. Wrightson and D. Levine, *Poverty and Piety in an English Village: Terling 1525–1700* (New York, San Francisco and London, 1979), p. 18.

Index